# CRITICAL SOCIAL THEORIES

# CRITICAL SOCIAL THEORIES

## An Introduction

### Second Edition

*Ben Agger*

**Paradigm Publishers**
Boulder • London

Copyright © 2006 Paradigm Publishers

First edition copyright © 1998 by Westview Press, a Member of the Perseus Books Group

Published in the United States by Paradigm Publishers, 3360 Mitchell Lane, Suite E, Boulder, CO 80305 USA.

Paradigm Publishers is the trade name of Birkenkamp & Company, LLC, Dean Birkenkamp, President and Publisher.

**Library of Congress Cataloging-in-Publication Data**

Agger, Ben
  Critical social theories : an introduction/Ben Agger.—2nd ed.
    p. cm.
  Includes bibliographical references and index.
  ISBN 1-59451-206-X (hardcover : alk. paper)—ISBN 1-59451-207-8 (pbk. : alk. paper)
  1. Sociology—Philosophy.  2. Sociology—Methodology.  I. Title.
  HM585.A46 2006
  301.01—dc22

                2005028078

Printed and bound in the United States of America on acid free paper that meets the standards of the American National Standard for Permanence of Paper for Printed Library Materials.

Designed and Typeset by Straight Creek Bookmakers

10 09 08 07 06  1 2 3 4 5

*For Oliver and Sarah*

# Contents

# Preface to the Second Edition

Since the first edition of this book was published in 1998, the world has changed in significant ways. Social life, both here and abroad, has become more polarized, hierarchical, and conflicted. Inequalities have become deeper. These are precisely the issues addressed by critical social theories, which have become even timelier. I assess the impact of these changes on critical social theories in my new concluding chapter.

The deepening of conflict has been manifested on several fronts. The global gap between rich and poor countries and regions has widened. The privileged nations deal with the impact of digitality and media culture on social and personal life. The poor countries, especially in Africa, deal with AIDS and hunger. "Globalization," which is really another name for world capitalism, has further divided the east and west as well as the north and the south. Underdeveloped countries lag far behind in economic development, and they have runaway population growth as well as high infant mortality. They are also breeding grounds of despotism. At home, so-called red and blue states are increasingly polarized. Born-again Christianity has become both a political platform and a social agenda, while urbanites on both coasts remain traditionally Democratic. In world economies everywhere, there is a growing gulf between the professional-managerial class and unskilled and nonunionized service workers, frequently nonwhite and young, who work at dead-end jobs and even in sweat shops. These service workers are fungible labor and their jobs are outsourced. This is a trend also occurring in universities, where managerial academic administrators chip away at tenure and deploy many part-time instructors who can be hired and fired at will. Finally, on the intellectual front, there is a growing gap between positivists and nonpositivists, especially in the social sciences such as sociology. Positivists continue to control the academic disciplines and graduate curricula, but nonpositivist theorists and qualitative scholars, as I document in chapter 9, are becoming an important intellectual counterforce as they both insist that quantitative methodology is not a royal road to truth and practice a public sociology. The critical social theories have played an important role in fortifying this antipositivist counterforce.

These growing inequalities and conflicts challenge sociology and the other social sciences to be socially and politically relevant and to not lapse into abstraction and obscurity. At issue, as it has been since the mid-nineteenth century when Marx debated Adam Smith about the nature of capitalism, are the paradigms with which we should frame our particular analyses and diagnoses. Critical social theories are broad-gauged and not piecemeal; they generalize at the risk of missing ground-level detail; they are political in the sense that they want to use social-science knowledge to change the world, much as Marx and Engels did in the eleventh thesis on Feuerbach.

Three years after the first edition of this book appeared, Islamic-funda-mentalist terrorists crashed airplanes into the World Trade Center towers and into the Pentagon. A plane destined for the White House was brought down by struggling passengers. In the aftermath of 9/11 American patriotism and xenophobia have flourished, and President Bush has embarked on a cam-paign of military adventurism laced with unilateralism. The United States has very few friends in the world, and one of its only allies in the war in Iraq (rapidly approaching a Vietnam-like quagmire) is England, which has been the site of recent terrorism. It is difficult to imagine that a value-free social science can find any warrant after 9/11, when everything seems politicized and people are taking sides. A sociology that ignores the issues imbedded in 9/11, such as globalization, uneven wealth across countries and regions, the role of religion in everyday life, the viability of the nation state, and the fate of the project of modernity, is doomed to irrelevance. Critical social theorists challenge positivists to address these and other issues of the day, developing a public sociology more interested in broad civic issues than in methodological refinements. Instead of having to apologize for politicizing one's sociology in these times, scholars should have to explain why their sociologies aren't political (which, as Jacques Derrida explained, they always already are).

It is fitting that the second edition of *Critical Social Theories* is being issued by a publishing house called "Paradigm." Thomas Kuhn used the term *paradigm* in his *Structure of Scientific Revolutions* to refer to broad understandings of, and assumptions about, the physical universe. Of interest to such paradigms are the nature of motion, mass, matter, time, and space. You cannot prove one paradigm correct or incorrect; you can only bring their basic assumptions to light and debate them, much as Einstein began to do when he published his first paper on relativity in 1905. Critical social theories constitute a paradigm, although a paradigm embodying difference and debate; they develop a model of the social universe grounded in analyses of inequality and conflict, and they aim for a better society in which these fundamental differences have been overcome.

In this second edition, I continue to defend the idea that the most interest-ing writing and teaching in contemporary sociology and the related social sciences address themselves to "paradigms," models of social being, social action, and social justice. And in my new concluding chapter, I reach back to the 1960s for insights and inspiration with which to strengthen a paradigmatic critical sociology in these post-9/11, digital, global times. I draw from the 1960s New Left in formulating the program of a "next" left inspired by C. Wright Mills's and Tom Hayden's examples of a critical public sociology, both of which stem, I contend, from early Marx, who remains perhaps the most important critical sociologist of all. In Marx's 1843–44 "early manuscripts," he did for social theory and social science what Einstein did for physics in 1905; he changed its foundational assumptions, stressing that people can be free to enjoy their work, their communities, their bodies, and nature. Alienation can be overcome, especially if we don't assume that it is our fate. Sorely lacking today is utopian vision, aiming high and not accepting things as they are, or as they appear to be. This second edition is a contribution to utopia, for which we find resources in the continuity between early Marx and the early SDS.

# Acknowledgments

The idea for a second edition of *Critical Social Theories* was suggested to me by Dean Birkenkamp. Dean is more than a good editor and publisher; he is a colleague with whom authors develop and discuss ideas. This is rare indeed in publishing today, which is why authors clamor to publish with Paradigm.

I am grateful for feedback I received from readers and adopters of the first edition of the book. Their enthusiasm for a book that introduces critical social and cultural theories in an accessible way motivated me to consider doing a second edition. My students have also responded well to the book, which attempts to clarify and apply complicated concepts. People remain interested in critical approaches to social science and humanities because there is so much wrong with the world and because positivism provides no solutions. Indeed, as I argue herein, positivism is part of the problem because it does not spark utopian imagination, which is urgently needed in these times.

My kids, Oliver and Sarah, one approaching junior high and the other in high school, keep me laughing and hopeful. My wife, Beth Anne Shelton, is a rare combination of a nonpositivist empiricist. She appreciates theory, as long as it makes sense and is grounded. Our forthcoming book, *Fast Families, Virtual Children,* is our own effort to understand our kids' worlds in light of the large structural issues of work, family, and media culture.

Julie Kirsch has done another great job of editing on this project, untwisting my prose when necessary!

# CHAPTER I

# The Disciplinary
# Positioning of Theory

## CRITICAL SOCIAL THEORY
### AND THE CRITIQUE OF POSITIVISM

This book introduces readers to the varieties of critical social theory. It also attempts to deepen the theoretical understanding of professional social theorists. The book both surveys original theoretical writings and cites secondary literature. The rapid burgeoning of secondary literatures in critical social theory reflects growing interest in critical theory, within and beyond sociology. In my own teaching, I have felt the need for a text written in accessible prose that addresses all of the current varieties of critical social theory. Because I could not find a book of that kind, I decided to write one. I have kept this book relatively brief, recognizing that it will serve as a supplementary text. Although each chapter is comprehensive, I omit extraneous detail. My bibliography is quite extensive in order to guide further reading.

This book has three possible audiences. It is directed at student readers at the upper-division undergraduate and graduate levels. It is intended for professional social theorists interested in how these critical social theories can be unified around some common themes. Finally, it addresses mainstream sociologists curious about recent theoretical developments. Critical theory, postmodernism, and feminist theory increasingly abound at the national and regional meetings and even in the journals; they are current even if sometimes controversial. These varieties of critical social theory deserve to be given a book-length introduction and not simply relegated to chapters in omnibus sociological theory textbooks, which range from Auguste Comte to Herbert Marcuse.

This is a book about—and against—the end of social theory. It is an argument for the continuing viability of social theory, especially in an age characterized by some as postmodernity. Necessarily, this book is personal—it is my account of where social theory is heading and should be heading. I am purposely selective: I omit large chunks of what passes for social theory today, such as rational choice theory, network theory, and ethnomethodology. I instead examine critical theory, postmodernism, feminist theory, multiculturalism, and cultural studies as examples of critical social theory. I explain each of those traditions, integrate them where possible, and demonstrate their empirical applications.

Although this book is directed at readers uninitiated into the theoretical traditions under discussion, I also make arguments. Among my arguments are the following:

1. It is more than ever necessary to explore and explain society using what Jean-François Lyotard (1984) calls "grand narratives"—analyses that paint with a broad brush and attempt to explain interrelationships. I do not agree with postmodern theorists such as Lyotard that we should not deploy these comprehensive theories because they might lead to oversimplification and even political authoritarianism. Although postmodernism provides valuable insights into language, culture, and power, we need not refrain from constructing comprehensive social theories of the kind attempted by Karl Marx, Max Weber, and Talcott Parsons.

2. Sociological theory as a distinctive canon of thought typically including the work of Comte, Emile Durkheim, Weber, Marx, and Parsons is giving way to social theory—a broadly interdisciplinary project comprising activities of people in the social sciences and humanities who are inspired by various European perspectives on the human sciences and culture. People interested in "theory" read many of the same sources: Michel Foucault, Jacques Derrida, the Frankfurt School, French feminism. We use many of the same terms—*discourse, hegemony, subject position*. This combination of theoretical developments represents one of the most exciting advances in contemporary intellectual life. Although this book is certainly meant for students and practitioners of sociological theory, I attempt to expand the body of work typically considered under that rubric. I argue that the specialized project of sociological theory is increasingly constrained by its disciplinary framework. At the same time, I recognize that many theorists, especially in sociology, respect the disciplinary division of labor and believe that sociological theory as a distinctive body of thought is relatively self-contained and clearly demarcated from other theoretical orientations and traditions.

3. Many of these European perspectives share common assumptions, which allow them to be synthesized—hence, my term *critical social theory*. People combine these influences in different ways. Many do not believe that all of these perspectives can be reconciled, especially where postmod-

ernism so obviously stands opposed to the totalizing project of Marxist social theory. Although the reader can treat the chapters in this book as relatively discrete units introducing each of the substantive critical social theories, throughout I synthesize these views, integrating them around certain unifying themes without effacing their differences.

4. The theoretical perspectives covered here are applicable in empirical social research. Some of them have already triggered empirical applications. I am not a positivist who attempts to test theory, instead recognizing that data are theoretically constructed; I do not believe positivism exhausts available theories of knowledge. Hence, we can apply critical social theories in empirical research without pretending to "verify" or "falsify" them. In chapter 8, I explore actual and possible applications of critical social theory.

In the rest of this section, I develop my third argument, stated above, about how all of these theories share common features that allow one to synthesize these perspectives into an overarching critical social theory. Of all my contentions, this argument for unity will prove the most challenging, given what people ordinarily take to be differences among critical theory, postmodernism, multiculturalism, feminist theory, and cultural studies. One can make weak and strong cases for synthesis. A weak case simply suggests common generic features of the varieties of critical social theory covered in this book. A stronger case would go further and attempt to build a unified critical social theory out of these diverse theoretical perspectives. In this chapter I make the weak case, identifying certain theoretical commonalities among these perspectives. As I move from theory to theory in the course of this book, I present a stronger case for substantive interchangeability among these theories.

It is not necessary for readers to accept *either* of these cases in order to profit from the book. As I have said, readers can treat each chapter as a more or less freestanding unit that describes a particular theoretical orientation. However, I want to consider both weak and strong cases for synthesis. The weak case (for a generic critical social theory) is heuristically useful; it helps the reader recognize certain common theoretical features of each perspective that enable one to characterize them as instances of critical social theory. The strong case is substantively useful because it advances the project of critical social theory by borrowing insights from each perspective that, taken together, build a better theory. The risk involved in the strong case is that it effaces theoretical differences among the perspectives.

What I am calling the weak case is actually an argument that all of the theories presented here have common features that allow them to be distinguished from other categories of theoretical perspectives. Nicholas Mullins (1973) has already proposed a format for identifying theories and theory groups in American sociology. Most standard introductory sociology text-

books group theories into structural functionalism, symbolic interactionism, and conflict theory. I have criticized this tripartite approach for,
among other things, conflating conflict theory and Marxism and ignoring
theoretical perspectives such as feminist theory (Agger 1989c). In any case,
there is a good deal of arbitrariness in grouping theories together and, indeed, in identifying intellectual perspectives as theories in the first place.
For example, it is arguable that rational choice theory (Elster 1986; Coleman 1990; Coleman and Fararo 1992; Carver and Thomas 1995; Green
and Shapiro 1994) is more an empirical perspective than a full-blown theory. One could say essentially the same thing about ethnomethodology
(Garfinkel 1967; Mehan and Wood 1975). There is no definitive way to resolve these issues apart from making good arguments about what constitute theories and theory clusters.

I treat critical social theory (CST) as a theory cluster, although I stop
short of offering a full taxonomy of theoretical clusters in sociology and
other social sciences. For a theory to be considered a critical social theory,
it must have the following features:

1. CST opposes positivism. It argues that knowledge is not simply a reflection of an inert world "out there" but is an active construction by scientists and theorists who necessarily make certain assumptions about the
worlds they study and thus are not strictly value free. Furthermore, CST
opposes the positivist notion that science should describe natural laws of
society, believing on the contrary that society is characterized by historicity
(susceptibility to change).

2. CST distinguishes between the past and present, largely characterized
by domination, exploitation, and oppression, and a possible future rid of
these phenomena. It links past, present, and future by arguing that the potential for a better future is already contained in the past and present. In
this sense, CST endorses the possibility of progress. This future society can
be realized through concerted political and social action. The role of CST
is to raise consciousness about present oppression and to demonstrate the
possibility of a qualitatively different future society. Thus, CST is political
in the sense that it participates in bringing about social change. Yet it is not
simply or mechanically agitational: It steps back from society in order to
appraise it and then offers its insights and analyses to people and groups
involved in social movements.

3. CST argues that domination is structural. That is, people's everyday
lives are affected by larger social institutions such as politics, economics,
culture, discourse, gender, and race. CST illuminates these structures in
helping people understand the national and global roots of their oppression.

4. In this vein, CST argues that structures of domination are reproduced
through people's false consciousness, promoted by ideology (Marx), reifi-

cation (Georg Lukacs), hegemony (Antonio Gramsci), one-dimensional thinking (Marcuse), and the metaphysic of presence (Derrida). Today false consciousness is fostered by positivist social sciences such as economics and sociology that portray society as governed by intractable laws, suggesting to people that the only reasonable behavior involves accommodation to these allegedly fixed patterns. CST pierces this false consciousness by insisting on the power of agency, both personal and collective, to transform society.

5. CST argues that social change begins at home, in people's everyday lives—sexuality, family roles, workplace. In this sense, CST avoids determinism and endorses voluntarism.

6. Following Marx in this sense, CST conceptualizes the bridge between structure and agency as dialectical. That is, although structure conditions everyday experience, knowledge of structure can help people change social conditions. CST builds this dialectical bridge by rejecting economic determinism.

7. By connecting everyday life and large-scale social structures, CST opposes the notion that eventual progress lies at the end of a long road that can be traversed only by sacrificing people's liberties and even lives. By focusing on the dialectical connection between everyday life and structure, CST holds people responsible for their own liberation and admonishes them not to oppress others in the name of distant future liberation. CST rejects revolutionary expediency, arguing that the dictatorship of the proletariat or other privileged vanguard groups quickly becomes a dictatorship over the proletariat. Liberty is not to be won through the "expedient" sacrifice of liberties and lives.

None of the theories considered here explicitly endorses all seven of these themes. For example, postmodernists rarely use the term *domination* in their writing. I am interpreting the theories as instances of critical social theory by addressing their commonalities, thus helping readers view them as more similar than different. This is important in order to build a comprehensive theory that preserves their diverse strengths. The risk in this strategy is that we blur their boundaries so much that we lose sight of their specificity and differences. To stress "commonality" already assumes that we can blend theories in order to create a total (or totalizing) theory, a premise more familiar to Marxists than postmodernists. One could reasonably say that my interpretation of the theories treated in this book as more similar than different reflects my own Frankfurt School/Hegelian-Marxist biases about the merits of comprehensive social theory.

Critical social theory's critique of positivism is its central and most enduring feature. Positivist tendencies in the social sciences since the Enlightenment provoked critical social theory, beginning with Marx. Comte's notion that sociology (his neologism) should attempt to become "social physics" by describing naturelike social laws freezes the present into ontological ice, portraying such historical patterns as capitalism, racism, sexism, and the domination of nature as inevitable and necessary. Marx attempted to unfreeze these representations of social nature through what he called ideology critique. For him, this was directed largely to religion and to bourgeois political economy. As I argue later, some of the most important developments in critical theory since Marx have involved the incorporation of insights from literary and cultural theory, including both postmodernism and feminism, that allow the original Marxist critique of ideology to be extended into the critical analysis of a whole range of ideological discourses, all the way from mass media to education and architecture.

The term Marxists use to pierce the static representations of a lawful social universe is *historicity*, which refers to the historical fluidity of social patterns. The historicity of society suggests that past and present patterns, though they appear intractable, can in fact be changed through concerted political and social efforts by oppressed people. In *The Communist Manifesto* (1967), Marx and Engels sketched the possible historical role of the working class in overthrowing the capitalist market economy and what they called its logic of capital. Marx wrote *The Manifesto* and other works such as *Capital* to suggest the possibility of historicity—and hence of social change. Although *The Manifesto* was more polemical than *Capital*, both books deployed historical and social analysis in order to challenge static representations of alleged capitalist "laws" that, like natural laws, cannot be changed.

This is not to imply that there *are* natural laws somehow outside of history. The postpositivist philosophy of natural science since Albert Einstein and Werner Heisenberg suggests that natural science is neither devoid of philosophical constructs nor incapable of studying the world without necessarily changing it. The model of natural science emulated by positivist social scientists can be contested. If natural science does not describe a lawful, timeless universe, neither can social science attempt to do so. Critical social theory is firmly grounded in postpositivist notions of science as a thoroughly historical, philosophical, and political activity. This does not mean that critical social theorists renounce objectivity—description and discussion of the world within which science is situated. Marx was a social analyst who addressed the world objectively *and* critically.

The critique of positivism addresses positivism's metaphysical view of history, its freezing of history into the allegedly eternal patterns of the present. Following Marx's lead, critical social theorists portray history as a horizon of possibilities constrained but not determined by the past and present. In particular, they regard emancipation from capital, patriarchy, and racism as possible, given their view of people's capacities for cooperation. Emancipation is predicated on people's ability to *recognize* "historicity," the impermanence of domination. In this sense, critical social theory is a critique of ideology, notably the positivist representations of various social laws.

This is not to deny that there is a certain positivist strain within Marxism itself, perhaps even within Marx's own body of work. Engels, V. I. Lenin, and Joseph Stalin developed alleged socialist laws that closely paralleled capitalist notions of lawfulness in their invariant qualities. Engels in his essay "Socialism: Utopian or Scientific?" placed himself within the theoretical tradition supposedly laid out by his friend and collaborator Marx. Nonpositivist Marxists argue that Engels was unfaithful to Marx's dialectical view of history in his attempt to reduce Marxist theory to historical materialism (which Stalin later called dialectical materialism). In particular, the critical social theorists argue that Engels ignored Marx's crucial stress on the dialectical relationship between empirical conditions and human consciousness. Without "true" consciousness of their own possible emancipation, people only reproduce the present in their everyday behaviors. For example, if workers behave as if capitalism is eternal, enacting the subordinate roles prescribed for them in bourgeois economic theory, capitalism *becomes* eternal, constituting what the sociologist Robert Merton (1957) called a self-fulfilling prophecy. By the same token, if women behave as if male supremacy is everlasting, it becomes everlasting, regardless of how objectionable male supremacy is.

In this sense, nonpositivist Marxists and all critical social theorists argue against any postulate of social necessity on the ground that the conception of "necessity" ignores human freedom. There is a strong existentialist strain in critical social theory, going back to Heidegger, Friedrich Nietzsche, and the French existentialists such as Jean-Paul Sartre, Maurice Merleau-Ponty, and Simone de Beauvoir (see Poster 1975). In his book *Being and Nothingness* (1956), Sartre suggested that the evasion of historicity is "bad faith" on the part of human beings who thus avoid their own responsibilities for making decisions. Later, in *Critique of Dialectical Reason* (1976), a more explicitly Marxist work, Sartre indicated that this does not mean that everybody possesses abundant or equal efficacy but only that a view of the social world that altogether ignores voluntarism reproduces the existing society. Of course, some people have "more" freedom than others, given their privileges like wealth and education. But Sartre's existentialism suggests that everybody, even political prisoners and the homeless, possesses an ineradicable core of freedom, the recognition of which is truly liberating in the sense that it can lead to socially reconstructive activities once people join together to overcome their common opponents.

Critical social theory's critique of positivism is optimistic in that it stresses people's basic existential freedoms and hence their opportunities for political mobilization. This critique of positivism is not idealistic or unrealistic, however, for it recognizes that the choices we make are constrained by the past and present—our social class, gender, race, religion, and national origin, all of which inform our personal biographies. The notion that people are completely determined by their social fate is owed to Durkheim's discussion of "social facts" at the beginning of his book *Rules of Sociological Method* (1950), a founding document of sociological positivism. Although Marxism certainly takes account of various social and economic influences on people's behavior and consciousness, Marxists and critical social theorists stress that consciousness can transcend social conditions in the sense that the mind is always free, even if it is highly influenced by prevailing ideologies, including positivism itself. In this sense, people can engage in their own critiques of ideology or consciousness-raising, as the American women's movement since Betty Friedan's *Feminine Mystique* (1963) emphasized: Liberation begins at home, in one's private reflection and everyday life.

Positivism, then, is a form of ideology, as religion and bourgeois economic theory were for Marx. *Ideology* (see Gouldner 1976, 1979, 1980) here refers to any organized belief system that represents social change as impossible, even if it suggests modes of individual betterment within the frame of reference of the existing social system. For example, in post–World War II society many accept the inevitability of capitalism, in return for which they are promised modest personal betterment such as job promotions and abundant consumption. To be effective in reproducing people's conformist behaviors, ideologies must not be sheer illusion but must in some respects correspond to "reality" as people experience it. Thus, for Americans who read the newspaper and watch television news it is very difficult to imagine different, better social systems in light of the ways in which the former Soviet Union—"communism"—is portrayed as illiberal and irrational. Life as middle-class citizens of capitalist democracies know it is demonstrably preferable to life under illiberal regimes, hence validating claims about the inevitability of capitalism. It is not as if ideologists simply conjure up wild claims about reality that bear no relationship to our everyday experiences. Rather, ideologies are subtle attempts to portray the present as both rational and necessary, especially given the apparent alternatives, past and present.

It is far easier to believe that capitalism, patriarchy, and racism are ineradicable, even "necessary," than it is to defend radical alternatives, whether socialism, feminism, or anticolonialism. After all, people have not yet created workable alternatives to capitalism and authoritarian state socialism of the variety found in the former Soviet Union and other Eastern bloc countries. Marx used the concept of historicity to demonstrate that the future is not preordained by the past, to be divined by social metaphysicians who read the past for its supposedly invariant patterns. The concept of historicity did not guarantee a benign outcome such as socialism but simply suggested that the constraints imposed on action by the past and present are not complete and that with will, knowledge, and tenacity, people can break the fetters of precedent and custom in order to realize heretofore utopian dreams of freedom and justice. It takes theoretical leaps of faith to make a credible case for a future that is fundamentally discontinuous with—different from—the present. One cannot simply rely on precedent to seal this case, especially where precedent suggests precisely the opposite, namely, that the future will be a continuation of past and present perfidy and misfortune.

One cannot "prove" that socialism or gender and racial equality are possible and practicable. No science will clinch this case, even the dialectical science of positivist Marxists such as Engels. The future is a risk, a choice, framed by the past, the legacy of which is difficult to overcome. But critical social theorists, even if they cannot prove the possibility of a radical alternative to the present, are certain that the past and present do not neatly extend into the future without any slippage. No societal scenario is determined by social laws, whether capitalist or socialist, simply because social laws do not exist. In their absence, choice prevails, albeit not the unconstrained choice of liberal individualism that portrays citizens as consumers set loose in the cafeteria of commodities and political options.

On one reading, then, critical social theory points out the ample impediments to freedom. On another equally credible reading, though, critical social theory uses the concept of historicity to demonstrate that freedom exists, even if only in embryonic, underdeveloped form, refusing lawful representations of the social universe that ultimately descend to fatalism. This second reading establishes that critical social theory opposes left- and right-wing positivism, renouncing all concepts of social lawfulness because such concepts forget history and renounce agency. One does not have to be a critical theorist to reject the concept of social laws, although most critics of this concept embrace various tenets of critical theory, notably the stress on agency. Certain qualitative sociologists such as ethnomethodologists and symbolic interactionists, who stress the socially constructed nature of society, do not necessarily accept critical theory's critique of domination. What they have in common with critical social theorists is the idea that people create their own meanings as well as institutions.

## INTERDISCIPLINARITY:
### FROM THE SOCIOLOGICAL TO THE SOCIAL

Increasingly, social scientists who oppose positivism embrace various theses of critical social theory, especially as the influence of the Frankfurt

School, postmodernism, feminist studies, and cultural studies grows. Symbolic interactionists such as Norman Denzin (1991a, 1995) blend the themes of these different approaches into a version of critical social theory that not only opposes positivism but combines the traditional descriptive agenda of qualitative sociology with the more theoretical agendas of German and French social theory. The ongoing theory explosion across the humanities and social sciences merges the critique of positivism and certain critical-theoretical themes of social and cultural analysis into an interdisciplinary project that opposes not only positivism and neoconservatism but the nineteenth-century German model of the departmentalized academic division of labor. In this sense, the critique of positivism overlaps and informs the critique of disciplinarity (Klein 1990, 1996), which aims to remake the whole intellectual and academic landscape in ways quite unrecognizable to traditional scholars in both the humanities and social sciences. All of these developments, taken together, represent a new scholarship bridging the humanities and social sciences. The new scholarship springs from various European intellectual developments in social, political, cultural, and interpretive theory since World War II, including critical theory, postmodernism, feminist theory, and cultural studies.

This is not to exaggerate the influence of the new theoretical scholarship. Traditional scholars who accept positivism, disciplinarity, and conservative social and cultural perspectives abound. Yet it is impossible to walk into any academic bookstore or sample any graduate-level course catalogue in the humanities and social sciences without being struck by the abundance of work and teaching in critical theory, postmodernism, feminist theory, and cultural studies. In its reportage the *Chronicle of Higher Education* trumpets many of these themes without necessarily embracing them. It is clear that these developments are increasingly difficult to ignore, even if one does not accept many, or even any, of them. Dissertations, books, journal articles, conferences, courses, faculty jobs, and grant proposals are being produced from within the frameworks of the new scholarship, providing models for students and scholars dissatisfied with traditional disciplines, epistemologies, and curricula.

The new scholarship puts traditionalists on the defensive, especially now that supporters of the new scholarship have acquired cachet and graduate students. With its convoluted constructions and fads, postmodernism is easy to ridicule. In my former sociology department, a cartoon lampooning postmodernism circulated among quantitative empiricists, who do not study postmodern theory but rather react to it viscerally as a serious threat to their hard-earned legitimacy as scientists. Others (e.g., Bloom [1987] and D'Souza [1991]) oppose multicultural theory for politicizing the university, failing to acknowledge that academic life has always been political, even—especially—when people like Weber argued that one could be free of values. Still others (Fish 1995) contend that politicizing literary and cultural criticism tends to efface the necessary line between critique and action. Attempting to avoid politics in the name of remaining free of values is the most political stance of all, as Max Horkheimer and Theodor Adorno argued in *Dialectic of Enlightenment* (1972).

The new interdisciplinary scholarship poses profound challenges to traditional conceptions of sociological theorizing inasmuch as it calls into question the disciplinary identity and territoriality of sociology. No longer can we safely assume that sociology is clearly separate from neighboring disciplines like political science or anthropology. Nor can we assume the separability of the humanities and social sciences where, for example, the study of culture is concerned. (Cultural studies [see Agger 1992a] is a thoroughly pandisciplinary project, bridging concerns of people in English and sociology departments.) This is not to suggest that interdisciplinarity is the death knell of traditional disciplinary identities. For some, interdisciplinarity is simply an occasion for scholarly endeavors across disciplines that otherwise remain safely separated by substance and method. In most universities interdisciplinary centers are gathering points for disciplinary scholars who share common interests in projects such as cognitive science, Asian studies, and women's studies. These centers need not prompt thoroughgoing rethinking of traditional disciplines but can proceed outside of disciplines and departments as para-entities with relatively short life spans (perhaps equivalent to the duration of the grants that support them). I am not "against" this sort of work but simply acknowledge that many disciplinary scholars and administrators who support and even engage in occasional interdisciplinary research projects do not necessarily call into question the fundamental rationale of their home disciplines but rather treat interdisciplinary scholarship as an occasion for getting grants, calling conferences, and producing publications.

In this book I address sociologists and sociological theorists who accept the separable disciplinary identity and territorial boundaries of sociology as established by the founders such as Comte, Durkheim, and Weber and social theorists who believe that critical social theory is a genuinely pandisciplinary project requiring the abandonment of traditional disciplinarity. The insights of critical social theory can inform traditional sociological theory (e.g., in the study of culture and gender) without challenging the very existence of sociological theorizing and of sociology generally. Or as I prefer, critical social theorists can develop a social and cultural theory so comprehensive that it reveals sociological theory to have become overly fragmented and insular. Sociological theorists cannot understand the world adequately without plundering other disciplines and methodologies for concepts, constructs, and data *that render traditional disciplines obsolete.* Social theory broadens sociological theorizing in the sense that it identifies

*the social* in venues traditionally beyond the compass of sociological understanding—in literature and art, popular culture, the gendered behaviors
and discourses of everyday life, the adornments and gestures of the body,
domestic labor. This is not to suggest that mainstream sociology has simply
ignored art, culture, and sexual politics but to suggest that the best ways to
study them are not found in contemporary sociology. The best critical sociology in many universities is taking place in English and comparative literature departments, geography departments, women's studies programs,
law schools.

The broadening of sociological theory into pandisciplinary social theory
involves not only the deployment of methods and topics heretofore off-limits to sociology but also the abandonment of positivist theories of knowledge, which have been central to sociology since the late nineteenth century. Critical social theory not only learns from other disciplinary sources
and methods but applies these approaches in nonpositivist ways, challenging the contemplative and hence conservative posture of mainstream sociologists who seek to discover and describe laws of social motion. Thus, the
transition from sociological theory to social theory has both methodological and political components. A person interested in the social as opposed
to the sociological values total structural understanding, which can liberate
the imagination and lead to transformational political practices, more than
the advancement of a singular discipline. Such a person's intellectual identity is not defined by allegiance to discipline and the norms of professionalism that frame career advancement in traditional academia but rather by a
commitment to total structural understanding, necessarily expressed in
nonpositivist, hence "critical," ways. What is *critical* about critical social
theory is precisely this idea that knowledge exists in history and can
change the course of history if appropriately applied. Critical social theorists do not define themselves in terms of their contribution to the advancement of singular disciplines, within which they advance their own professional careers through vita building and networking. Rather, they develop
total structural understandings that transcend disciplinary differentiations
or, better said, that plunder numerous disciplines and methods for approaches to the social.

In sociology, professionalism has been central to the development of a
highly differentiated discipline increasingly subdivided into specialty areas,
methods, theories, and institutional orientations. Critical social theory is
not opposed to professionalism per se, in the sense that professionalism democratizes science and knowledge in crucial ways, but rather regards professionalism as an inadequate goal for intellectuals, who, according to critical social theory, have a primary allegiance not to discipline but to the
development of comprehensive structural understandings of the social. Professionalism and positivism have gone hand in hand since Comte,

Durkheim, and Weber in the sense that the founding sociologists believed that by imitating the "hard" natural sciences like physics they would legitimize the emerging discipline of sociology in the university. Professional sociologists embraced positivism because they saw that professionalism and positivism have been intertwined for natural scientists, psychologists, and economists. Even today certain self-styled "mainstream" sociologists argue that sociology must become more scientific and grant-oriented in the fashions of the natural sciences in order to gain professional legitimacy at a time when sociology is increasingly viewed by cost-conscious university administrators as a throwback to the 1960s, when American sociologists were involved in the antiwar and civil rights movements. Some argue that professionalism will be the salvation of sociology departments that successfully demonstrate that they support universities with grant money and shed light on useful societal applications in the realm of social and political policy.

I am not "against" grants or policy relevance as such. However, this approach to sociological professionalism endorses a positivist conception of sociological research and theorizing that has significant political consequences. The more sociologists imitate natural scientists in what they take to be their value-free approach to knowledge, the less sociologists can take license in developing large (but perhaps empirically untestable) models of the social world from which they can derive relevant insights for social activism within the framework of new social movements theory. On the disciplinary level, positivist sociologists who seek to enhance their professionalism and hence their institutional stature oppose the "politicization" of their discipline on the ground that this will bring sociology further disrepute in these fiscally challenged times.

This implies that allegedly value-free positivist social science is not already political. It also implies that the most important aim for academic sociologists should be legitimacy—the valorization of swimming in the mainstream as opposed to struggling against the current. Both of these implications can be challenged, and critical social theory does. First, critical social theorists argue that value-free positivist sociology affirms the present social order by intending only to represent its ahistorical, lawful patterns, which are then generalized into the social fate of capitalist modernity. Thus, value freedom is a political stance in that it pretends to eschew values, thus reinforcing the status quo. Second, although critical social theorists also value legitimacy as a way of obtaining political and intellectual leverage, they do not regard legitimacy as the highest or most important aim, especially where it may compromise truth. In other words, critical social theorists value professional competence and institutional legitimation; these are means to an end—critical insight and thus social change. Jürgen Habermas in his introduction to his two-volume *Theory of Communicative Action* (1984, 1987b) argues that critical theory needs to compose itself with an eye toward its legitimation in the university. But this is not simply to attain professional standing, without which sociology cannot claim to be a science, but to gain access to power and influence. As a Marxist of sorts, Habermas recognizes that the Adorno-like posture of detachment is no longer feasible, given the powerful forces of institutional integration and political absorption. But Habermas does not want to be a professional as much as to have his ideas taken seriously across traditional disciplines whose vocabularies he has mastered in order to make himself understood.

To be sure, my erstwhile empirical colleagues did not busily "test" Habermas's ideas—or even read him. His *Theory of Communicative Action* remains an underappreciated work of critical social theory, in spite of its engagements with Parsons, Durkheim, and speech-act theory. But it is undeniable that mainstream sociological theorists have begun to read and appreciate Habermas's efforts to address the relationship between what he calls system and lifeworld, even if they do not share his basic political stance, which derives from the original Frankfurt School's revision of Marxism. Habermas's efforts to address mainstream sociological theory in its own terms have borne the fruit of his recognition and even citation by neofunctionalists and others with whom he is in dialogue. This is at least a modest victory for Horkheimer and Adorno's former student, who recognizes that his mentors forfeited academic legitimacy by refusing to play by the rules of organized academia, Nietzscheans that they were.

Critical social theorists who study the social and not narrowly the sociological seek professional legitimacy in order to gain critical and political leverage. They do not reduce intellectual life to political orthodoxy, as leftists since Lenin have done. Political correctness thwarts thought, whether it comes from the orthodox left or from postorthodox multiculturalists. Like mainstream sociologists, liberals who oppose the supposed politicization of academia tend to conflate critical social theory, orthodox Marxism, and multicultural identity politics in order to defend their self-proclaimed professional objectivity. This is wrong on two scores: First, critical theory, orthodox Marxism, and multiculturalism are quite different when it comes to their conceptions of the link between intellectuality and politics. Second, as I said above, professional objectivity conceals deeper value commitments to the present social order, which positivists attempt to represent lawfully and ahistorically as the social fate of modernity. Most critical social theorists position themselves *against* all political orthodoxies that reduce thought to cant, formula, recipe. The theorists of the original Frankfurt School such as Adorno, Horkheimer, and Marcuse developed their particular versions of critical theory in counterpoint to orthodox Marxism, which minimized the role of consciousness and denied the autonomy of theoretical work. Their version of critical theory argued for the relative autonomy of consciousness

and theory precisely in order to generate political critique as a way of rein-
vigorating class struggle and other postproletarian modes of resistance (or
new social movements, as Habermas later called them).

Critical social theorists responded to the eclipse of class struggle, which
Marx and Engels in *The Communist Manifesto* originally viewed as the
moving force of world history. This is not to say that critical theorists endorsed this eclipse. They identified themselves as Marxists, albeit ones who
took a fresh look at "late" capitalism, which came into being after the
Great Depression and matured after World War II. The Frankfurt School's
critical theory wended its way between an orthodox Marxism that refused
to revise Marxism empirically in response to the expanding roles of the
state and culture and the liberal academic professionalism and positivism
that professed not to be political at all, following Weber's (1946) famous
essay on the exclusion of politics from academic objectivity ("Science as a
Vocation"). The Frankfurt theorists endorsed objectivity but argued that
this did not necessarily require science to abdicate its own constitutive role
in social history. Social science and social theory were to liberate the imagination and thus aid social groups in overthrowing domination and oppression. This conception of critical social science and social theory stands
sharply at odds with the liberal positivist professionalism of mainstream
sociology in the sense that it conceives human liberation as the highest purpose of intellectual activity.

Habermas has taken pains to argue that this critical conception of social
science and social theory is not opposed to what he calls the project of
modernity, which began with the Enlightenment. Indeed, he contends that
critical social theory, conceived as communication theory and ethics, fulfills the project of modernity by further rationalizing social life in ways anticipated but not completed by Weber. Although I have argued that Habermas unnecessarily divides instrumental and communicative rationalities,
much as Kant did, thus restricting the field of human liberation to communicative projects but leaving technology and its domination of nature un-
touched, he masterfully reconceptualizes Marxism in ways that give it empirical and political purchase in the present. Far from abandoning
modernism and modernity, Habermas argues that Marx was a modernist
and that the project of modernity can only be fulfilled in a Marxist way, albeit in terms that deviate significantly from the Marxist and Marxist-
Leninist frameworks of the early twentieth century. Habermas supports the
Enlightenment's program of universal liberation and rationality *through* (a
reconceptualized) Marx.

This commitment to the Enlightenment and modernity should absolve
critical social theorists such as Habermas of the charge that they are Luddites, antimodernists, anarchists. Far from wanting academic life, including
social science and social theory, to be reduced to didactic political educa-

tion, Habermas wants to open intellectual life to genuine debate and diversity, which he theorizes in terms of his communicative ethics. Although the characterization of left academics as intolerant supporters of "political correctness" is largely hype promulgated by 1980s neoconservatives, many critical social theorists are especially hard on purveyors of multicultural identity politics, especially those who derive from postmodernism. (This is not to deny that one can formulate a genuinely radical and "promodernist" postmodernism but simply to defer that discussion until later.)

Professionalized liberal positivists, including many U.S. sociologists, conflate all theoretical heterodoxies, especially where they argue that one must defend the disciplinary project of sociology against the wild men and women who would "politicize" sociology and social science at a time when respectable sociologists are fighting a rearguard action against budget-slashing university administrators. These professional positivists marginalize all thought and research that do not conform to the strictures of allegedly value-free quantitative empiricism. This effaces nuances: Habermas (1987a) takes postmodernism to task; Fraser (1989) urges Habermas and Foucault to be more explicitly feminist. It also fails to recognize that critical social theories embrace rigorous analysis, objectivity, professionalism, even disciplinarity. Critical social theorists differ from professionalized positivist sociologists most sharply in arguing that the aim of knowledge is enlightenment and hence liberation, not the enhancement of personal professional credentials or the advancement of one's discipline. Critical social theorists refuse Comte's model of the hard sciences as a metaphor for their own work because they believe that positivism eliminates historicity and hence the possibility of large-scale structural change. Critical social theorists are unashamed to be seen as political, especially when they agree with Horkheimer and Adorno in *Dialectic of Enlightenment* that the pretense of freedom from values is the most impregnable value position of all, embracing the present as a plenitude of social being and denying utopia.

It is ironic that positivist sociologists in the United States who attempt to entrench their discipline in the university by emphasizing its resemblance to the hard sciences, including both positivist quantitative method and grant-worthiness, also argue that sociology should articulate what are called policy implications, especially when a Democrat is president. Applied sociology suggests state policies in realms such as health care, aging, social welfare, work and family, and crime. Positivist sociologists claim that sociology pays its own way by emphasizing its real-world applications suggested in the narrow technical analyses proliferating in the journals. Many positivist journal articles formulaically conclude with short excursuses on "policy" in this sense (see Agger 1989b for a deconstructive reading of such journal sociology). This segue into policy analysis both legitimizes sociology in the state apparatus (e.g., public research universities) and helps sociology avoid a more radical politics—the notion of policy implying moderate amelioration of social problems and not thoroughgoing change. As well, the discussion of policy enhances the grant-worthiness of sociological research, which has become a hallmark of academic professional legitimacy.

Thus, the shift from the *sociological* to the *social* on the part of critical social theorists who support interdisciplinarity is threatening to disciplinary positivists because it augurs the politicization of social theory and social science at a time when some believe sociology must put definitive distance between itself and its 1960s engagements. The tired stand-up line of sociology's critics that *sociology* alliterates with *socialism, social work,* and *the sixties* represents this preoccupation with the legitimation of sociological disciplinarity and explains why interdisciplinary approaches to the social are so threatening.

The social is accessible to all comers, whether they are from disciplines like sociology or from interpretive disciplines such as English and comparative literature. It is no accident that scholars in these interpretive disciplines are at the forefront of the new scholarship, as I called it above, inasmuch as they are involved in their own political struggle against the canonical literatures of male occidental culture. (See, for example, Eagleton's [1983] excellent theoretical and political introduction to new varieties of literary and cultural theory.) The politicization of the canon in the interpretive and cultural disciplines has gathered powerful momentum in the wake of postmodernism, French feminism, multiculturalism, and other versions of critical theory. The interpretive disciplines and sociology are moving in opposite directions: Interpretive scholars and cultural critics laud the politicization of the canon, whereas positivist sociologists want to vanquish politics. Leading U.S. literary programs such as Duke's are awash in these new theoretical movements that stress the obsolescence of canonical approaches to the study of literature and culture. (Duke's sociology department, by contrast, is largely positivist.) In these venues, politics is not a scourge to be eliminated but an opening to new ways of seeing, writing, and teaching. Suddenly, with the influx of these new European and feminist influences, traditional approaches to "representation" (depicting the world) in both art and criticism could no longer be trusted. Postmodern literary and cultural theory blossomed in a postrepresentational era, precisely the opposite of what was happening in positivist sociology, which clings more tenaciously than ever to representation—achieved through quantitative method—as the supposed salvation of an embattled discipline.

Not all versions of postmodernism qualify as either social or critical theory. However, as Fredric Jameson (1991) has argued in *Postmodernism, or, the Cultural Logic of Late Capitalism,* postmodern theory has the potential for new forms of neo-Marxist social and cultural analysis pertinent to late capitalism. Foucault, Jean Baudrillard, and Derrida make way for critical theories of the social, especially where they make possible the critical analysis of cultural discourses and practices that closely resemble and deepen the Frankfurt School's analysis of the culture industry. And postmodern theory has made it nearly impossible for people in interpretive and cultural disciplines to approach texts as if the "meanings" of those texts could be disclosed to presuppositionless, essentially positivist readings. Postmodernists drive home the point that reading is itself a form of writing, of argument, in the sense that it fills in gaps and inconsistencies in texts through strong literary practices of imagination and interrogation. Few today can approach the act of reading or writing about reading in the same secure way that they could read texts before postmodernism, before representation was interrogated as a deeply theoretical and political project in its own right. (Hence, the representation of primarily white men in the literary canon is now to be viewed as a deliberately exclusionary practice from the perspective of those "others" silenced and ignored by canonical texts.)

A significant number of sociologists and anthropologists (e.g., Brown [1987], Richardson [1988, 1990a, 1990b, 1991a, 1991b], Denzin [1986, 1989, 1990, 1991c], Aronowitz [1990], Luke [1989, 1990], Fraser [1984], Kellner [1989a, 1989b], Marcus and Fischer [1986], Rosaldo [1989], Behar and Gordon [1995]) draw from postmodernism in reformulating both social science research and theory in light of postmodernism's powerful challenge to positivist theories of representation, writing, and reading. However, it is clear that most American sociologists and others in neighboring social science disciplines not only mistrust but deplore the postmodern turn for its alleged hostility to science and hence objectivity, rigor, disciplinary legitimacy, quantitative method, and grant-worthiness. When I chaired a sociology department, I noticed that on applications from and letters of recommendation on behalf of candidates for faculty positions, some of my colleagues would circle words such as *postmodern* and *feminist*, reading these as code for dreaded politicization and antiscientism.

For its part, a good deal of postmodern literary and cultural theory has been averse to social analysis, in spite of its criticisms of the posturing of New Criticism, which attempted to seal off the text and hence its interpretation from sullying social and political influences. But I maintain that one of postmodern theory's most important if insufficiently realized contributions to critical social analysis is precisely the promise of a reformulated scientific method that not only acknowledges the crisis of representation, of presuppositionless writing and research method, but embraces it as the occasion for multiple new forms of writing and reading, typified by what the Russian critic Mikhail Bakhtin (1978, 1994) called polyvocality. Post-

modernism need not eschew either natural or social science if we concede
that method in itself does not solve intellectual problems but is merely one
text of argumentation among many others. Indeed, a postmodern approach (see Agger 1989b or Aronowitz 1988) embraces quantitative
method without fearing its imperialism, especially where theorists acknowledge that method is polyvocal and neither inherently quantitative
nor qualitative.

Much of this discussion will be familiar to postpositivist philosophers of
science (e.g., Thomas Kuhn), who have long recognized that science is in-
determinate and hence frustrates representation. It is ironic that positivist
sociologists are half a century behind these philosophers of science in their
own self-understanding. Positivism continues to be hegemonic in U.S. sociology for the reasons mentioned above (such as desire for institutional legitimacy and opposition to radical politics). Increasingly, though, sophisticated sociological methodologists who read broadly are beginning to
recognize the postmodern and postpositivist challenges as legitimate, if not
ultimately persuasive. They recognize that there are no such things as
"facts" that imprint themselves photographlike on science's journal page.
By the same token, sociology cannot simply discover pure laws, which are
necessarily fraught with indeterminacy or what Marxists call historicity.

Critical social theory draws from the postmodern emphasis on the discursive nature of knowledge. It also draws from the postpositivist philosophy and history of science, which extends from early-twentieth-century relativity theory (e.g., Heisenberg's principle of indeterminacy) to Kuhn's
history of science. Although neither postmodernism nor postpositivism is a
substantive social theory in its own right, both postmodernism and postpositivism inform critical social theory's stress on the historicity of knowledge and science. Critical social theory deconstructs supposed laws of capitalism, patriarchy, racism, and the domination of nature, arguing that
positivism has frozen these social facts into our alleged social fate—domination. Indeed, critical theorists argue that positivism is no longer simply a
theory of knowledge but has become an important new ideology in late
capitalism that counsels adjustment to the everyday, which is experienced
through invariant cultural and epistemological categories as fundamentally
unalterable. In this sense, critical theory makes use of postpositivism in order to supplement Marx's original theory of ideology. Where Marx understood ideology to be organized belief systems such as religion and bourgeois economic theory that close the door on fundamental social change
while providing for personal betterment, the Frankfurt School understood
ideology also to be a representation of the world that collapses given ap-
pearances into invariant essences (laws), precluding critical thought.

Critical social theory theorizes the sociological as a realm of domination,
first mapped by Durkheim in his *Rules of Sociological Method* (1950), in

which he defined social facts as instances of the external determination of social behavior. In defining social facts this way, Durkheim assumed that people's behavior was fated to be "caused" by impinging social forces in modernity. Marxism, the first critical social theory, parted company with Durkheim precisely here: Marx argued that it is possible to create a social order in which people are not ruled by social facts such as capitalism, patriarchy, racism, and the domination of nature. That is, where Durkheim and Comte suggested that we could explain people's behavior in terms of operating social laws, Marx argued that there are no social laws that operate invariably but only historical patterns such as capitalism that can be changed. Thus, Durkheim's search for social laws ignored that history can be changed through concerted human effort.

Durkheim mapped out a discipline—sociology—devoted to the depiction of social facts. He was interested in the apparent cause-and-effect relationships between social facts, which methodologists call variables. For example, Durkheim's study of suicide attempted to plot the relationship between people's religious affiliations and the rate at which they commit suicide. By relating variables (representing social facts) in this way, Durkheim sought laws of social behavior and social organization—in terms of the suicide example, Durkheim discovered that Catholics have lower suicide rates than Protestants. If this sort of relationship held up in other venues of social organization, one might conclude generally that people's degree of alienation varies inversely with their degree of integration into their community or communities. Although his book *Suicide* stopped short of suggesting definitive social laws, his famous model of sociological research, relating the "variations" in variables (social facts) in the way I just described, supposedly prepared the way for the inference or establishment of social laws.

Durkheim and those who have followed in his methodological tradition believed that researchers could come closer to understanding the lawfulness of the social world by accumulating additional evidence about the relationships between variables such as religion, social class, level of education, age, race, family size, and political orientation. That is, through what Kuhn (1970) called "normal science" sociologists would pile fact upon fact, study upon study, within the frame of reference of the dominant paradigm (research literature) of the time. They would thus gradually begin to approximate social laws binding once and for all. Kuhn's objection to this approach is that the piecemeal accumulation of evidence does not lead to major scientific breakthroughs. Only massive paradigm shifts, through theoretical and even metaphysical speculation, create real scientific breakthroughs. Once a new paradigm is established, researchers busily engage in normal science that improves knowledge within the new paradigmatic frame of reference. Kuhn suggests that science (e.g., statements of "law") is historically situated, and thus he casts doubt on the original sociologists' attempts to arrive at invariable statements of cause and effect somehow independent of the particular paradigms within which such cumulative research is carried on.

Marx objected to the notion of social causality because he believed that people can make their own history and thus uproot traditional patterns of domination and determination. Kuhn objects to causality because, he argues, science is framed historically by prevailing paradigms, which may change when evidence collected by normal scientists can no longer be explained within the prevailing paradigm. Both Marx and Kuhn implied that Durkheim and positivist sociologists of his ilk ignored *history*, notably the future, which may be inconsistent with the past and present for either political (Marx) or paradigmatic (Kuhn) reasons. Durkheim appeared to ignore the future because as a modernist who accepted the Enlightenment's optimism about mastering society and nature through industrialization, he assumed that modernity was close to its end point—Western capitalism. Like Comte and Weber, he believed that Western society was proceeding along an evolutionary vector, unfolding from simple and mythical to complex and rational. Although Durkheim and Weber noted the prices exacted by this evolutionary progress, such as anomie, alienation, and the disenchantment of culture, they disagreed with Marx that we could rupture the continuum of capitalist progress, after which all bets were off as to the established patterns of social cause and effect.

Neither Durkheim (in *Division of Labor in Society* [1956]) nor Weber (in *Theory of Social and Economic Organization* [1947]) was completely sanguine about the future or ignored social problems of the present. Each was more acutely aware of social problems, conceptualized as the costs of inevitable progress, than are many later empirical sociologists who dispense with speculative issues of the philosophy of history and instead occupy themselves with the technical details of quantitative data analysis. A casual reading of articles in *American Sociological Review* reveals that apart from the obligatory concluding comments on social policy, most articles are larded with technical and methodological details that border on mathematics. Nearly completely absent are the grand theoretical and historical speculations found in Comte, Durkheim, and Weber.

Whereas the founders delved into the philosophy of history, ethics, and comparative sociology, never failing to keep the issue of the ultimate purposes of modernity clearly in view, latter-day positivists dispense with this speculative narrative and instead engage in a nearly wordless methodological narrative, which rests on mathematical and figural displays. I characterize this contemporary version of sociological positivism as *hypersociologism*, which stands in contrast to the grand positivism of the founders. At least in rhetorical and narrative sweep, this grand positivism resembled

Marx's own speculative perspective on history and society, even if it differed with his on epistemology, ethics, and values.

The sociological founders and Marx all placed great emphasis on history and historical analysis; hypersociologists experience a peculiar amnesia whereby the only valid intellectual past is contained in the last five or ten years of journal citations in their own specialized subfield of investigation. Durkheim, Weber, and Marx had deep and broad cultural and intellectual formations, whereas latter-day hypersociologists are expert only in the short history of their own substantive problems. Keeping up with the literature is all that is required of hypersociologists, who left the large questions of the founders behind in graduate school, in the obligatory courses on theory that, even at the time, appeared to have little intellectual value for their subsequent research careers.

Critical social theorists who broaden the focus of investigation from the sociological to the social want to reclaim history and thus historicity—the possibility of a qualitatively different future. They oppose the deliberate amnesia of hypersociologists as well as their blinkered disciplinarity that does not reward reading and writing out of discipline or even out of their own subfield. Professional apprenticeship for hypersociologists largely involves learning how to use computers in order to manipulate and analyze quantitative data. My hypersociological colleagues shun history, culture, and politics not because they are lazy but because those types of knowledge and experience do not translate well into a successful professional career, which rests on publication in refereed specialist journals and appropriate professional networking and conferencing.

Still, Weber and Durkheim are canonized as sociological founders; even Parsons has been revivified by Jeffrey Alexander (1982, 1985). Parsons is an unlikely canonical figure because although he was not a technically obsessive hypersociologist, his writing lacked the richness and historical sweep of Durkheim, Weber, and Marx. Nevertheless, compared to the number crunchers coming out of graduate school today, Parsons was a sage. These founders are recognized as deep thinkers, although they are viewed with nostalgia because hypersociologists contend that sociology has greatly "advanced" in the meantime—meaning it has become methodologically sophisticated. Although this technical sophistication is hailed as the necessary growth stage of a mature science, hypersociologists recognize that something has been lost in the transition from grand founding sociology to the technically detailed hypersociology of the present. Hypersociologists do not feel that they can "afford" to engage the sweeping questions about modernity, bureaucracy, and rationality raised by the founders lest their discipline backslide into prescientific mushiness and lose hard-won institutional legitimacy.

C. Wright Mills addressed this transition from grand theory to what he called abstracted empiricism in his *Sociological Imagination* (1959).

Lauded for its conception of creative sociological imagination necessary to vitalize research projects, this book is a staple of many introductory sociology courses. Neglected is Mills's biting critique of hypersociology as well as his "plain Marxist" politics (as he characterized his posture in his widely ignored book *The Marxists* [1962]). Mills was particularly hard on the aimless empiricism driven by a methodological agenda that builds careers and enhances what I (Agger 1989c: 70–72) have called the science aura of mainstream sociology. If he were alive today to update his critique of abstracted empiricism, which he formulated at a time when computer sociology was in its infancy, he could strengthen his argument considerably, perhaps even incorporating elements from discourse theory. Discourse theory allows me to deepen his critique of abstract empiricism into a critique of hypersociology, which treats methodologically invested journal sociology not only as *substance* (topic choice, level of analysis, political implications) but also as *rhetoric* (driven by technique, dispassion, the segmentation of literature review into framing introduction dropped after that initial stage setting). Hypersociology, as I call it here, advances the agenda of what Mills labeled abstracted empiricism into a postmodern era of sociology, in which traditional narrative becomes much less important to journal science than the figural and mathematical workings of method.

This preoccupation with technique, translated into the visual gestures of journal science, conjures up the image and aura of scientificity—what is required of writing to be regarded as science. Mills understood that U.S. sociology was losing its original concern with social problems and historical analysis in its drive to become a respectable science discipline. This troubled Mills, as it troubles critical social theorists today, because he wanted sociology to help change the world—to provoke critique, to stimulate social activism. Mills's unashamed political agenda would be rejected by current hypersociologists, who believe that major strides have been made since the 1950s in legitimating scientific sociology in the university.

What, then, is the appeal of his book today? Why do hypersociologists assign it to students and hold it up as an example of good sociological writing even when they dislike aspects of its critique of sociology's pretension to be a science? The answer, I believe, lies in Mills's clear sense of disciplinarity, his view that sociology is worthwhile and must be defended. The major difference between Mills's critique of sociology and my own is that Mills did not recognize fully the disabling, narrowing effect of discipline: Mills thought that sociology could be reformed and refocused. (Of course, as I indicated above, sociology at the time he wrote *Sociological Imagination* had not proceeded very far toward mathematics.) Today there is little reason to expect that hypersociologists will abandon their methodological obsessions, striving for sciencelike legitimacy, and fixation on grants, given their dominance in the discipline. In the late 1950s, it was still an open question whether sociology would move toward science or manage to integrate grand theorizing with its middle-range research efforts. Thus, Mills did not fully appreciate the way that sociology's disciplinarity was narrowly confined to the sociological, which Durkheim defined in terms of people's determination by impinging social forces, hence robbing sociology of utopian efficacy. In this narrowing of sociology to the study of social determination, the potential for what Mills called imagination—and hence freedom—was lost. Critical social theorists attempt to broaden social science and social theory from the sociological to the social precisely in order to introduce a utopian element to social research, suggesting the possible overcoming of domination.

## POSITIVE, INTERPRETIVE, AND CRITICAL THEORIES

This book is concerned with critical social theories. In this focus I exclude consideration of two other classes of social theories, which deserve mention here. Positive theories attempt to formulate lawful understandings of the social universe, following Comte's first sketch of sociology as a science and further elaborated by Durkheim, Weber, and Parsons. In particular, these theories attempt to explain the causal relationships supposedly governing the social world. For the most part, these theories are built out of the findings of particular researches, gathering them together into a generalizable pattern. Particular researches "explain variance," as methodologists call it, in the dependent variable. That is, they try to assess the relative contributions of particular independent variables to the variation in a dependent variable. For example, a researcher might propose to explain variance in the divorce rate (the dependent variable) produced by differences in people's social class and race (the independent variables). Positive social theory assumes that social laws govern these sorts of relationships between dependent and independent variables. Sociologists hope that enough empirical research, conducted rigorously according to the current protocols of scientific methodology, will eventually produce these social laws. Positive social theory assembles these findings into general patterns of social explanation, perhaps, in terms of the aforementioned example, elaborating a large-scale theoretical understanding of the relationship between family dynamics, reflected particularly in the divorce rate, and class and race. Positive social theory attempts to account for the social world "as it is," that is, as sociologists find it.

Since Parsons, who drew upon Comte, Durkheim, and Weber, this has been the dominant mode of sociological theorizing. Merton, Parsons's student, characterized this theorizing as middle-range, indicating that theory does not initially grapple with large questions of social causation but builds up from lower levels of generalization made possible by empirical research. This notion of positive theory very much accepts a cumulative model of the progress of science, drawn from studies of the history of natural and physical science before the pioneering work of Kuhn, who radically reformulated the history of science not as a smoothly linear progress of cumulation but as a discontinuous series of paradigm shifts. Kuhn thought that theorists (paradigm builders) create scientific progress, whereas positivists contend that progress is largely achieved through ground-level empirical research, which accumulates into larger patterns. A name sometimes given to a particular type of positive social theory is theory construction, emphasizing not that theory constructs the world, as a postmodernist might say, but that theory is constructed out of cumulative empirical research.

Positive social theory differs from critical social theory in that positive theory attempts to formulate social laws explaining variations in social behavior, whereas critical social theory rejects the concept of social laws and instead attempts to explain social history in order to gain insights into how history can be changed. Where positive theorists emphasize causal explanation, critical theorists emphasize historicity, the susceptibility of social data to be viewed in the light of their possible transformation. Positive theory purports not to be political, nor to engage in partisan advocacy. It stems from Comte's first representation of sociology as a form of social physics, Durkheim's concept of social facts as instances of external determination, and Weber's strictures on objectivity in the social sciences. Critical social theory argues that all theories are political in the sense that they make far-reaching assumptions about the nature of social phenomena that necessarily imply particular conceptions of the good life. (For example, Marx's assumption that people are defined by their labor leads the way to his utopian conception of disalienated labor.) Critical social theory is not ashamed of its political commitment. It argues that political commitment need not subvert rigorous objectivity, viewing the world "as it is," leading to passionate critique and organized social change.

Positive theorists respond that critical social theory undercuts sociology's scientific legitimacy, which has been hard-won given current academic conceptions of sociology as a "soft," social-problem-oriented discipline. Critical social theorists do not place a high value on disciplinary legitimacy, especially in that they argue that disciplinary thinking is increasingly outdated because of the interdisciplinary nature of knowledge today. As well, critical social theorists believe that they are rigorously objective in their analyses, refusing to wear rose-colored lenses through which they view the world unrealistically. Following Marx's and Engels's eleventh thesis on Feuerbach, critical theorists contend that the aim of knowledge is to raise consciousness and thus to contribute to social change. For positive theorists, the aim of knowledge is the formulation of social laws. Following Comte, they claim that knowledge of these laws of evolutionary progress allows stewards of the state to fine-tune society as it occasionally wanders off course en route to mature modernity.

Although positive theorists are probably in the majority today in U.S. sociology, critical social theorists have been increasing in number since the 1960s, when the war in Vietnam and the outbreak of other new social movements such as the civil rights movement and women's movement politicized a younger generation of sociologists who believed that sociology should play a role in social change. C. Wright Mills's work, noted above, and Alvin Gouldner's *Coming Crisis of Western Sociology* (1970) were important statements of the critical position, breaking ranks with Parsonian-era social theorists who accepted the positivist conception of sociological theory. During the 1980s other important intellectual and social developments in European social and cultural theory, such as postmodernism and French feminist theory, refreshed critical social theory. These European influences on American social theory have broadened the conception of sociological theory into social theory, a topic I take up later in this chapter. Although the social movements of the 1960s waned in the retrenching period during the presidencies of Ronald Reagan and George W. Bush, these European developments in interpretive theory, discourse theory, and cultural theory have provided another powerful challenge to positive social theory and positivist empirical research. These European influences are only beginning to be metabolized in U.S. sociology, as some theorists (Denzin [1994]; Richardson, Brown, and Clough [1992]; and Seidman [1991a, 1991b, 1994a, 1994b]) develop various themes in postmodern-feminist critical theory.

Positive social theorists have been scandalized by postmodernism in particular. They reject postmodernism not only because postmodernism challenges the positivist concept of representation (knowledge and words simply mirroring the world out there) but also because postmodern theory challenges sociology's disciplinarity. Postmodernists argue for a genuine interdisciplinarity of topic and method such that people could engage in cultural studies and gender studies across disciplines as diverse as English and anthropology. In this sense, postmodernism threatens sociology's identity as the discipline that studies the social laws impinging on people's behavior, as first laid out by Durkheim. Finally, postmodernism is an esoteric, sometimes playful discourse that challenges the representational discourse of positive sociology. As much as anything, positivist theorists resent the *strangeness* of postmodernism, its way of turning the discursive tables such that words no longer reflect things. Derrida in particular troubles positive sociologists, as he challenges the positivist notion that words have singular meanings and referents and can be deployed to convey science's intentions fully. A journal editor who asked me for a "comment" on a published article admonished me to write in "plain English," knowing that postmodern social theorists regard all language as capricious and thus use it ironically, dialectically, and playfully. The editor well understands that postmodernists wreak havoc with traditional sociological discourse by calling into question the politics of representation. Postmodern theorists argue that words do not clearly or cleanly represent the world but rather conceal and confuse meaning as much as clarify it, requiring writers and readers to recognize that word choice not only conveys the writer's values but also reflects them.

French feminist theory has been conceived within postmodernism's frame of reference. French feminists such as Luce Irigaray (1985), Hélène Cixous (1986, 1988), and Julia Kristeva (1980) argue that language is gendered, requiring cultural analysts and theorists to take close looks at the subtly engendering effects of words, including scientific ones. The feminist critique of positivist science continues to build. Feminist critics believe that positivism is a male project that reflects and reproduces male values of control and clarity, which these feminists say are inimical to the creation of a culture and language within which women thrive. Feminist innovations in the philosophy of science and methodology are also quite challenging to positive social theory, which has always regarded the gender of science as a nonissue (Reinharz 1992). Although it is certainly possible to develop a feminist conception of science that does not abandon the project of science altogether but rather formulates a gendered version of it, the feminist critique of "male" methodology has politicized methodology in ways unimagined by traditional positivists.

The three most recent versions of positive social theory, all of which have taken up the challenge posed by an emerging postmodern-feminist version of critical theory, are neofunctionalism, rational choice theory, and exchange theory. *Neofunctionalism* is the term used to refer to Jeffrey Alexander's reconstruction of Parsons's structural functionalism in a way that co-opts aspects of Marxian theory and thus defuses Marxist politics. Alexander and others formulated neofunctionalism at a time when the Soviet Union was collapsing and Marxism was rapidly losing legitimacy, both in the United States and abroad. Some of Alexander's statements during the 1990s, such as a review essay on British cultural studies in *Contemporary Sociology* (Sherwood, Smith, and Alexander 1993: 370–375), the American Sociological Association's journal of book reviews, clearly express his studied antileftism.

One of neofunctionalism's particular foci is the so-called micro-macro link, the linkage between personal and interpersonal everyday life and large-scale social structures. This was one of Parsons's main topics in *The Structure of Social Action* (1937) and *The Social System* (1951). Parsons, like his neofunctionalist followers, argued that it is possible to conceptualize both personality systems and social systems in terms of the same patterns of integration, suggesting that social order is simultaneously achieved on personal and societal levels. Habermas (1984, 1987b) takes exactly the opposite position, arguing that what he calls the dynamics of lifeworld and system increasingly collide in late capitalism. Although Habermas addresses Parsonian theory in *Theory of Communicative Action*, he disagrees with Parsons's assumption that personality systems and societal systems integrate themselves in similar ways. Instead, he conceives of late capitalist social structure as threatening the well-being of individuals, especially their ability to formulate shared cultural meanings in everyday life.

Another variety of positive theory afoot today, rational choice theory is borrowed largely from economics, notably the work of Chicago economist Gary Becker (1976). James Coleman, a Chicago sociologist, has attempted to introduce fundamental principles of bourgeois economic theory into sociological theory (e.g., his lengthy *Foundations of Social Theory* [1990]). Rational choice theorists argue that social behavior can be explained in terms of "rational" calculations individuals make about the choices confronting them in everyday life. These "rational" calculations involve the weighing of contrasting costs and benefits. Thus, for example, Becker has argued that couples decide to allocate the burden of housework and childcare to the spouse who earns the least amount of money. This ignores domination and exploitation, instead suggesting that people rationally choose their lots. At an existential level, perhaps it could be said that people choose their situations freely. But this ignores the vast differences in resources and opportunities with which people enter into their supposedly rational calculations and negotiations about feasible courses of action (see Friedman and Diem 1993).

Rational choice theory, even more than functionalism, intends to be an antidote to critical social theory, especially postmodernism, because it implants economic theory squarely within sociological theorizing. This has the supposed advantages of injecting sociology with "hard" economic reasoning and borrowing from a discipline with greater cachet in the university. Similarly, the third variety of positive theory current today, exchange theory, borrows from another "hard" and prestigious discipline—psychology—as well as from economics. A social-psychological perspective owed to the work of George Homans (1950), exchange theory suggests that society can be reduced to a series of exchanges between individuals who, like the actors of Becker and Coleman, pursue their rational self-interests. People enter into exchanges because they seek to maximize their resources, much as economists theorize people enter the marketplace in order to increase their utilities. Homans suggested that people's exchanges are, in the aggregate, balanced, everyone "winning" in their exchanges with others. Exchange theory has been applied to analyzing the contemporary family, with spouses conceived as involved in a series of exchanges that benefits themselves as individuals and the family as a whole. For example, the wife "exchanges" her stint of housework and childcare (as well as sex) for her share of the so-called family wage, primarily earned by the husband. Like rational choice theory, exchange theory ignores exploitation, suggesting that people freely enter into exchanges and inevitably derive benefits from them.

Neofunctionalism, rational choice theory, and exchange theory oppose critical social theory by appearing tough-minded, rigorous, scientific. As well, they draw from disciplines that are seen as exemplars of the most legitimate sciences. As such, they are seen to transcend politics and ideology, hence earning legitimacy for sociology at a time when sociology is undersupported by academic administrators who either identify sociology with the fractious 1960s or believe that sociology has been balkanized into applied disciplines and subdisciplines such as social work, medical sociology, criminology, and social psychology, thus losing its center. Positive social theorists argue that sociology *has* a center, which is positivism—a theory of knowledge that pursues laws. Supposedly, the methodological engine of sociological positivism is quantitative method, borrowed from the positive natural sciences such as physics and biology and from the hardest social sciences such as economics and psychology.

It is crucial to understand that positive social theories blame critical social theory for delegitimating sociology during a time it needs all the institutional help it can get. Postmodern feminists are seen to prolong the adolescent leftism of the 1960s, when students demanded power and sociologists marched against the war in Vietnam. Critical social theorists who borrow from difficult European theoretical discourses are even more threatening than the marching leftists of the 1960s because they speak esoteric languages that make few concessions to the supposedly "plain English" of positivism. But even a casual glance at the leading American sociology journals suggests that journal science is as demanding and technical as postmodernism, critical theory, and French feminism. Journal science is driven by methodological technique, inferential statistics, mathematical modeling, and research design accessible only to expert readers.

Even more menacing than the politics of critical social theorists are the discourses and writing styles of these theorists, which are difficult and different. Midwestern sociology departments such as those of Michigan, Wisconsin, Ohio State, and Penn State control the discipline. Midwestern empiricism, which I also call hypersociology, follows a corporate model of sociology whereby teams of researchers, sometimes at different institutions, analyze large data sets, write grant proposals, and publish their methodologically driven work in so-called mainstream sociology journals. These hypersociologists advance their careers by publishing narrow, coauthored and multiauthored papers that provoke further technical refinements and hence produce additional publications. This kind of sociological research assumes a common intellectual frame of reference (midwestern empiricism, positivism), common discourse (quantitative method), and official publication outlets (*American Sociological Review, Social Forces, Social Science Quarterly, Journal of Health and Social Behavior, Demography*). The busy empiricists who work in this vein oppose critical social theory both because they oppose its politics and because they do not tolerate discursive difference. They ridicule critical social theory as the apotheosis of midwestern empiricism, rejecting its politicization, its abstruse language, its empirical irrelevance, and its mode of book publication.

Although positive social theories do not exactly fit the mold of factory-like hypersociology in the sense that they are frequently not based on data, they are much closer to the concerns of midwestern empiricists than are critical social theories. Neofunctionalists, rational choice theorists, and exchange theorists are positivist and antipolitical and have strong disciplinary identities, even though they borrow from other, "harder" disciplines for legitimacy. These positive social theories often yield empirical applications, especially in the case of rational choice theory, which underpins demography, and exchange theory, which underpins social-psychologically oriented family sociology. Indeed, one reason quantitative empiricists, who normally disdain theory, affiliate themselves to one or another of these versions of positive social theory is that neofunctionalism, rational choice theory, and exchange theory frame ordinarily atheoretical empirical research. These perspectives do not pack much theoretical punch but allow empiricism to be conducted without intrusion by grand theory and yet with the appropriate legitimation of theoretical framing. (Empirical journal articles, especially the most methodologically driven ones, need to claim some theoretical contribution in their opening sections, where they review the current literature in the field.)

Interpretive theories try to understand social action on the level of the meanings that people attach to it. Unlike positive theories, they do not attempt to produce social laws valid once and for all. Unlike critical theories, they do not attempt to mobilize social activism by revealing society to be a fluid field of sometimes contradictory social forces that can be redirected, given theoretical understanding and political mobilization. Whether interpretive theories are "closer" to positive or critical theories depends on which features one emphasizes. For my purposes here, interpretive theories are quite similar to critical theories in that both sets of theories define themselves largely through their differences with positivism about the existence of social laws. Although interpretive theories do not attempt to enter the political fray the way critical theories do, they nonetheless reject the notion of a sociology modeled on the natural sciences. Indeed, they oppose such efforts, drawing from what is called a neo-Kantian tradition that separates sciences of nature and studies of culture and consciousness. Neo-Kantian interpretive theorists believe strongly that sociology should not try to resemble social physics (Comte) but should instead seek to shed light on the meanings that people attach to their actions in everyday life.

Although interpretive theory derives from Weber's attempt to understand social action "on the level of meaning," as he termed it, using techniques of systematic *Verstehen* (empathy), interpretive theorists differ on the extent to which they embrace Weber's essentially positivist conception of social theorizing as an objective, value-free activity. Some interpretive theorists (e.g., symbolic interactionists from the so-called Iowa School) conceive of interpretive sociology as a valuable buttress to quantitative survey research. These interpretive theorists argue that interpretive work can even contribute to lawful understandings if conducted rigorously enough. But other interpretive theorists (e.g., ethnomethodologists, social phenomenologists, social constructionists) strongly disagree with this positivist bent and instead deploy interpretive sociology as a counter to survey research, which, they argue, not only fails to understand the meanings people attach to their lives and actions but also mistakenly models social science on the predictive physical sciences, hence violating the central tenet of neo-Kantianism.

Interpretive theorists such as Denzin and Patricia Clough argue that interpretive theory mixes well with cultural studies and feminist theory. For these theorists, interpretive theory is virtually a branch of critical theory (or perhaps better said, critical theory is a branch of interpretive theory). (Denzin [1992] is a good example of this critical interpretive approach, as is Clough [1992]; see also Holstein and Miller [1993].) Interpretive theorists in the more critical tradition believe that it is useful to link people's activities in everyday life to the large-scale social structures that their action creates (and that necessarily constrain action in capitalist, sexist, and racist societies). Critical social phenomenologists (e.g., Paci [1972], Piccone [1971], O'Neill [1972]) have argued that social phenomenology is an interpretive theory especially useful to understand the connections and conflicts between micro- and macro-levels, tracing domination down to the so-called lifeworld—everyday life as it is experienced by people—and thus showing at once how deeply people are manipulated and manipulate themselves and how social change needs to spring from this subjective and inter-subjective level if it is to have lasting significance and proceed democratically. Marcuse's *Essay on Liberation* (1969) makes much the same point from within the Frankfurt School's critical theory. In that book, Marcuse argued that social change needs to begin at home; if it does not do so, if liberty is sacrificed to the prospect of distant future liberation, then social change merely replaces one authoritarian order with another, albeit in the name of a new ideology. Although Marcuse was not an interpretive theorist per se, his work on the New Left and Freudian Marxism (1955) closely resembles the more critical themes in social phenomenology, social constructionism, and ethnomethodology.

Interpretive theories' preoccupation with everyday life is a defining feature of feminism, which holds that the personal is political. That is, feminists argue that what goes on in people's kitchens, nurseries, and bedrooms is political, at once reflecting and contributing to political and economic dynamics outside the household. Feminist ethnographers (Clough 1994) and feminist ethnomethodologists (Smith 1987, 1990a, 1990b) trace these connections between everyday life and social and political structures, contending with male theorists such as Marcuse and Habermas that liberation must spring from everyday life and remake it. Perhaps the most powerful source of interpretive theory today is feminism, affecting a wide range of theoretical statements in and beyond sociology.

Most interpretive theorists compose their work in ways that richly describe and draw from people's everyday narratives. In this sense, it is somewhat misleading to characterize much interpretive work as theoretical. Like positive theories, interpretive writings draw upon theory but have depth and detail usually lacking in critical social theory. This is at once a strength and a weakness: It is a strength in the sense that it gives sociology access to everyday life, which is not only a vital empirical resource for social research but also a necessary political platform for social change, as both Marcuse and feminists have pointed out. It is a weakness in the sense that many interpretive narratives fail to contribute to explanatory theory; they describe but do not analyze social life. Harold Garfinkel's ethnomethodology is much more descriptive than Dorothy Smith's interweaving of feminist theory, ethnomethodology, and Marxism. A rough rule of thumb is this: The more theoretical interpretive writing is, the more critical (in a political sense) it tends to be. Some interpretive studies (e.g., Denzin's *Images of Postmodern Society* [1991c]) combine these two modes, moving back and forth between explanation and description.

Perhaps the fundamental difference between interpretive theory and critical social theory is that interpretive theorists almost always dispense with the concept of false consciousness, which is a staple of Marxism and many critical social theories. Interpretive theorists argue that it is arrogant for social analysts to suppose that people have "false" consciousness about their lives. They argue that analysts must not arrogate to themselves the right to decide whether consciousness is true or false. Rather, interpretive theorists treat all narratives as having truth value in that they represent people's attempts to describe and make sense of their own lives. For their part, critical theorists argue that this introduces an irresolvable relativism, preventing interpretive theorists from dealing effectively with ideology and hegemony that structure consciousness and thus produce political quiescence.

Marxist critical theorists retain the concept of false consciousness. Postmodern critical theorists and many feminists tend to reject the sharp polarity of true and false consciousness presented by Marx, and yet they do not descend to the sheer relativism of many interpretive theorists, who simply accept as true what people say about their own lives. Instead, postmodernists and feminists analyze the discourses of everyday life (e.g., advertising) as sources of power and control that are in a sense foisted on people, who confront them as inescapable structures of culture and consciousness. For example, although Foucault did not embrace Marx's notion of false consciousness, he understood certain discourses of criminality and sexuality as agents of discipline and punishment that constrain people by limiting their conceptions and experience of what is possible. In other words, people's narratives about their lives to some extent reflect the definitions and discourses of reality given to them. Consciousness is not mechanically manipulated, as some species of Marxism imply, but develops in a dialectical interplay between experience and language that borrows from prevailing conceptions of reality and yet reflects people's own free imaginations.

This discursive formulation of consciousness helps explain why some sociologists such as Denzin merge interpretive theory and postmodernism into a version of critical social theory capable of understanding people's domination and also their opportunities for resistance and liberation. Although some of Denzin's writing deals with people's narratives, he provides enough structural explanation, via discourse theory and cultural studies, to frame his presentation of these narratives in ways that reveal them to be simultaneously "true" and "false." That is, people's narratives about their lives can be read to reveal both the ways in which they have been socialized to accept "reality" as defined for them by dominant ideologies and institutions, and the ways in which they creatively resist and transform these definitions. Like Denzin in his mix of interpretive theory and critical postmodernism, feminist theorists such as Clough and Smith stress that women tell important stories about their lives that can be heard to contain both falsehood and truth, reflecting mystification and socialization on the one hand and their own feminist imaginations on the other.

In this book, I stress the bonds rather than the differences between interpretive theories and critical social theories. Although, as I said above, certain interpretive traditions like Iowa School interactionism do little to contradict the basic emphases of positivism, interpretive theorists increasingly draw from postmodernism and feminist theory to produce sophisticated understandings of the discourses that structure people's lives. This blend of interpretive theory and postmodern-feminist discourse theory increasingly takes the form of cultural studies, which I examine in Chapter 6.

# CHAPTER 2

# The Politics of Grand Narratives I

## Theorizing Postmodernity

### LYOTARD'S CRITIQUE

Jean-François Lyotard's *Postmodern Condition: A Report on Knowledge* (1984) is a useful guide to the central assumptions of postmodern social theory. Although by now there are many treatments of postmodernism and postmodern theory worth consulting for general overviews and critiques (e.g., see Best and Kellner 1991; Harvey 1989; Agger 1989a, 1991), Lyotard's book is a relatively accessible statement of the postmodern position. Lyotard joins other important postmodern theorists such as Derrida, Foucault, and Baudrillard in developing a social theory of postmodernity that represents one of the most interesting and controversial varieties of critical social theory. In the preceding chapter, I discussed the blending of interpretive theories and postmodern theories as a key development within social theory. In this chapter I concentrate on Lyotard, although I outline assumptions common to all postmodern critical theorists.

At the outset, it is important to note that postmodernism includes but is not limited to postmodern social theory. I am interested in postmodern social theory mainly as a variety of critical social theory. Postmodernism began as an architectural and aesthetic movement that was dedicated to intermingling architectural styles, embellishing modernist architecture (e.g., gigantic rectangular skyscrapers that were the staple of Western urban design in the 1960s and 1970s) with borrowings from earlier periods (e.g., Greek, baroque). This postmodern aesthetic movement made certain assumptions about society and social change that provided the basis for the literary and cultural theories of Lyotard, Derrida, Foucault, and Baudrillard. These postmodern writers share a mistrust of the Western portrayal of evolutionary progress as culminating in modernity, characterized by rationality, science, and objectivity. Nietzsche and Martin Heidegger are important philosophical influences on the postmodernists in their critiques of the Enlightenment. Nietzsche and Heidegger also influenced the Frankfurt School's critique of civilization.

It is useful to disentangle the web of architecture, art, literary theory, and social theory composing what people usually call postmodernism into three themes or varieties: postmodern architecture, art, and design, which I just mentioned (see Portoghesi 1983); postmodern literary and cultural theory, sometimes represented by the activity called deconstruction (see Chapter 3 of this volume as well as Culler 1982); and postmodern social theory, which relies on the other two varieties of postmodernism for historical antecedents and intellectual influences but is primarily concerned with analyzing society using tools afforded by the postmodern critique of society and existing social theory (see Ryan 1982, 1989; Dews 1987). Lyotard, Derrida, Foucault, and Baudrillard contribute mainly to the second variety of postmodernism, although Lyotard, Foucault, and Baudrillard have also written directly about postmodern social theory. Examples of postmodern social theorists include Fredric Jameson, Stanley Aronowitz, Douglas Kellner, Timothy Luke, and Nancy Fraser. Within U.S. sociology, Norman Denzin, Richard Brown, and Laurel Richardson have been influenced by postmodern assumptions in their theorizing and empirical work, which largely involves the deconstruction of existing texts and cultural practices. One of the readiest empirical applications of postmodern critical theory lies in the realm of cultural analysis and media studies, a growing movement frequently termed "cultural studies." Another interesting application of postmodern theory is in the realm of the philosophy of social science and research methodology, involving postmodern perspectives on the nature of truth, narrative, and ethnography. This has been especially evident in recent feminist work on gender and culture (e.g., Richardson).

All of these types of postmodern work, and especially postmodern literary, cultural, and social theory, theorize postmodernity in terms of its insufficiencies and opportunities (Hassan 1987; Huyssen 1984, 1986). David Harvey's *Condition of Postmodernity* (1989) is a useful guide to writings on postmodernity, which he conceptualizes as a distinctive stage in the development of modernity. The prefix *post-* in the word *postmodernity* connotes the idea that we are now in a stage of civilization somehow beyond the condition of modernity theorized by most Western social theorists, including Comte, Durkheim, Weber, and Marx. The *post-* prefix further suggests that prior understandings of modernity fail to address unprecedented developments in our present stage of civilization. In this sense, postmodern social theory attempts to theorize these developments, drawing on theories of modernity and improvising new understandings.

According to postmodern social theorists, the stage of postmodernity is characterized by:

- *Globality:* Nations and regions are increasingly interconnected in ways that blur the distinctions between so-called developed (or First World) and underdeveloped (or Third World) nations and regions.
- *Locality:* Global trends impact directly on people's local environments, making it possible to comprehend global dynamics by studying their local manifestations.
- *End of the "end of history":* Modernity, as theorized by proponents of the Enlightenment, is not the final stage of history, issuing in a postindustrial era in which everyone's basic material needs are satisfied and thus group conflict and ideological contest disappear. Instead, postmodernity is a stage of history discontinuous with the smooth path of capitalist evolutionary progress as sketched by proponents of the Enlightenment and by the founding sociological theorists and bourgeois economists.
- *"Death" of the individual:* The bourgeois concept of a singular, stable subjectivity clearly differentiated from the outside world is no longer tenable in postmodernity. Instead, the self or subject has become a contested terrain, with permeable boundaries between it and the external world. Following the postmodern psychoanalyst Jacques Lacan (1977, 1982), postmodern social theorists conceive of people not as stable or singular subjects but as occupants of shifting subject positions.
- *Mode of information:* The mode of production, in Marxist terms, is now less relevant than what Mark Poster (1990) calls the mode of information, notably the ways in which postmodern societies organize and disseminate information and entertainment.
- *Simulations:* Baudrillard (1983) argues that so-called reality is no longer stable and cannot be grasped with traditional scientific concepts, including those of Marxism. Instead, society is increasingly "simulated," conjured, in images and discourses that substitute for people's experience of a hard-and-fast reality. Advertising is one of the primary vehicles of simulation in this sense (Goldman and Papson 1995). Simulations also tend to take on lives of their own, overpowering the "reality" of the things that they purport to describe. Foucault (1977, 1978) has studied discourses of criminology and sexuality as sources of social control and domination.

- *Difference and deferral in language:* In postmodernity, according to Derrida (1976, 1978, 1981), language is no longer positioned in a passive representational relationship to "reality" such that words can clearly and cleanly describe the existing world. Instead, language, including writing, is a muddy, ambiguous medium that necessarily defers clear understandings indefinitely. Thus, people's attempts to clarify ambiguity and misunderstanding simply raise new aspects of ambiguity and misunderstanding, creating an infinite regress that imperils the positivist notion of a thoroughly objective discourse of science. In this sense, the reading of texts (through deconstruction) is a creative activity that supplies missing or ambiguous authorial meaning. This empowering of deconstructive reading changes the hierarchical relationship between writing (no longer seen as a primary activity) and reading or criticism (no longer seen as a secondary or derivative activity).
- *Polyvocality:* Bakhtin suggests that everything can be said differently, indeed in multiple ways that are not inherently superior or inferior to one another. Thus, science becomes one among a number of competing, contrasting, and/or supplementary "narratives" that has no privileged epistemological status (i.e., a superior status as a theory of knowledge).
- *The demise of analytical polarities:* Traditional polarities (e.g., proletariat/capitalist class; women/men; Third World/First World) are no longer viable, given the plurality of people's various subject positions.
- *New social movements:* There are multiple grassroots movements for progressive social change, including but not limited to movements of people of color, environmentalists, women, gays, and lesbians (Habermas 1981b). In postmodernity these movements do not necessarily fit the traditional grid of Marx's bipolar analysis of class conflict, suggesting new theories of social change.
- *Critique of grand narratives:* Lyotard argues that the grand narratives or large stories of history and society told by Marxists and others who derive from the Enlightenment need to be abandoned in a postmodern, plural, polyvocal world. He suggests that these large stories do not adequately capture local and interpersonal differences and variety. Moreover, they tend to imply or suggest authoritarian political outcomes, consistent with their millennial conceptions of history. Lyotard favors instead small stories about social problems told by people themselves at the level of their local lives and struggles.
- *Otherness:* Postmodern theorists argue against the marginalization and subordination of groups, people, and practices most theorists of

modernity consider "other," notably including women and people
of color.

Probably the most important single contention of postmodern theorists
is that progress is a myth. This borrows from Nietzsche's denunciation of
the Western myth of progress, unfolding linearly from simple to complex
stages—lower to higher, preindustrial to postindustrial, eastern to western,
southern to northern, rural to urban. Postmodernists do not scorn the
achievements of modernist progress per se, such as health care, industrial
production, transportation, universal education. Rather, they regard
progress not as a social law but as a contingent outcome of intersecting, interacting social forces that do not necessarily extend smoothly into the future. At the heart of postmodernism is a profound ambivalence about
modernism and modernity—cities, capitalism, global communications,
computers, space exploration. Postmodernists stress both the costs and
benefits of modernity. Perhaps most important, they do not regard
progress as inevitable, spreading outward centrifugally from the United
States to more primitive global societies.

It is tempting to read this concept of postmodernity as an abandonment
of Western values such as freedom, justice, and the abolition of material
scarcity. Postmodernism has been roundly criticized (e.g., Rorty 1989) for
its relativism, its refusal to take sides, and its neglect of objective truth. It is
said that postmodernism is at once antirational and antiscience. Although
these are possible outcomes of a postmodern position on civilization, postmodernists (e.g., Jameson) are for the most part progressive, even leftist, in
their social values. They advocate social change but contend that social
change has been inadequately framed by Marxism and liberalism. There
are intriguing parallels between the work of various postmodern theorists
such as Derrida and the theorists of the Frankfurt School, notably Adorno
and Horkheimer. The first generation of the Frankfurt theorists, confronting the fascist death camps as the epitome of machine-age "civilization," were highly skeptical that the traditional Western concepts of
progress, even those found within Marxism, adequately captured the de-
monic forces unleashed by mythology, which, they argued, had not been
vanquished by the Enlightenment but continued to coexist with the forces
of reason in a volatile admixture (e.g., the Nazis structured their death
camps along "rational" organizational principles, almost like factories).
Although Adorno favored rationality and was politically progressive, he
was ever alert to the dangers of simplistic, ideological thinking that reduced human liberation to programs and slogans. Like Derrida, he stressed
the pitfalls of an arrogant, uncritical faith in reason that neglects the ambiguity and uncertainty of the human condition. Above all, he cautioned
against blind faith—in principles, systems, science. Indeed, one of the cen-

tral themes of Horkheimer and Adorno's *Dialectic of Enlightenment* (1972), their elliptical statement of first-generation critical theory, is the way scientism (the belief that science will solve all social problems) itself becomes a form of myth if it pretends to be free of values.

I remarked earlier that postmodernists such as Derrida and the Frankfurt School theorists had common roots in Nietzsche, who could be seen as the first postmodernist. Nietzsche not only declared God dead; he also criticized impostor gods such as science and philosophy. Although postmodernists and critical theorists do not embrace his notion of a superman, or overman, capable of rising above the mundane travails of everyday life in an act of heroic transcendence, these theorists take inspiration from his dialectical critique of the Enlightenment, which he traced all the way back to Socrates. Nietzsche anticipated the postmodern disenchantment with linear Western rationality, if not the more progressive implications of postmodernism and critical theory viewed as examples of critical social theory.

Occasioned by a crisis of faith in Western rationality and science, the concept of postmodernity as discontinuous with earlier capitalist development is consistent with urban experience today. Crime is chronic; the economy swings wildly from cycle to cycle; although the cold war has ended, renegade nations brandish nuclear weapons and engage in bloody skirmishes; AIDS spreads unchecked; race relations have if anything worsened; homelessness abounds; the gap between rich and poor people, groups, and nations widens. All of these and more are symptoms of a crisis of modernity that challenges social theorists to come up with new understandings of the present and future. Without these understandings, the idea of progress, achieved in a late or even final stage of modernity, would appear ridiculously ungrounded in light of local, national, and global developments. Whereas G. W. F. Hegel characterized reading the morning newspaper as the prayer of the realist, suggesting a stability and continuity of events, today reading the newspaper is an exercise in stoic fortitude, what with the atrocities and irrationalities dominating the headlines.

And these events do not occur only in far-off lands such as Somalia or Bosnia. Packs of teenagers roam New York City's Central Park, looking for joggers to terrorize. Children commit murder. Parents murder their own children. Motorists shoot other motorists. Beneath the level of these sensational events, U.S. society is falling apart. Public schools are bad and getting worse, sites of violence and warehouses of the urban poor. Our cities' infrastructure of roadways, bridges, sewers, and buildings is eroding. Garbage piles up. The homeless huddle in subways and over warm-air grates. The national deficit is so enormous that federal spending to solve these and other social problems has been cut back to the bare minimum. Meanwhile, the prison population grows as incarceration reproduces a criminal class. Virtually the only federal and state expenditure that is increasing today is for new prisons and prison personnel. Violence is so routine that we have become inured to it, ritually equipping our homes and cars with security systems. Women take self-defense classes as the incidence of rape and violence against women rises. Americans buy guns in record numbers, believing that they are in mortal danger, even in their homes. Meanwhile, poverty afflicts over 20 percent of Americans, who cannot feed or clothe their families. Infant mortality in the United States is higher than in most other Western countries. The teenage pregnancy rate is rising, in spite of the threat of AIDS. Black unemployment in some cities is at or near 40 percent. Although certain minorities have begun to ascend the various ladders of mobility, the lot of African Americans is worsening because of both structural and interpersonal racism (see Wilson 1996).

Even the middle class is pinched and failing. Baby boomers have worse jobs and homes than their parents; they can afford fewer children and vacations. The cost of higher education is spiraling out of reach. Urban housing in desirable fast-track cities is beyond the means of the middle class, who are forced to commute from distant suburbs. The stresses associated with making and maintaining families and holding down two jobs in a bad economy are acute for many couples. Time and money are scarce and growing scarcer.

Seen in light of these developments, "modernity" is not all that it is cracked up to be. Postmodern theory addresses disappointment and the resentment it breeds. In contrast, modernity theory always assumed a happy outcome. Today most people dislike their jobs (if they have jobs); few find sufficient solace in their family lives (if they have family lives). Modernity theory simply missed the possibility that industrial capitalism would fail to solve both social and personal problems. Comte, Durkheim, and even the sophisticated skeptic Weber believed that the overcoming of material scarcity would eliminate social problems, thus producing general happiness. Although Weber and Durkheim acknowledged the possibility of disappointment, this was a marginal concern given their overall conviction that capitalist modernization was not only rational but necessary.

Marx, too, thought that modernity would solve social problems and make people content. However, modernity for him was socialism and communism, not capitalism. Although Marx had a much more acute understanding of human alienation than other modernists, he did not doubt that the end of capitalism, which he characterized as a stage of prehistory, would solve people's problems (which he believed stemmed from the alienation of their labor power under capitalism). Although most critical social theorists agree with Marx that alienation can be reduced if not altogether eliminated under alternative social, economic, gender, and race arrangements, critical theorists who derive from the Frankfurt School have a much more ironic and even tragic conception of humanity. These critics of alienation do not tie the end of alienation to the sheer advance of modernity, as if "more" (cities, commodities) will eliminate suffering.

In this sense, then, postmodern critics, even if they oppose capitalism, as most of them do, reduce the utopian ambitions of Marx. With a variety of existentialists and phenomenologists (all influenced by Nietzsche), post-modernists and Frankfurt School theorists believe that life is tragic, issuing in disappointment and ending in death. Critical social theorists demonstrate that this tragic foreboding need not cancel attempts to liberate; rather, they argue that one can appreciate the limits to liberation imposed by such things as nature, the mortal body, and the existence of other people without reducing efforts to bring about progressive social changes that make life more bearable and fulfilling. Indeed, postmodernists advance the quite reasonable argument that it was precisely the grandiose ambitions of the Enlightenment and of modernism that inflated people's expectations about the fruits of modernity and thus led them to experience disappointment when their dreams were not fulfilled. Had the philosophers and social theorists of the Enlightenment been less grandiose, less Promethean, in their ambitions (and in the "grand narratives" they told about progress), people would have accepted disappointment as an inevitable concomitant of the attempt to win liberation and thus reduce their emancipatory aims to manageable proportions.

Given the rampant problems and perils of modernity, it is almost inevitable that people today scale down their expectations as well as abandon the eschatologies and ideologies of universal liberation stemming from an image of the conquest of nature that animated the Enlightenment. Postmodern theorists view postmodernity as an era in which all bets are off as to the likelihood, let alone inevitability, of progressive social change (see Sloterdijk 1987). This newfound skepticism can segue into conservatism and neoconservatism, where disappointment about the aims of the Enlightenment leads to an embrace of irrationalism. For the most part, though, the postmodern theorists mentioned in this and the next chapter are decidedly not conservatives or irrationalists.

## MODERNITY "OR" POSTMODERNITY?

Having conceptualized a postmodern stage in the development of capitalist modernity, postmodern theorists risk implying a clean break between the modern and postmodern. The adjective *post-* is troubling inasmuch as it implies a "beyond" to modernity that postmodern theorists do not necessarily intend (see Habermas 1981a; Agger 1996). Indeed, as Andreas Huyssen argues, modernity can be perceived as already containing a postmodern moment or postmodern tendencies. I think this is precisely what

Lyotard, Foucault, Derrida, and Baudrillard intended, making their concept of postmodernity more complex than meets the eye in the sense that the postmodern is not clearly separated either temporally or structurally from modernity. Marx made the telling point that capitalism already contains within it the seeds of a possible socialism. Indeed, Marx dismissed those he characterized as "utopian socialists," who imagined socialism as a qualitative rupture with capitalism that bore no relation to it but created a kind of countersociety from the sheer will of its utopian participants. Instead, Marx argued that socialism must be produced structurally out of the "contradictions" of capitalism, giving rise to transformational social movements seeking to bring about a new social order.

Marx maintained that what Habermas was later to call the project of modernity could be fulfilled within modernity, albeit in a phase of modernity qualitatively different from—and better than—the phase that preceded it. Marx embraced modernity, although his followers have argued that theorists such as Weber who also embraced modernity did not envision a future stage of modernity—socialism—in which bureaucracy, hierarchy, and state power would melt into air. In this sense, then, one might say Marx and Weber agreed on the fundamental issue of whether modernity is "good" and disagreed only on how far modernity would unfold. By the same token, postmodern social theory does not necessarily oppose the modern (e.g., industry, health care, universal education, transportation, electronic media) but simply the possibility of different phases and phrases of modernity from within its own frame of reference. That is, postmodernists do not abandon the modern so much as reformulate a multiplicity of possible modernities, some of which do not conform to the modernity of the present. Postmodernity, then, is a phase of modernity in which modernity's most acute contradictions, tensions, and tendencies are magnified, allowing us to recognize that modernity is not a monolith that must be embraced or opposed in total (see Agger 1994b).

Thus, postmodern social theory need not pose the modernity-postmodernity relationship as an either-or relationship (although sometimes postmodern writers like Kroker and Cook [1986] appear to do precisely that). Instead, modernity is expanded to include possibilities, both good and bad, unforeseen by the earlier modernists, who had a simplified view of the project of modernity. Weber did not foresee television, the internet, AIDS, or women's liberation, to name only a few "postmodern" developments. This leaves open the crucial question of which social phenomena are deemed modern as against postmodern. These things are not easy to identify, especially where apparently postmodern developments such as global television (e.g., CNN) spring out of modernity (e.g., American television of the 1950s).

One might say that social phenomena, processes, and behavior are genuinely postmodern where they emerge from "modernity" but were not necessarily predicted by modern theorists from Comte to Weber and Parsons. That is, postmodernity extrapolates modernity in ways unanticipated by the original modernists. Whether Marx is a modernist or even a postmodernist is an open question; I think he was postmodern in important ways—for example, in forecasting a possible stage of development beyond capitalism, which until now bourgeois social theorists had assumed to be the economic framework of modernity. In positing a society beyond alienated labor, Marx gave voice to qualitatively new forms of association and institutions that bourgeois modernists never imagined. At the same time, Marx may have been surprised to hear that he was a postmodernist, rejecting the implication of the *post-* prefix that his conception of the future was utopian—unrealizable within the trajectory of capitalist modernity. Nevertheless, Marx's visionary conception of global capitalism found in *The Communist Manifesto* and elsewhere ("all that is solid melts into air," anticipating Baudrillard's notion of simulations) suggests many postmodern themes (see Berman 1982).

Determinations of the break between the modern and postmodern aside (for, after all, definitions cannot do our thinking for us), it is important to understand that most postmodern thinkers do not love or hate postmodernity or view it as something entirely new; rather, they approach it—the emerging present, what Jameson and Stanley Fish call the "postcontemporary"—as a new constellation of problems and possibilities. For example, in his *Postmodernism, or, the Cultural Logic of Late Capitalism* (1991; it expanded his 1984 *New Left Review* article of the same title), Jameson further develops his conception of Marxism from within postmodernity, suggesting to readers that he is neither *against* postmodernism nor *for* it. Rather, he takes postmodernity and postmodernism seriously, as cultural and intellectual developments of our time that cannot be ignored.

In the preceding chapter, I addressed reasons why mainstream American sociologists dislike postmodernism or, better, are afraid of it: It is "different" and can be difficult. Similarly, theorists of both right and left persuasions reject it because it is trendy, endorses the present condition of postmodernity, opposes Marxism, and licenses relativism. Too few approach postmodern social theory as a set of empirical propositions about the social world that enhance modernist social theories, both Weberian and Marxist. To theorize postmodernity, to view it as a distinctive stage of social history at once continuous and discontinuous with modernity (or, better said, with modernities, for there are many) does not require the theorist to abandon social criticism, Marxism, liberalism, democracy, values, distinctions, science, reason, clear writing! Although one can point to postmodernists and postmodernisms that abandon some or all of these things, especially clear writing, these are exceptions to the general rule that postmodern theory is a serious contribution to critical social and cultural theory today that grapples with phenomena simply unexplained by traditional modernist social theories.

Admittedly, a good deal of work that claims to be postmodern *is* trendy, flashy, and insubstantial. There is no escaping that *postmodern* is a buzzword adorning all sorts of cultural, social, and political commentary and analysis. One finds reference to postmodernism in the newspaper and *Newsweek* as well as in exotic theoretical works. It is clear that postmodernism moves products in the marketplace of ideas and fashion. But that is no reason to condemn or reject postmodern theory as a significant contribution to our understanding of the social world, especially where it has been demonstrated by leading postmodern thinkers that postmodern theory does good work in the realms of theorizing and deconstructive analysis.

Although I have written about postmodernism as fad, I, like Jameson, have also tried to learn from postmodern theory, especially where its central insights appear to follow from and enrich Marx, Marxism, and critical theory. Michael Ryan's *Marxism and Deconstruction* (1982) is but one good example of work that allows critical theory and postmodernism to cross-fertilize, producing interesting theoretical hybrids. One problem in writing about postmodernism is that the word *postmodernism* functions as what postmodernists call a signifier—it represents something else, notably a whole decadent, dispirited, disillusioned worldview according to which anything goes. Not only is postmodernism condemned as fad and fraud; it is regarded as nihilist, which makes it seem intellectually disreputable in certain quarters. As a signifier, the word *postmodernism* suggests suspicious motives on the part of the user, unless the user condemns it outright.

One of the most serious treatments of postmodern theory is Steven Best and Douglas Kellner's *Postmodern Theory* (1991). As does Kellner (1989c) in his book on Baudrillard, Best and Kellner manage to deconstruct postmodernism into a historically situated set of propositions about society that can be dealt with accessibly and rigorously. Kellner's engagement with postmodernism, like Jameson's, is seen to signify his conversion, whereas in fact almost the opposite is true, given his rather unsparing critique of postmodern theory as a betrayal of the critical theory of the Frankfurt School. Engagement with postmodernism types one as an acolyte or deeply disturbs self-proclaimed postmodernists, who believe that postmodernism can be engaged only from within its own frequently nonlinear frame of reference.

One problem with the reception of postmodernism, as well as with the reception of engagements with postmodernism, is that people who write about postmodernism are often read to endorse a strong version of the break between postmodernity and modernity. I have suggested above that most postmodern theorists themselves endorse what is in effect a weaker version of this break, suggesting that postmodernity is simply the latest stage in the development of modernity, manifesting some of modernity's internal inconsistencies. It is notable that neither Foucault nor Derrida claims to be postmodernist; at most, they might acknowledge engaging postmodernity or the postmodern moment. Detractors of postmodernism wrongly portray postmodern theory as an ism, when in fact one of the defining features of postmodern theory is its aversion to system, ideology, dogma. In this light, then, postmodern theory is not necessarily an endorsement of postmodernity but simply an address to it. With Jameson, Aronowitz, Kellner, and Terry Eagleton, I take postmodern theory seriously because I recognize that original theoretical writings about modernity, even by Marx, are somehow inadequate to explain and thus criticize what is transpiring today. Similarly, opponents of deconstruction often add the suffix -*ism* to deconstruction, thus giving it the appearance of ideology or at least program.

In examining the writings of postmodern theorists themselves, we find that they take varying positions on the break between postmodernity and modernity. Baudrillard in *Simulations* (1983) appears to suggest that the society of simulations is a qualitative break with societies based on material production and thus on a more traditional Marxist concept of ideology. It is also true that Baudrillard views postmodernity as emerging out of modernity, albeit eventually reaching a point where material production is replaced by simulations as moving forces and thus points of critical intervention. Foucault, by comparison, nowhere suggests that postmodernity is a radical break with modernity. Indeed, both Foucault and Derrida deploy postmodern theory to analyze modernity differently than before. Although Foucault concentrates on empirical issues of social control achieved through discourse analysis and Derrida on deconstructive readings of philosophies that show the limits of what he calls logocentrism, both work within the framework of modernity using postmodern theoretical insights that issue in social, cultural, and philosophical analyses demonstrating how modernity has been inadequately understood by modernist theorists, even Marx. Again, to read these theorists as postmodern*ists*—as ideologists, in effect—is to allow terminology (e.g., the word *postmodernism*) to do work beyond its capability. In positivist terms, to call these theorists postmodern*ists* simply misrepresents their "real" positions. (A postmodern reading of these postmodern theorists would abandon the notion that writings can be "really" read as meaning this or that. All readings are valid; each of them produces a different text under consideration, hence becoming a significant text in its own right.)

For his part, Lyotard (1988) does not embrace postmodern*ism* but takes the weaker view that postmodernity is contained by modernity, which needs to be read in new ways, notably by less-than-grand narratives. This is one of the important ways in which most postmodern theorists, even those who eschew postmodern*ism*, differ from most modern theorists. Most postmodern theorists tend to reject the sweeping stories of history (grand narratives) that reduce the flux and flow of social life to a singular or a few axial structural principles such as capitalism, male supremacy, or racism. Although none of the postmodern writers under discussion here or in the next chapter endorses capitalism, sexism, or racism, none believes that society can be reduced to monocausal structural explanations. For Lyotard, such explanations simplify the complexities and varieties of social life, failing to acknowledge the fact of incredible human diversity reflected in people's differing class, gender, race, religious, and national subject positions.

Grand narratives such as Marxism speak with only one "voice," yet, postmodern theorists argue, narratives come in many voices, classes, colors, and genders. Postmodern theorists disagree with traditional Marxists that people who experience oppression do so for reasons that are largely common, such as their class positions. A distinctive characteristic of postmodern theory is the embrace of diversity in moral, ethical, and methodological terms. In this sense, most postmodernists are also poststructuralists—that is, they reject the sweeping structural explanations offered by Marx. Although postmodernism is more a social and cultural theory and poststructuralism more a literary and textual theory, their overlap, especially in the work of Derrida, is substantial. (Best and Kellner [1991] examine some of these points of contact, as I do somewhat differently in an article on the sociological implications of poststructuralism, postmodernism, and critical theory [Agger 1991].)

## RATIONALITY AND SCIENCE

This issue of the utility of grand narratives in postmodernity leads to other important epistemological questions postmodern theorists raise. In opposing structural grand narratives such as Marxism, Lyotard challenges not only the rhetoric of modernist theories (e.g., the issue of sweeping versus narrow explanations) but also the very project of a social science, especially when modeled on the natural sciences. Although it could reasonably be argued that social scientists' attempt to duplicate the alleged positivism of the "hard" sciences fails to comprehend that philosophers of natural science are now postpositivist in their own self-understanding, certain postmodern writers oppose not only positivism, the target of all critical social theorists, but *all* versions of science, both natural and social, for their attempts to generalize about the world. In this sense, these more radical postmodernists might argue that attempts to explain and understand must proceed only through small narratives that do not extrapolate knowledge of particular situations, phenomena, and events into generic explanations.

That is, certain postmodern theorists hold up to critical examination the project of science itself as a vehicle of modernity.

Is postmodernism antiscience? If so, is postmodernism irrationalist? Perhaps more important, is postmodernism *necessarily* averse to science and reason? Postmodernism's debt to Nietzsche could well lead people to believe that it is both antiscience and irrationalist, as well as antimodernist. In the preceding section, I pointed out that the modernity-postmodernity relationship is not necessarily disjunctive if we conceive of postmodernity as the latest stage of modernity that cannot be adequately explained using modernist social theory. Similarly, even though postmodern theorists reject positivism, they are not necessarily antiscience or irrationalist. Lyotard in *The Postmodern Condition* (1984) suggests that chaos theory could exemplify a postmodern approach to science. It is very important here, as in the case of the Frankfurt School's critical theory, to disentangle positivism and other versions of science (Agger 1976). Although postmodern theory occasionally rejects the whole configuration of modernity, including industrialization, science, and occidental rationality, it is more common to find postmodern theories and approaches to knowledge that reject positivism but embrace nonpositivist versions of science.

There is a strong and growing movement in the social sciences (e.g., see Rosenau 1992) to incorporate postmodern understandings into both theory and research. Postmodern theory and methodology have made significant inroads in anthropology, history, sociology, and political science. Especially in anthropology postmodern approaches to fieldwork, in particular those involving narrativity and interpretation, challenge positivist and other approaches to theory and method that have dominated these disciplines. Far from inhibiting or being opposed to empirical research in these social science disciplines, postmodernism has invigorated them.

Postmodern theory can both criticize positivist method, in this case journal writing in sociology, and formulate alternative modes of postmodern exposition, including the presentation of figural and quantitative analyses. Such literary features as reflexivity, irony, invitation to dialogue, and acknowledgment of authorial presence and values can characterize new, nonpositivist approaches to the scripting of a postmodern social science that democratizes knowledge and fosters critical theorizing. There is no reason to disqualify quantitative social science from its postmodern reformulation as a more self-conscious and reflexive text. Methodology is merely one text, one type of rhetoric, that like all forms of rhetoric attempts to persuade readers of its validity and veracity. Seen this way, method loses the special privilege given to "social physicists" and "social arithmeticians" since the Enlightenment. Indeed, my deconstructive reading of journal science in mainstream sociology reveals that positivism is less an explicit epistemological doctrine in contemporary U.S. sociology than a rhetorical strategy advanced by the lavish figural and numerical displays dominating the journal page in *American Sociological Review, Social Forces,* and *Demography* (Agger 1989b, 1990). The real text of this sort of sociology is not the reasoned analysis supporting figural pyrotechnics but the pyrotechnics and techniques themselves. Suddenly, sociological prose becomes marginal to the powerful quantitative subtext composed according to certain literary norms learned in graduate school and through imitation.

Journals are an important convention in sociology that produce all sorts of value for academic careers. It may be disturbing to those who edit and publish in these journals to view their sacred texts as governed by literary conventions that in their nature could as well be changed or dropped altogether. As well, any approach to method as a rhetorical text and not sheer technique poses serious challenges to positivist hegemony in sociology and other social science disciplines attempting to gain the stature of the hard sciences. But these criticisms only make the point that method is text-, rhetoric-, argument-, and value-laden (see Feyerabend 1975). There is nothing "wrong" with method; it is simply one text among many that must compete to get its voice heard and its arguments (once revealed as arguments) accepted. For example, regression analysis in sociology, elaborately figured and tabled, supports the secret contention that sociology should seek to describe laws—to explain variance, in methodological parlance (see Diesing 1991).

It is true that postmodern theorists are often hard on science and rationalism much in the way that Nietzsche was. But their critics sometimes forget that Nietzsche called for a gay, or happy, science (*fröhliche Wissenschaft*) and not the abolition of science. In the same vein, Marcuse, following his reconstruction of Marxism via psychoanalysis in his *Eros and Civilization* (1955), calls for a "new science" in *An Essay on Liberation* (1969), a cognition that liberates what Sigmund Freud termed the "life instincts" (Eros). The French critic Roland Barthes (1975) celebrates "the pleasure of the text," the way in which writing and reading take liberty with words not capriciously but because words and figures in their nature are "undecidable," in Derrida's terms—they do not fit neatly to things in the world but are already in the world themselves and thus create as well as reflect meaning. Barthes, like all the postmodern theorists, recognized that writing is a strong practice, an act of artifice. Accordingly, language is not inert, found only in dictionaries and thesauruses, but replete with what philosophers call constitutional efficacy. The problem with positivism in science and the New Criticism in literary analysis (see Fekete 1978) is that both disempower the text, reducing it to mere reflection of nature and meaning, respectively. But Barthes's notion of pleasurable textuality can be extended beyond literature to science, much as Marcuse tried to do via a Nietzschean and Freudian version of critical theory.

As for the issue of whether postmodern theory is irrationalist, it is useful to examine what people who criticize postmodernism intend by the terms *rationalism* and *rationality*. Many postmodern theorists believe that they are rationalist, although they would expand the concept and domain of rationality in such a way that their theory could best be seen as postrationalist, not irrationalist. That is, they incorporate elements of Western rationalism but attempt to go beyond this rationalism (without regressing behind it). The Frankfurt School theorists do much the same thing: Marcuse in his reformulation of a Freudian-Marxist "rationality of gratification" that does not pit life against death instincts and Adorno in his critique of Western rationalism's domination of nature. The important issue here, then, is not setting up a clear polarity between rationalism and irrationalism but expanding the continuum of rationality to include types heretofore neglected or excluded by dominant theories of rationality.

Lyotard, Foucault, Derrida, and Baudrillard do not contest the material and intellectual gains Western "rational" societies have achieved since the Enlightenment and industrial revolution. Nor did Marx. But they extend Western rationality beyond its historical mooring to a stage of industrial capitalism that is evolving at such a rapid rate as to make prior understandings of capitalism, both Weberian and Marxist, somewhat problematic. As I discussed above, most postmodern theorists conceptualize postmodernity as a stage *within* modernity, albeit one that requires new theoretical understandings. Similarly, they do not think of rationality as "bad" but only as limited, excluding other modes of cognition, theory, science, culture, and language found both in non-Western societies and in earlier historical epochs. It is not a question of somehow turning back the clock so that we return to a putative golden age; postmodernists and Marxists believe such a time never existed but is merely postulated as ideology. Rather, we need to broaden and deepen theories of rationality so that we include marginalia left out of or denigrated by Western philosophical systems since the Greeks.

Such marginalia include the whole history and culture of non-Western societies that have been subordinated to the West in virtually all theories of modernity. (Although Marxism developed various understandings of nonoccidental societies, such as the concept of the "Asiatic mode of production," Marxists did not fare much better than bourgeois theorists at understanding nonoccidental societies and rationalities.) One of the most interesting new areas of critical theory and cultural studies involves the examination of colonialism and postcolonialism (e.g., see Said [1978] and Spivak [1988]). Such marginalia also include women, gays and lesbians, people of color, nonpositivist epistemologies, and all manner of subordinated people, groups, and practices. In excluding these marginalia from modernist conceptions of rationality or by subordinating them, we narrow rationality too much. Postmodern theory interrogates otherness. In *Gender, Culture and Power* (Agger 1993), I argue that this conceptualization of otherness is the underlying theoretical logic uniting Frankfurt critical theory, postmodernism, and feminism. I propose a unified theoretical logic encompassing these three theoretical orientations based on the understanding that civilization has been marked by the differential assignment of value to central and marginal people, groups, and practices, including epistemological, discursive, and cultural practices. On this understanding, domination proceeds according to discourses and practices that construct "others" as less valuable than members of the dominant center (who control the discourses of value).

Rationality, then, is constructed within a framework from which certain people have already been excluded or in which they are subordinated. The Greeks, for example, defended an active concept of public citizenship, from which democratic theory (e.g., Arendt 1958) has drawn its concept of publicity. Yet for the Greeks, women and slaves could not by definition attain citizenship. Thus, the Greek concept of democratic rationality that sustained the Enlightenment and survives today at least as ideology contains aspects of what a postmodern reading might consider irrationality, notably the arbitrary exclusion of women and slaves. Another example of the perspectival nature of rationality is the way in which Weber defended bureaucracy as a rational form of organization, arguing that modern organizations require hierarchies of command and a division of labor. As Marcuse (1968) notes in a 1964 paper on Weber, Weber's concept of bureaucratic rationality disqualifies noncapitalist modes of social and economic organization, such as workers' control. In effect, Marcuse argues, Weber's concept of bureaucratic rationality functions ideologically where it remains silent on and thus appears to disqualify antibureaucratic modes of social and economic organization that do not require regression behind industrialization. A postmodern reading of Weber suggests that Weber's seemingly objective account of organizational rationality is inflected by procapitalist assumptions and values.

Postmodern theorists have not yet worked out a more inclusive concept of rationality; nor for that matter have they developed an adequate theory of knowledge including a concept and practice of science. Heretofore, postmodern theory has functioned largely as a critique of modernity's institutions and ideologies, including positivism and rationalism. That postmodernists engage in critiques of this sort has led some to conclude that deconstruction is purely a destructive activity and cannot suggest positive reformulations of values and practices. I do not believe that this is necessarily the case, given postmodern theory's potential to combine with neo-

Marxist critical theory and feminist theory, both of which have more deliberate political programs than does postmodernism. That deconstruction has functioned as social and cultural critique does not preclude postmodern theorizing about positive social, economic, and cultural alternatives. That postmodern theorists like Derrida have devoted themselves primarily to critical readings of other philosophical and literary works does not prevent them from developing substantive social theories that contain both positive and negative elements, both construction and critique. In this sense, then, postmodern theory in its critique of notions of rationality that have explicitly or implicitly marginalized "others" suggests the possibility of rationalities that refrain from this sort of decentering and thus serve the interest of liberation.

## THE END OF THE SOCIAL?

Sociologists suspect Lyotard and Baudrillard of endorsing the thesis of the end of the social, which is highly challenging to sociological conventional wisdom. The notion of the end of the social suggests that meaningful social experiences and interactions are increasingly eliminated in postmodernity. Instead, people hole up in their private spheres, into which meaning is broadcast by the omnipresent electronic media such as the Internet that, in Baudrillard's terms, "simulate" reality, which no longer has hard-and-fast coordinates. Thus, the project of a social science is doomed inasmuch as the realm of the social ceases to comprise the traditional institutions of family, religion, economy, politics, education, and culture that are susceptible to empirical analysis but is rather a "simulacra," as Baudrillard terms it—a fiction formulated by Madison Avenue and Hollywood to convince us that modernity has not vanished into postmodern hyperspace.

Media analysis is a staple of postmodern cultural studies, which is premised on this notion of the simulation of the social (see, e.g., Fiske [1982, 1987], Kellner [1995], Ryan and Kellner [1988], Denzin [1991b, 1991c], Rachlin [1988]). Numerous examples come from television, which has been a favorite theoretical target of critical social theorists, including Kellner (1990), Luke (1989), and Mark Crispin Miller (1988). Robbed of the authentic experience of the bourgeois family, in which parents and children congregate around the dining table and reminisce about their days at work and school and thus bond together, family members gulp down solitary fast-food meals and then consume the simulation (imagery) of family from television shows. Family has been a favorite simulation of Hollywood since *Leave It to Beaver* and *Ozzie and Harriet* in the late 1950s and early 1960s. *The Waltons* and *The Cosby Show* dominated the 1970s and 1980s. All of these shows televised an idealized image of happy family life into living rooms in which the idea of family was being assailed from all sides. Instead of serving as havens in a heartless world (Lasch 1977), families were being torn apart by expectations they simply could not fulfill. Divorce, desertion, spouse and child abuse, careerism, time pressure, infertility, and geographic mobility all undercut the bourgeois family at a time when people increasingly want the family to provide them with satisfactions they do not gain in the workplace. Thus, television and movies simulate family for people who watch together but do not experience the "reality" of family firsthand.

The end of the social, in this case the family, is at once evidenced by its simulation (e.g., heartwarming situation comedies and dramas about fictive families) and accelerated by it. Although there is nothing inherently wrong with television from the vantage of critical social theory, television falsely compensates people for experiences not attained in the "real" world. As narcotic, television leaves people empty, even though it helps companies sell products and keeps people off the streets and thus out of trouble. Postmodern proponents of cultural studies do not disdain popular culture, as the Frankfurt theorists sometimes appeared to do, but on the contrary take it seriously, both as a source of discipline and possible critical insight. Ryan and Kellner's important book *Camera Politica* (1988) demonstrates the liberating insights afforded by Hollywood film. The original Frankfurt School's notion of the "culture industry," although still apt in an era of the end of the social, is overly mechanical and elitist. Popular culture can be reformulated from below: Community television stations, small presses, progressive newspapers and magazines, feminist film, and even books of critical theory written accessibly demonstrate that the popular is a relevant political venue at a time when cultural politics matters more than ever.

In this light, then, I prefer to treat the notion of the end of the social as a hypothesis and not a thesis—something to be investigated and not assumed. The postmodern notion of the end of the social, like the Frankfurt School's (Horkheimer 1974) notions of the decline of the individual and eclipse of reason, describes a tendency rather than an iron law. There *is* a tendency for social action to be replaced by privatized experience, for (in Habermas's terms) the system to dominate people's lifeworlds. The public sphere, valorized by the Greeks (albeit leaving out women and slaves), is increasingly obliterated by centralized institutions of capital, culture, and control whose long arms invade not only our homes and lives but our experiences and imaginations. This was an argument Marcuse forcefully made, albeit without postmodern phrasings, in his *One-Dimensional Man* (1964).

The strong version of the idea of the end of the social would rob sociology and social science generally of any subject matter. If people did not participate in activities situated within public institutions such as family, economy, and politics, sociology's traditional assumptions about how these and other institutions influence behavior, impart values, and afford meaning would have to be abandoned. Seen in this light, the postmodern thesis of the end of the social would put a whole discipline out of business. But I believe that most postmodern theorists treat the concept of the end of the social hypothetically, as a set of tendencies possessing a certain momentum that can be reversed. In large measure, the concept of the end of the social responds to the new and unprecedented ways in which global postmodern media of information have displaced traditional institutions like family, religion, and education as sources of meaning. Of course, Weber warned about precisely this development when he talked about the "disenchantment of the world" by rationality and science, lamenting (but treating as inevitable) the loss of meaning occasioned by thoroughgoing social rationalization. In this sense, it could be said that Weber anticipated postmodernity.

Weber helped to found sociology, even though he predicted the growing disenchantment of the world that postmodernists call the end of the social. Marx, too, anticipated the growing rationalization of the world in his concept of commodity fetishism, which later Marxists such as Lukacs (1971) termed "reification"—the reduction of human relations to relations between objects. Like Weber, Marx believed that this tendency toward reification could be reversed, although, unlike Weber, he argued that only a socialist revolution would begin to effect this reversal. (Weber theorized that capitalist bureaucratization was inevitable—"rational," as he termed it.) Neither Weber nor Marx foresaw the extent to which the social—human initiative, shared meaning, public discourse—could be eliminated through what Habermas later called "the colonization of the lifeworld." Marx was closer to Habermas's understanding of the end of the social, which did not quite approximate the strong postmodern version of the thesis. Of course, there is variation in the extent to which theorists of modernity emphasize alienation, privatization, and the loss of meaning, ranging from Durkheim at one pole to Baudrillard at the other.

A key implication of the idea of the end of the social is the abandonment of structural "narratives" such as liberalism and Marxism that purport to explain all manner of social phenomena. Instead, people are seen as dispersed into a wide variety of subject positions from which they speak polyvocally about their experiences and meanings. One cannot talk of "society," "institutions," "structure," or "ideology" as if these large abstractions have existences apart from individuals. This idea of the end of the social resembles poststructural critiques of structuralism, which emerge in many ethnographies of social life from the vantages of people's multiple class, race, and gender subject positions. Postmodern proponents of the end of the social do not necessarily agree that sociology must abandon all narratives about social life once it abandons structural narratives. Postmodern social science on this view would replace the disengaged analytical voice of the grand narrator with the engaged, experiential voices of small narrators ensconced in everyday life.

Indeed, scientific sociologists who embrace the concept of social structure as well as the "grand" scope of sociological narratives would probably balk at the idea that science is a narrative at all. To call science a narrative, as all postmodernists would do, is to reduce science to a prescientific storytelling that enjoys no epistemological privilege. For their part, postmodernists do not think that they abandon sociology simply because they replace grand narrator (structural explanation) with small narrator (experiential ethnography). They view the "small" sociological discourse *as* sociology, indeed as superior to the abstract analytical sociology that replaces actors and experience with structures and functions. Indeed, this has been the thrust of a host of phenomenologically and discursively oriented critiques of structural sociologies since Harold Garfinkel published *Studies in Ethnomethodology* in 1967. Ethnomethodology, social phenomenology, social constructionism, and symbolic interactionism all embrace the small narrator, albeit without necessarily using postmodern terminology.

Seen in this way, the idea of the end of the social need not scandalize sociologists if those sociologists acknowledge ethnomethodological alternatives to structural sociology. Garfinkel has not been as threatening to mainstream sociologists as postmodernists both because Garfinkel wrote relatively accessible prose and because he spent more time elaborating his new method of sociological analysis than he did criticizing the very idea of a structural social science (although his implication was quite clear to those who paused to listen). Ethnomethodologists and phenomenologists can still be found in U.S. sociology departments, but most of them have adopted the identity of postmodernism, especially those who are feminists and do work on gender. Many feminist sociologists (e.g., Stacey [1990]) deploy postmodern approaches to the study of gender, rejecting grand (male) narratives in favor of small (female) ones and still retaining a sociological identity. The question of whether one's work is genuinely sociological depends on the values, both political and epistemological, of the reader. Anti-postmodern sociologists who reject the idea of the end of the social, and with it the replacement of grand with small narrators, privilege a particular, typically positivist version of structural sociological explanation. Postmodern sociologists argue that their own narratives are sociological, albeit different from traditional Weberian, Parsonian, and even Marxian narratives.

The guardians of disciplinary sociology want to control the definition of appropriate sociology in order to keep outsiders out. At present there is an increasingly tense battle being waged in "mainstream" sociology over the nature of the sociological identity (see Lemert 1995). Postmodern sociologists, many of whom are feminists, critical theorists, and proponents of cultural studies, challenge sociologies of modernity. Postmodern "voices" are becoming louder, threatening positivists as never before (Seidman 1994a, 1996). At stake is the definition of what constitutes a legitimate science. Positivists cling to a narrow, causal, structural version of science because they fear losing hard-won disciplinary legitimacy. They oppose postmodernism because they think it would imperil their scientific legitimacy and thus cause sociology to lose ground to harder disciplines, as I discussed in my opening chapter. Although positivists still control sociology in the United States, their hold is weaker than even ten years ago, largely because the postmodern challenge has become compelling. In this chapter I have argued that postmodern theory does not necessarily abandon science but reformulates it in terms appropriate to the "end of the social" in postmodernity. Indeed, in this way postmodern theory and research constitute an important version of critical social theory, notably in its critique of positivist assumptions about the role and voice of the narrator.

# CHAPTER 3

# The Politics of Grand Narratives II

## From Derrida to Difference Theory

### DERRIDEAN DIFFERENCE

In the preceding chapter, I examined Lyotard's critique of grand narratives as a way of defending the notion that postmodernism offers a powerful version of critical social theory. I addressed some of the theoretical contributions of postmodernism. Finally, I argued that postmodern theory does not deny the scientific project of sociology and other social sciences, especially if the concept of the "end of the social" is treated as a working hypothesis. In this chapter I further explore contributions of postmodern theory, especially in the realm of multiculturalism and difference theory, one of the most powerful articulations of postmodern themes.

I begin this chapter by exploring Derrida's (1973, 1982, 1986, 1988) contribution to social and cultural theory, demonstrating the connection between his epistemological critiques and what I (Agger 1994a) call difference theory. I then discuss Foucault's (1972, 1980) contributions to difference theory and identity politics in light of my examination of postmodernism's essentially neoliberal post-Marxist politics. I contend that postmodern difference theory underpins what is typically called multiculturalism, which I treat as the academic and curricular manifestation of certain key postmodern tenets regarding narrativity, new social movements, and the trinity of class/race/gender. I rejoin this theme again in Chapter 8, where I examine the empirical applicability of critical social theory.

Derrida's main contribution to philosophy is his criticism of what he calls the "metaphysics of presence," which, he argues, began with Plato's privileging of speech over writing. Although this is an obscure foundation of Derrida's philosophy that has been challenged for its historical and philosophical inaccuracy, it is a heuristic device Derrida uses to establish important claims about—and against—Western philosophy. Derrida argues that the metaphysics of presence (which is virtually synonymous with positivism) falls victim to logocentrism, a privileging of oral speech over writing. Derrida argues that logocentrism is wrongheaded because it implies that through oral speech and other rationalist epistemological techniques such as science, the knower can achieve perfectly lucid knowledge of the world, which in effect becomes present to the knower. Through oral speech (reason, science, etc.), one can communicate these findings without ambiguity inasmuch as the person with whom one is speaking (on this model of oral speech) can hear one speak and ask for clarifications, leading to complete understanding. Logocentric theorists of knowledge do not doubt that one can use languages, including writing, science, and mathematics, that convey these lucid and complete understandings of the world (even if one moves from speech to writing).

Derrida suggests that no language, either spoken or written, is a perfectly transparent vehicle for conveying meaning. Instead, language utilizes dichotomies, based on a generic dichotomy of "presence" and "alterity," that simplify the complexity of reality and conceal secret hierarchies. When people pose these apparently clean dichotomies, they define alterity in terms of presence and thus subordinate alterity, albeit secretly. For example, the dichotomy of masculinity/femininity defines femaleness in terms of its difference from (alterity to) maleness, which in effect becomes the master term. Women are not-men, not only different from and subordinate to men but derived from them. Once one confronts these dichotomies in language, one recognizes that these apparently clean and exhaustive dichotomies fail to do justice to alterity, or otherness, because they define alterity only in terms of its absence (or lack) with respect to presence—here, femaleness with respect to maleness (see Weedon 1987; Sedgwick 1990).

And it is not only that language fails to escape these dichotomies that obscure otherness: Following the linguist Saussure (1983), Derrida argues that language is essentially a system of "signifiers" (symbols) that acquire their meaning not from their correspondence to a world they purport to represent but only in terms of their internal relations of "difference." Thus, the word *cat* has meaning not with reference to fuzzy, four-legged beasts who are domesticated as house pets; after all, one could call these beasts "fish" or "apples." Rather, *cat* has meaning only in reference to other signifiers (e.g., *dog*) from which it differs. This understanding of the inherent instability and arbitrary qualities of language robs logocentric discourses such as reason and science of the ability cleanly to represent discrete objects in the world, to which they have a clear and stable connection. Meaning is a product of linguistic difference rather than of language's representational correspondence to the world. Thus, meaning is rendered problematic and, with it, the ambition of Western logocentrism to create a rational language and knowledge that achieves perfect "presence" before the world and thus conveys meaning completely and without distortion.

Derrida underpins difference theory in the sense that his epistemological critique of Western philosophy and theory depends on the notions of difference and deferral as well as undecidability, all of which I explore here. *Difference* characterizes people's attempts in speech and writing to differentiate the meanings of various "signifiers." That is, words and concepts acquire meaning only in relational reference to other words and signifiers that convey meaning differently from them. For example, the cultural notion of masculinity (see Pleck 1981) holds meaning only inasmuch as masculinity is differentiated from the not- or nonmasculine, notably the feminine (which, for its part, acquires significance only in relation to its difference from the masculine). Thus, sociologically, the very notions of man and woman stand in relation to each other and have meaning only with reference to the other term. To be a "real man" is to be nonfeminine. To be a "real woman" is to be nonmasculine. Seen in this way, manhood and womanhood are not characterized by invariant biological or social essences but only in terms of what they are *not*, which is "other" to them. In our patriarchal culture, men are dominant over women, which means that gender difference tends to be characterized not only by difference but by inequality (see Lorber 1994). That is, to be a man has priority over being a woman, which is historically and culturally defined by the absence of male qualities (e.g., for Freud, by women's lack of a penis). By deconstructing the different or differential meanings of terms such as *man* and *woman*, we can uncover different distributions and relations of power between occupants of the different subject positions called "men" and "women."

*Deferral* refers to the way in which the definition of terms (such as *man* and *woman*) is never fixed or stable but elusive, given the "deferring" as well as "differing" nature of language. For example, in attempting to define a term such as *deconstruction*, the clarification of the meaning of the term necessarily takes place through language that itself needs to be deconstructed. Thus, definitions achieve clarification at the price of requiring new clarifications. According to Derrida, deferral is a feature of language inasmuch as language never lays itself open to definitive, final understandings but remains continually elusive. Understandings achieved through words create new problems of meaning, for which the only solution is more language. This is no lasting solution, given language's indeterminacy, ambiguity, even opacity.

This leads to Derrida's third central term, *undecidability*, which refers to the lack of any privileged textual vantage from which these problems of meaning can be permanently solved—outside of language, as it were. This concept of undecidability powerfully dislodges the argument for pure objectivity, or value freedom, as theorists of knowledge call it. Derrida argues against every absolutism that pretends to resolve issues of meaning and truth through discourses that do not court the confusions of difference and deferral. Every philosophical system is undecidable in the sense that its root terms and concepts are not impervious to deconstructions that unearth their assumptions and ambiguities. Every system, no matter how apparently unassailable by deconstructive excavation, is circular in the sense that one must make certain arbitrary assumptions in order for its reasoning to unfold. "Facts" are never cleanly or wholly represented to the eye of knowledge because the account of facts, with which positivists hope to ground their knowledge, necessarily proceeds through languages (including methodology) that are never free of ambiguity, difference, and deferral. Positivism attempts to replace language with mathematics but fails, inasmuch as every act of representation, including mathematics, necessarily assumes certain things that it cannot subject to interrogation outside of its own language game, as Ludwig Wittgenstein (1976) called it.

Philosophical systems are undecidable in their own terms. They suppress various assumptions and problems in order to get on with the business of analysis and argument. This book, for example, is necessarily undecidable in the sense that it does not discuss each and every one of the literary conventions (tropes) I use to guide my assumptions and political interests. Nor do I cite every possible source on each theoretical orientation. Nor do I consider every problem with each theory nor suggest all of their possible empirical applications. Readers may disagree with my interpretations of the theories in question—even, here, with my account of Derrida. For me to tackle every single one of these issues would make this a longer book than any publisher would publish. Indeed, I would never finish writing it because I would always find a problem to be addressed, a caveat to be appended, a term to be defined and refined. Writers hope to anticipate aspects of the undecidability of their arguments in order to lay bare the theoretical logic underlying their work, being as clear as possible about their meanings and about the possibility that they may be misread or misunderstood. But this becomes a process of infinite regress, a vain search for a foundation of argument and reasoning so solid, so unassailable, that everyone will agree that it represents a zero point from which no regress is possible or necessary.

Theories of interpretation have been notoriously unsuccessful at stipulating interpretive approaches that "solve" undecidability, hence producing definitive readings. Biblical exegesis occupied theologians and philosophers concerned to explain what the Bible "really" meant. Interpretive differences caused such serious conflicts that new sects and churches were founded on their basis and holy wars fought. Hermeneutics, or the study of interpretation, is an important philosophical outgrowth of literary theory, beginning with Bible study. Scholars such as Hans-Georg Gadamer (1975) have devoted whole careers to establishing the grounds on which interpretation may be conducted and disputes settled. Indeed, Habermas (1971, 1992) elaborates his critical theory in part with reference to developments in hermeneutics, emerging in his important debate with Gadamer about the nature of truth and interpretive method (see Teigas 1995).

Derrida attempts to settle hermeneutic problems by suggesting that they are in principle unresolvable, once we appreciate the undecidable nature of writing. The principle of deconstruction, as Derrideans call it, suggests that all texts unravel once subjected to careful enough probing of their linguistic, philosophical, and ethical lacunae—omissions, blind spots, glosses, suppressions. Although it is widely thought that deconstruction is simply a method for analyzing texts, it is really Derrida's notion that all texts "deconstruct" themselves by engaging inevitably in literary acts of omission, glossing, and suppressing. Deconstruc*tion* is the interpretive activity bringing these self-deconstructing moments of texts to light; Derrideans argue that deconstruction occurs at the level of texts' *subtexts*, the underlying or underneath writing that never quite surfaces and that contains evidence of texts' undecidability—questions unasked or unanswered, problems not posed, assumptions covered over or glossed.

One problem with viewing deconstruction as interpretive method is that it may imply that deconstructed texts are in fact purged of their muddiness and undecidability through deconstructive technique. But Derrida is saying more that texts deconstruct (themselves) than that they can be deconstruc*ted* by readers, although both seem to be true in light of his own assumptions about difference, deferral, and undecidability. Deconstruction is a property of all texts, including ones that purport to deconstruct others' arguments. The once-deconstructed text still deconstructs, albeit in ways different from the way in which it first deconstructed. For example, my attempt to interpret Derrida may lay bare things he did not say (but assumed), and yet I need to be deconstructed, too, for my own silences and segues. A book that purports to explain critical social theories itself needs to be explained, which is what will happen when teachers teach it and students study it. There is no *Urtext*, no foundational writing, that will make such primers unnecessary because, as I said, such a text could not be completed, hence published, given the infinite regression involved in explaining "everything" in terms that do not trade on "everything."

Lovers of truth, clarity, and plain language may despair of ever getting at this *Urtext* beyond which interpretation becomes unnecessary (see Gellner

1959). They suppose that at a certain point we can stop debating the meanings of words and simply get on with analysis, including sociological analysis. Although we can never stop debating and deconstructing the meanings of words, at some point we can act *as if* we can stop debating these meanings, even if that pretense is false. For example, this book is being written in such a way that it will not need elaborate interpretations by learned scholars who translate my prose into a clearer, less deconstructible one. I recognize that Derrida is difficult for most sociologists and that my goal is to make him simpler and then to demonstrate his empirical applicability (e.g., see Rosenau 1992). My discussion of him does not assume much prior knowledge about Derrida, although this is not to say that this book does not assume certain prior knowledge, for example, about the nature of Marxism, sociological theory, sociology as a discipline, the nature of academic life, the English language, and a certain vocabulary (see Bourdieu, Passeron, and de Saint Martin 1994).

Positivist methodologists suppose that we can cut through these quandaries of undecidability by subjecting our concepts to "empirical testing." A former colleague lamented that my work did not "test" deconstructive concepts through survey research. But Derrida's point is that empirical testing is already undecidable in the sense that it is a self-deconstructing nest of conventions, glosses, and subtexts that solves some problems of meaning but in the process creates others. For example, empirical elaboration of concepts used in this book might make issues clearer for sociologists who do quantitative research. But empirical testing, whatever that might mean, would surely muddy things for readers such as I, who view the pages of journal science as exotica. Reading reads in terms of what it knows, although it learns from writing and thus is itself transformed. Derrida believes that writings produce readings just as readings produce writings in their own images, that is, in terms of the conventions they adopt in order to make themselves understood or to understand. For example, some readers may find this chapter very puzzling, whereas they found the prior and following chapters quite clear, requiring little further explication. They may understand this in terms of their own prior understandings and backgrounds, or they may blame this on the clarity of my exposition and commentary. They may even blame (or praise) Derrida! In any case, nothing will automatically solve the problem of meaning apart from more attempts at meaning.

Anglo-American positivist philosophy has tried to solve the problem of meaning either with mathematics or with clarity, whatever that might mean (Whitehead and Russell 1962). This is yet another pursuit of an *Urtext* that Derrida would ridicule as undecidable. Neither method nor a thesaurus solves intellectual problems, except spuriously, in terms of the prevailing conventions of the moment. Accessibility is not a good philosophical rule of thumb inasmuch as readers come to texts with different backgrounds and dispositions. Graduate students in English and philosophy will treat a discussion of Derrida much differently than will sociologists trained in Durkheim and Weber, let alone quantitative method. Sociologists might simply declare Derrida irrelevant to sociology, whereas philosophers interested in Continental philosophy or humanists interested in literary and cultural theory might accept Derrida as a relevant and even conventional topic but not understand why a sociologist would want to discuss him or to assess his relevance for sociology.

Thus, one would conclude from a Derridean perspective that *there are many Derridas*, not the singular one represented by his books (or published interpretations of him). There are as many Derridas as there are readers, which does not mean that every Derrida is as good as every other, for all purposes. One can still evaluate readings of Derrida in terms of their interpretive competence, although "competence" is an undecidable text and not a criterion that stands on its own, outside of language and perspective. A competent sociological exposition of Derrida might differ from a competent literary-theoretic exposition of his work. The multiplicity of Derridas does not necessarily confound interpretation if readers and writers can accept the simultaneous possibility of objectivity and undecidability. There *is* a Derrida who lives and works in France and has a certain literary history and politics but who eludes any particular text by or about him. Readers frustrated by the multiplicity of Derridas might have wanted to ask *him* to explicate himself, and that would certainly have provided an interesting opportunity for his own version of himself, adding to his oeuvre. But even that would not solve the riddle of Derrida, for his account of himself and of his meaning would be no more decidable, no more clairvoyant, than any other account. One would still labor to penetrate his self-analysis, grappling with its ambiguities and ellipses. At a certain level, his own account cannot be trusted.

My argument here is that Derrida's analysis of difference can be put to the uses of critical social theory where difference implies a political and ethical agenda of the tolerance of differences as well as a theoretical logic that does not privilege a singular theoretical logic above all others (see Brown 1987). Rather, a Derridean critical theory would attempt to understand the multiplicity of oppressions in terms of the voices of their narrators while recognizing that these narrators tell stories that are themselves undecidable—not necessarily "the last word." Derrida does not privilege the voices of oppressed narrators over elite narrators (such as theorists) because, for him, narration is narration—that is, all narratives enjoy the same susceptibility to deconstructing and thus being deconstructed. At the same time, Derrida does not privilege elite narratives over the narratives produced by the oppressed (see Freire 1970), as theorists of modernity have almost always done. Derrida might say that all narratives provide insight into what is happening to people and why, as well as insight into their modes of false consciousness. (A Derridean would probably not use the term *false consciousness* because it implies a singular true consciousness, but he certainly does provide for mystification, ignorance, forgetting, and muddled thinking.)

Foucault joins Derrida here, providing further support for a postmodern social theory rooted in the appreciation and amplification of difference (see Breines 1994). He argues that discourses are vehicles of oppression and liberation, conveying and transacting power. Like Derrida, he does not privilege elite theoretical discourses over the discourses of everyday life but argues that we can learn from all of them and that we must learn to speak many ("polyvocal") discourses. He pays special attention to professional discourses of criminality and sexuality because, he argues, these discourses construct the world in ways that then lead to the punishment of "deviants," such as criminals, women, and homosexuals. Foucault contends that professional discourses must be contested and new discourses developed. He rejects Marx's analysis of false consciousness and instead argues that power is universally distributed and has positive as well as negative uses. Thus, the ability to speak certain discourses empowers people and expresses their empowering.

Like Derrida, Foucault rejects the idea that there is a master principle of universal domination that needs to be addressed by a single theoretical logic such as Marxism (see Dews 1984). Inasmuch as people occupy many different subject positions and thus narrate their lives and worlds differently, advocates of radical social change must not seek a master discourse of enlightenment and liberation but must accept polyvocality as an end in itself. This resembles one of the traditional pillars of liberal democratic theory, especially the work of John Stuart Mill. It also resembles the more radical arguments of Habermas, who has tried to reground critical theory on the premises of what he calls communication theory. Habermas contends that people's urge to achieve consensus through discourse provides critical theory and radical politics with an overarching ethical framework. Although Habermas disagrees with what he takes to be Foucault's and Derrida's abandonment of the project of modernity, in many respects their stresses on discourse and communication are similar. More than Foucault and Derrida, Habermas believes that we can strive toward a single master discourse of enlightenment and rationality (what he calls the "paradigm of communication"), although he also strongly implies that unfettered communication in its very nature is polyvocal. That is, rational communication operates in many languages, preserving the various subject positions of all narrators who accept the rules of the game, which require them to respect others and others' narratives.

By now, most critical social theorists accept that Marx's two-class model of the world is simplistic because it fails to address the complexities of postmodernity or postmodern capitalism. Foucault and Lyotard more explicitly than other critical social theorists such as those of the Frankfurt School distance themselves from Marx because, they argue, Marx belongs to an earlier modernity no longer relevant to the present. But upon close examination, we can see that the French postmodern theorists and German critical theorists agreed on many points of substance, as I just indicated with respect to the issue of polyvocality. The French theorists distanced themselves from Marx because Marxism in France was monopolized by the French Communist Party, which was orthodox and authoritarian. The German critical theorists put less distance between themselves and Marxism because Marxism in Germany led a more academic existence and was not usurped by Stalinism. Postmodern theory was a reaction to French structuralism, an approach that can be traced backward to Durkheim and Marcel Mauss and forward to Claude Lévi-Strauss and Althusser. Postmodern social theory grew out of the poststructural epistemological critiques mounted by Derrida and other members of the *Tel quel* group in France, all of whom vigorously objected to the structuralist theories of knowledge and society developed by Althusser (1970). In combating French structuralism for its antihumanism (e.g., Althusser's notion of "history without a subject"), the poststructuralists and postmodernists tended to conflate or confuse Marx with subsequent French Marxism (see Callari and Ruccio 1996). By contrast, the Frankfurt School theorists, following Lukacs, showed that it is possible to read Marx not as a positivist who embraces iron socialist laws but rather as a humanistic alienation theorist (e.g., see Marcuse 1972). In order to disentangle themselves from Stalinism, which was fueled by structuralism (especially in the work of Althusser), the French theorists attempted to surpass Marxism.

In this sense, Foucault was a post-Marxist, as are other French theorists such as Ernesto Laclau and Claude Mouffe (1985). It is crucial to understand that post-Marxists are not necessarily anti- or non-Marxist, although some of them are. This issue is akin to the earlier issue of whether theorists who address postmodernity necessarily thus give up modernity theory. As I said in Chapter 1, some do and some do not. Theorists who map postmodernity as a fundamental break with modernity are also likely to abandon modernity theories, including Marxism. Theorists who view postmodernity as a stage of modernity are likely to position themselves sympathetically with respect to Marxism while arguing that Marxism needs to be surpassed both theoretically and politically. It is this strain of thought that I am calling post-Marxist and to which Foucault especially has made an important contribution.

## From Post-Marxism to Commodity Postmodernism

Many post-Marxists, including Foucault, spend a good deal of time disassociating themselves from Marx and Marxism. They intend to distance themselves from Althusserian structuralism, which was the dominant mode of French Marxism when poststructuralists and postmodernists began to write in the late 1960s and 1970s. The postmodern theorists did not oppose leftist causes. Indeed, they believed that Althusserian neo-Stalinist Marxism betrayed the left by endorsing Marxist-Leninist vanguard politics, which identified the French Communist Party as the harbinger of social change. Most Western Marxists (see Agger 1979) oppose Marxism-Leninism, particularly Lenin's (1932, 1969) vanguard model of socialism, because it sacrifices life and liberty and thus postpones democratic socialism indefinitely, as was evident in the former Soviet Union. Foucault and his postmodern allies opposed French Stalinist Marxism in the name of what they regarded as genuine liberation movements, including the so-called May movement in 1968, which was a loose coalition of students, unions, and various left splinter groups. Their post-Marxism and postmodernism were conceived in relationship to what they regarded as the impostor Marxism of Althusserian structuralism.

Seen in this light, postmodern theory does not necessarily oppose Marxist and neo-Marxist critical social theories, even though they appear to speak quite different languages. Above, I suggested that Habermas's communication theory echoes certain postmodern themes regarding discourse and polyvocality, even though Habermas himself (1987a) wrote a book expressing his differences with postmodernism. Although in defending the project of modernity against postmodernists Habermas believes that he is opposing postmodern social theory, I prefer to read Habermas's critical theory and postmodern social theory as allied critiques of authoritarian Marxism that together stress the necessity of new social movements springing from the grassroots of everyday life. In this sense, then, both Habermas and Foucault could be seen as post-Marxists sympathetic to Marx's original aims and theoretical critiques (although Habermas speaks a more explicitly Marxist language than Foucault because German Marxism was never straitjacketed by Bolshevik dogma).

This is not to gloss over all theoretical differences within French and German thought but simply to situate their projects differently as a way of explaining their somewhat different tenors and themes. However, when we consider the American reception of postmodernism and German critical theory (see Jay 1984a), it is clear that the postmodern theories of Lyotard, Derrida, Foucault, and Baudrillard are positioned in order to support a version of post-Marxism that is closer to liberalism than leftism and that has emerged as the curricular agenda of multiculturalism (see hooks 1990; Collins 1991; West 1993) in contemporary universities. Multiculturalism is an offshoot of the American reception of French postmodernism that understands itself to be a fundamental alternative to Marxism and proposes a new theoretical logic based on the trinity of class, race, and gender as separable and coequal dimensions of oppression and liberation.

The American reception of French theory has given rise to a version of postmodern theory that rejects fundamental axioms of critical social theory. This version of postmodernism posits a sharp break between modernity and postmodernity. And it rejects Marxism in total. It embraces multiculturalism and what one might call multicultural theory as an expression of what it takes to be postmodernism. There are many aspects of multicultural theory and politics that all critical social theories would accept, but multiculturalism is closer to liberalism than leftism in the sense that it encompasses an identity politics (Aronowitz 1992) falling short of the more radical goals of critical social theories. Although multiculturalism and multicultural theory often use postmodern language, I do not believe that any French theorist embraces the multicultural agenda if that agenda is construed to be a significant departure from the goals of radical social change, even if those goals are framed in post-Marxist fashion. In other words, American multiculturalism uses postmodernism in order to advance a political agenda probably more limited than the agendas of the French theorists themselves, Foucault notably included.

Although, as I discuss below, multiculturalism derives from a particularly liberal or neoliberal reading of postmodernism, post-Marxism can have radical implications. Indeed, the French theorists are more radical, more clearly leftist, than many of their American multicultural counterparts, who put distance between the leftist project and difference theory (see Aronowitz 1981). Post-Marxist in crucial respects, Derrida and Foucault are nevertheless more radical than many multiculturalists because they do not situate their postmodern theories in curricular debates about the politics of the canon (e.g., see Graff 1992; Jacoby 1994). Instead, their versions of postmodernism are intended to demonstrate the possibility of postpositivist, postrepresentational cultural criticism and analysis in a stage of late modernity not anticipated by Marx.

Thus, to be post-Marxist may mean only that criticism tackles problems of meaning, discourse, and politics Marx did not foresee (Derrida and Foucault), or it may mean that one abandons Marx's structural analysis of domination in favor of multicultural, neoliberal alternatives (Lyotard, Baudrillard). In Europe Derrida and Foucault are radicals, interrogating postmodernity and elaborating the possibility of postcontemporary cultural and political criticism. But in their American translation (see de Man 1986; Fish 1989; Grossberg et al. 1992) they have become neoliberals, multiculturalists, difference theorists. This is largely because there has never been a Marxist political or academic culture in the United States within which the French theorists could have been read subtly as opponents of dogmatic Communist Party structuralism and as proponents of the radical project of modernity, including the French New Left. Instead, the American reception of the French theorists has turned them into literary critics, post-Marxists, even theorists of curriculum (see Luke 1988).

French postmodern theory was intended to be critical social and cultural theory, conceived in the shadow of Marxism; American postmodernism is framed by the project of neoliberalism, which loses contact with Marxism and even joins forces with neoconservatism in order to bury leftism. Lyotard wanted to break with all grand narratives that seek a singular meaning to history, whereas postmodernism in the United States breaks only with Marxism (see Woodiwiss 1993). In important ways American postmodernism endorses the American project of modernity, which spreads capitalism globally, supports liberal democracy, and positions itself against the Soviet empire. As I have argued in *The Discourse of Domination* (Agger 1992b) and *Cultural Studies as Critical Theory* (Agger 1992a), postmodernism in North America has become not only a fad but an "affirmative" theory of late capitalist society and culture, celebrating, not criticizing, it. The word *postmodern* adorns advertisements and peppers journalistic reportage, intended to convey cutting-edge commodities and ideas (that are themselves commodified). Many critical studies of television and advertising (e.g., Hebdige 1988; Goldman 1992) address the commodification of postmodernism as a way to "move" both products and ideologies.

French postmodernism, composed in the intellectual shadows of Nietzsche, was a heartbeat away from Marxist critical theory, whereas American postmodernism celebrates the Americanized world city, global television, the internet, ephemera of fashion and style, the "end of communism," and other cultural, political, and intellectual trends. On this view, postmodernity is equivalent to the present, which capitalist ideology has always attempted to freeze into eternity by characterizing it as rational and necessary—social "laws." Postmodernism functions as ideology in this way, even though it claims intellectual derivation from critical postmodern theorists such as Foucault and Derrida. American commodity postmodernism, as one might term it, bears little relation to its European predecessor. Indeed, in crucial ways it opposes the social and cultural criticism mounted by the French theorists as a response to Marxist intellectual and political failures.

Western Marxism, embracing the heterodoxies of the Frankfurt School as well as Lukacs and Karl Korsch (1970), is at best a marginal movement, as Russell Jacoby convincingly argued in *Dialectic of Defeat* (1981). Soviet Marxism (Marcuse 1958) and the neo-Stalinist Marxism of the European and British lefts were, according to Western Marxists, travesties of Marx's original ideas, failing to incorporate his nonauthoritarianism, humanism, and democracy. Seen in this light, the French postmodern theorists were trying to replace a moribund Marxism of the Communist Party with new ideas that allowed them to criticize the latest stage of modernity and derive emancipatory strategies that make sense in that context. Oblivious to the socialist experience, American postmodernism did not intend to improve on Marxist theory and practice but rather celebrated its alleged demise, as the Berlin Wall crumbled and communism ended.

American postmodernists, intoxicated by Baudrillard, have virtually duplicated Daniel Bell's well-known theses of the "end of ideology" (Bell 1960) and "postindustrial society" (Bell 1973), arguing that ideological contestation and conflict have been surpassed now that our economy has supposedly become postindustrial, with goods aplenty. We can dispense with Marxism once capitalism advances technologically to a point that most spend their leisure time shopping, improving their homes, and taking vacations. In this light, Baudrillard's postmodernism is simply the latest articulation of postindustrialism, which has been largely discredited because of the deep recessions of the 1970s and 1990s and the continuing poverty of many Americans, especially African Americans. Bell was engaging in wishful thinking when he speculated that social problems and thus ideology would be eliminated under capitalism. Postmodernists are less prophetic than Bell was; they argue that we already inhabit postmodernity/postindustrialism, whereas Bell in the 1960s and early 1970s suggested that a genuinely postindustrial, postideological order lay in the future.

Foucault and Derrida are post-Marxist in that they believe that Marx cannot be neatly applied to the condition of postmodernity; commodity postmodernists, in contrast, disagree with Marx's political aims. They are closer to being neoliberals than leftists in the sense that they do not question the capitalist framework within which representative democracy has become a way of circulating political elites and legitimating the state apparatus that, as Marx recognized, functions as an "executive committee of the bourgeoisie." The *neo-* in neoliberalism refers to the shift from the democratic theory of John Locke and John Stuart Mill, which assumed an economic marketplace relatively unencumbered by the state, to post-Keynesian democratic theory, which recognizes that the state is a major fiscal player (see Rawls 1971; Ackerman 1980). As well, neoliberalism places greater emphasis on the competent political management of the economy and social problems and less emphasis on the rights of individuals.

The post-Marxism of neoliberal American postmodernism is really anti-Marxism and reflects cold-war-era opposition to the Soviet Union. Neoliberals are Americans first and liberals second. They conflate all possible Marxisms with the Marxism-Leninism of the Soviet Union, which sacri-

ficed lives and liberty to the alleged requirements of forced industrialization and the political consolidation of the Communist Party. Although the
French theorists were not pro-Soviet, they recognized that there could be
Marxisms and critical theories that maximized liberty and minimized authoritarianism. (For example, see the work of Cornelius Castoriadis [1984,
1987], who was conversant with postmodern theory, if not one of its proponents.) Commodity postmodernists who embellish neoliberalism with a
certain cosmopolitan cultural sensibility and fashionable irony simply assume that Marxism—the Soviet Union—has been vanquished by capitalism, which has thus proved its superiority. This is a pervasive assumption
in the neoliberal West, even though the Commonwealth of Independent
States (CIS) is reeling from high unemployment and threatened by neofas-
cist resurgence in the wake of the centrally planned economy and its authoritarian political superstructure.

As yet there is no evidence that the CIS or other Eastern European nations
that have undergone perestroika have successfully shifted to a market economy and a democratic political system. There is evidence that Western consumer culture has taken hold in these societies, misleading theoretically un-
sophisticated observers that McDonald's in Moscow heralds democracy.
This is not to endorse state socialism or the Berlin Wall but simply to indicate that the neoliberal commodity postmodernism that trumpets the "end
of communism" as the triumphal end of history achieved by Western capitalism has not yet made its case. As yet, the CIS remains dangerously destabi-
lized, both politically and economically. It is not at all clear what historical
progression is being followed in the CIS, in spite of neoliberal proclamations
that democracy is on the verge of breaking out all over.

## Multiculturalism: Difference, Narrativity, and New Social Movements

The most politically engaged version of American postmodernism is multiculturalism. Multiculturalism is a variety of difference theory (West 1988;
Collins; Lemert 1993) that draws from postmodernism the notion that
people's differences are more analytically important than their similarities
(Spivak 1988; Butler 1990). Following Ferdinand de Saussure, Derrida emphasized that words and concepts acquire meaning only in relation to
other words and concepts from which they differ. Multiculturalism begins
from this point of departure and goes on to develop a critique of existing
society and a concept of alternative societies fundamentally different from
that of Marxism and German critical theory. Multiculturalists celebrate
difference as a framework within which to appreciate many groups and

their distinctive narratives about their experience. What is more, postmodern multiculturalists deny the possibility of uniting groups' differences into common causes that begin to change overarching social structures.

Multiculturalism advances an identity politics according to which each oppressed group is encouraged to "narrate" its own experience of oppression, which is conceived as different from other groups' experiences of oppression. For example, the African American experience is different from the experience of white women. As well, multiculturalists argue that only members of the oppressed group can tell the story of their own oppression (e.g., see Anzaldua 1987, 1990). Others outside the group cannot speak for them inasmuch as they do not occupy that particular subject position and hence cannot know what it is like to "be them." The political aim of these multiple narrations is to produce narratives allowing members of oppressed groups to formulate coherent personal identities based on their membership in these groups. Although this resembles consciousness-raising in the original feminist sense, it differs from feminist consciousness-raising in that the accomplishment of multicultural identities is seen as an end in itself, not simply as a means to political mobilization that would require collaboration with members of other oppressed groups. The political aim of multiculturalism in this sense is to remake the self, which learns how to understand its own experience of oppression by reading and hearing narratives of other group members.

Critical social theories employ consciousness in order to achieve social change, recognizing that social change cannot take place behind the backs of individuals; multiculturalism, in contrast, makes the self its primary political agenda. This is the main way in which multiculturalism is closer to liberalism than to leftism. Multiculturalists view the good society in terms reminiscent of American pluralist images of Ellis Island as a real and figurative gateway to the American dream, which is the flourishing of individual initiative and the fulfillment of economic and social opportunities. Multiculturalists who attempt to "empower" minorities and women do so by enhancing their identities as valuable players in the American mosaic, as worthy as the founding Puritans.

Like Locke and Mill's liberalism, multiculturalism does not oppose the capitalist framework within which issues of mono- versus multiculturalism are cast (see Kann 1982). This is partly because multiculturalists, like liberals, oppose Marxism as illiberal—un-American—and partly because multiculturalists, drawing from a peculiarly American version of postmodernism, believe that people's subject positions are "inflected" (a soft word for *determined*) by race and gender as much as by class. Although no critical social theorist would disagree with this notion that race and gender are primary structuring elements of people's oppression, most critical theorists do not believe that race, class, and gender operate independently of each other in such a way that it is meaningful to talk about people's separable racial, class, and gender identities. In other words, according to critical social theorists, race, class, and gender do not function as separate variables fragmenting people into racial, class, and gender groups with unique identities but are so inextricably interwoven as to blur distinctions to the point of meaninglessness.

Critical theorists treat race, class, and gender as structures of oppression somehow "larger" than individuals who reproduce them. Multiculturalists view race, class, and gender as aspects of identity that influence ("inflect") experience, which can then be narrated by the person who occupies that particular subject position (see Healey 1995). In seeing race, class, and gender as individual-level characteristics that produce aspects of identity, the multiculturalist perspective is quite similar to Weber's approach to social stratification, which spawned the so-called status-attainment approach within U.S. sociology (see Blau and Duncan 1967; Featherman and Hauser 1978). This approach treats social phenomena such as class, race, gender, education, religion, and age as individual-level variables that can be evaluated for the contributions they make to the methodological explanation of variance. Sociologists who take this approach study the impact of class and race on the crime rate, for example, explaining certain amounts of variance in crime produced by class and race. As individual-level characteristics, these variables are "operationalized" into measurable quantities by methodologists, who translate class position into a combination of a person's level of education, annual income, and occupational prestige.

Marx viewed class as a structural feature of capitalism, depending on whether a person owns the means of production or is merely a wage laborer. Weberians view class as a set of individual characteristics that can be studied in order to explain the causal impact of class on other variables such as crime and life expectancy. Multiculturalists who follow in Weber's tradition separate class, race, and gender into individual-level characteristics that produce experiences that can be narrated by the occupant of a particular subject position. Although multiculturalism is explicitly influenced by postmodernism and not by Weber (see Hekman 1990 for an exception to this), its individualistic assumptions about the meanings of class, race, and gender are similar to Weber's. The difference between Weber and multiculturalists is that Weber wanted to assess the sociological effects of individual characteristics, whereas multiculturalists want to evoke the individual experiences of these characteristics, which a person then narrates in order to form his or her particular self. Although Marx understood that the structural reality of class position matters to the individual in the sense that it produces particular types of political consciousness conducive to class mobilization, he did not reduce class either to individual-level characteristics (e.g., annual income, level of education) or to individual experiences subject to narration. Indeed, Marx mistrusted people's experiences of class and the narratives they produce because he thought that ideological hegemony purposely distorts experience, thus protecting capitalism.

The word *reality* is anathema to postmodern multiculturalists, who argue that reality is equivalent to people's experience of it and not an objective construct to be imposed from outside of people's everyday experience (see Smith 1987). Nor should theorists arrogate to themselves the right to express or explain oppressed people's experiences to or for them. In fact, multiculturalists argue that the white male theorist cannot fully understand the selfhood of the oppressed person inasmuch as the theorist occupies a different, more privileged subject position. Thus, the theorist cannot impose his or her definition of reality on oppressed people, who experience "reality" directly and who thus have the greatest expertise in understanding racism, poverty, and sexism.

Multiculturalists worry that the oppressed are not only robbed of money, power, and dignity but also of their narratives, which express their very selfhood. For male leftist theorists with comfortable university jobs to "steal" the voices of the oppressed is seen as little different from the injustices they suffer in other spheres of their lives. Thus, multiculturalism restores the discourses of the oppressed in order to afford them identity, subjectivity, personhood. A critical social theorist would not gainsay the restoration of voice as an important stage in consciousness-raising and political mobilization. But the critical theorist would probably say that this is not an end in itself. Even more important, the critical theorist rejects the notion that people's experiences and hence narratives are so unique that others cannot produce them through sustained programs of empathetic imagination. Critical social theorists propose a rational universalism that postmodern multiculturalists reject, regarding such universalism as yet another veiled attempt by the dominant group to impose its own experiences and interests on the oppressed.

As before, there are productive points of contact between multiculturalism and critical social theory. Habermas has written about new social movements that replace or supplement the nineteenth-century proletariat. These movements include the women's movement, movements of people of color (e.g., the antiapartheid movement in South Africa), postcolonial social movements, the environmental movement, the antinuclear movement, and movements of national liberation. Habermas argues that critical theory must appreciate these diverse movements as they arise from people's local resistance to domination. Multiculturalists also recognize the diversity of new social movements, which stem from local experience and speak distinctive discourses. A difference between Habermas and multiculturalists is that Habermas theorizes universally about these diverse movements, stressing points of overlap (their democratic politics and opposition to bureaucracy) even while he is aware of their diversity. He does not abandon the effort to tell large stories about people's various smaller stories in the interest of developing an overarching critical social theory that makes sense of global dynamics.

Multiculturalists who advance the causes of new social movements based on class, race, gender, religion, and nation support many of the same movements as does Habermas. Unlike Habermas, though, they do not conceptualize the cumulative effects of the achievements of these social movements but champion them sui generis, in terms of the limited aims of each. The postmodern politics of identity defines effective social change as the achievement of selfhoods by group members who tell stories about their own lives and thus do not deny their identity as members of these racial, gender, and cultural affinity groups. All of this was foreshadowed in the women's and black-pride movements in the 1960s, although those movements did not theorize themselves in terms of postmodern affinity politics but strictly in terms of traditional U.S. liberalism and pluralism (for a critique, see Jacoby 1975).

One problem with identity politics, then, is that it views narrativity as an end in itself, not as a springboard to radical social change. Another is that it assumes group identities to be incommensurable, characterized by difference, although in fact Habermas, as I have said, demonstrates certain common structural features of new social movements (also see Boggs 1986). Once postmodern multiculturalists abandon grand narratives such as Marxism, they set themselves the difficult task of formulating the structural implications of new social movements that are centered around various versions of identity politics, especially where these social movements are primarily concerned to produce narratives enhancing and expressing victims' selfhood.


## Postmodernism as Critical Social Theory

In the previous chapter and in the first section of this chapter, I laid the foundation for a postmodern social theory. I suggested that neoliberal and multicultural postmodernisms do not constitute critical social theories in the sense that they do not mount radical challenges to the existing social system. Although critical theorists favor neoliberalism over authoritarianism and consider multiculturalism preferable to the myth of the melting pot, neoliberalism and multiculturalism reject fundamental axioms of critical social theory, notably its creative dialogue with Marxism about the possibility of radical social change in postmodernity.

In this final section of the chapter, I suggest ways in which postmodern social theory that does not celebrate commodity culture or advance an identity politics through curricular agendas in the university has become a legitimate version of critical social theory.

*Postmodern theory joins a dialogue with Marxism.* Instead of rejecting Marxism wholesale, for example, conflating it with the Marxism-Leninism of the former Soviet Union, postmodern theory builds creatively on Marxism and neo-Marxism. Jameson's work on postmodern culture in late capitalism is a good example of this engagement. Postmodernity is theorized as a "late" stage of capitalist modernity and probed for its contradictions and crises, much as Marx probed early market capitalism. In this sense, postmodernism (see Ashley 1997) directly contributes to the advancement of social theory by considering the ways in which theories of modernity, including Marxism, are no longer fully adequate to understand the present.

*Postmodern theory develops a deconstructive discourse theory capable of identifying and criticizing ideologies,* now found not only in doctrinal works such as bourgeois economic theory or religion but also in the dispersed texts of popular culture and advertising. The deconstruction of these popular discourses and practices reveals their hidden political agendas. It also suggests ways of reformulating cultural hegemony, notably by fostering grassroots efforts to make nonhegemonic films, publish critical books and newspapers, produce alternative television, and enhance cyberdemocracy. In Gramsci's sense, postmodern critical theory helps create counterhegemony by reformulating cultural practices, which have become potent forms of ideological persuasion.

*Postmodern theory empowers citizens who "read" to become authors who write,* hence building a democratic polity in which the Greek idea of active public citizenship is fulfilled. Derrida shows that reading is a strong practice that necessarily intervenes in texts in order to supply them with meaning and perspective. This epistemological and literary empowering can lead to political empowering, much as Paulo Freire in *Pedagogy of the Oppressed* (1970) argued that Latin American peasants create democracy by becoming literate.

*In placing a strong value on "difference," postmodern theorists help eliminate some of the blind spots of male modernist theorists,* notably about women and people of color. Instead of being treated as marginal, women, people of color, citizens of postcolonial societies, gays and lesbians, and various other "subalterns" (Spivak 1988) are now made central by postmodern critical theory, which not only speaks in their name but theorizes their oppression in common terms. Although postmodernists and other critical theorists may differ on the extent to which theory can create a single narrative that encompasses and explains all these aspects of oppression, postmodern social theory nonetheless makes the explanation and articulation of difference a central aim. This differs from multiculturalism in the sense that it not only "allows" various subalterns to narrate their lives and experiences but builds a critical social theory on the basis of evidence gathered from these narratives. It is not enough for subalterns to achieve voice; through this, they must come to control discourse, culture, and hence power. Fraser makes this argument nicely in her *Unruly Practices* (1989), in which she advances a feminist-postmodern version of critical theory.

For theorists to take postmodernism seriously as a body of theoretical propositions conceived in dialogue with Marxism and other modernist social theories, *commodity postmodernism must be opposed as an impostor version.* Far from heralding the postmodern moment, postmodern social theory criticizes the present as insufficient, albeit in terms that may differ from previous modernist critical theories, especially inasmuch as postmodernism takes popular culture seriously. In this sense, postmodern theory finds a middle way between the cultural mandarinism of the Frankfurt School, which disdained the popular as a manipulated region of false consciousness and false needs, and the celebratory postmodernism that glorifies the television show *Twin Peaks* and Nike advertisements. This is precisely the agenda of a critical cultural studies that takes the popular seriously as a region of political contest and ideological manipulation while seeking to transform everyday life by empowered readers/writers who author their own lives.

In this sense, *postmodern theory develops a concept of postmodern intellectuality that writes accessibly* without forsaking complicated concepts necessary to understand society. The Frankfurt School theorists and French feminists couch conceptual difficulty in challenging prose. Although postmodernism does not reject technical language per se, it argues that these esoteric languages can be demystified and democratized. This is one of the most powerful implications of the postmodern concept of narrativity, which suggests that individuals can tell their own stories and hence become powerful, as I noted above. But postmodern narrativity does not simply repeat the commonsense language and consciousness of everyday life, which is often stupefied by cultural hegemonists, but elevates the everyday into a sophisticated mode of theoretical understanding. In this sense, postmodernism lowers high theory and at the same time elevates narrativity into a public intellectuality—again, retrieving the Greek concept of citizenship so vital to all critical social theories' valuation of what Habermas calls "the public sphere."

*Postmodern theory suggests a postrepresentational theory and discourse of knowledge* that at once abandons positivism in the social and natural sciences alike and preserves the possibility of empirical science. Although there are antiscience strains in various versions of postmodernism and especially in postmodernism's articulation as deconstructive literary theory in certain American humanities departments, nothing requires postmodern theory to oppose science. Rather, postmodern approaches to both narrativity and interpretation suggest ways of writing and reading science in a postmodern vein, maximizing accessibility and bringing to light the assumptions that science discourse often conceals, thus opening science to dialogue and debate. In this sense, deconstruction "authorizes" the lifeless, leaden, third-person prose of conventional science writing, demonstrating that the science was written by auteurs with values, assumptions, perspectives, and blind spots. Karin Knorr-Cetina's *Manufacture of Knowledge* (1981), although not explicitly anchored in postmodern theory, demonstrates how a deconstructive analysis of the published work of scientists in a Berkeley laboratory as well as an ethnography of their own accounts of their scientific work brings to light ample evidence of "authorship." This style of analysis not only deconstructs science and makes visible its assumptions and values but also contributes to the sociology of science. Far from abandoning science, postmodern theory can invigorate science at a time when science is viewed as an incomprehensible, specialist activity that exists not for the sake of social betterment but simply to pad vitae, obtain grants, and build academic careers.

This deconstructive approach to science not only enables science to be read critically by "authorizing" science; it also suggests more self-conscious modes of scientific writing, whereby scientists lay bare their assumptions and rely less on technique, including mathematics and figural displays, to make their points and earn their legitimacy.

*Postmodern social theory need not abandon the ideal of progress but rather reformulates it within a framework less linear than the modernity theory that sprang from the Enlightenment.* Postmodern social theory does not view progress as an inevitable outcome of society's conquest of nature, industrialization, and the development of capitalism, including its extension into world markets. Postmodern social theory does not reject modernity (e.g., technology, health care, public education, etc.) but instead picks and chooses among modernity's benefits, also emphasizing modernity's costs (such as environmental crisis, poverty, prejudice and discrimination, imperialism and colonialism, the nuclear threat). In this sense, one can reinterpret Marx as a postmodern social theorist who valued technological, social, and political advances achieved by capitalism but viewed capitalism as an imperfect, even contradictory social system destined to negate its own gains by producing class warfare. For Marx, the resolution of these contradictions was to be found in socialism. But Marx did not foresee the extent to which capitalist societies could protect themselves against class conflict, notably through what the Frankfurt School called the culture industry (which produces cultural hegemony, false consciousness, and consumerism) as well as through an active state apparatus that both stimulates and manages the economy. Marxism is viewed as obsolescent by neoliberals and postmodernists who believe that one cannot separate Marx's analysis of alienation and his vision of a utopian, disalienated society from his own prediction of the imminence of the "expropriation of the expropriators." Western Marxists such as Lukacs and the Frankfurt School argue that one *can* make this separation, thus valuably retaining Marx's theoretical logic while revising Marxism in light of cultural, political, and economic developments that he did not foresee.

Jameson, Kellner, Aronowitz, Fraser, Luke, and David Ashley argue that one can use certain postmodern concepts in order to revise Marxist critical theory appropriately and thus reinvigorate the ideal of radical social change. In the following chapter, I discuss the Frankfurt School's critical theory, from which these theorists have drawn as they have attempted to blend postmodernism and critical theory. Although we all agree that critical theory offers the most comprehensive analysis of contemporary society, we acknowledge that postmodern theorists such as Foucault and Derrida help us better understand the newfound characteristics of ideology in a "media culture," as Kellner (1995) has termed it.

# CHAPTER 4

# The Critical Theory of the Frankfurt School

## PERIODIZING CAPITALISM AFTER MARX

The theorists of the Frankfurt School (formerly called the Institute for Social Research, founded in 1923; see Jay 1973; Schroyer 1973; Held 1980) developed an important version of neo-Marxism called critical theory. Theodor Adorno, Herbert Marcuse, Max Horkheimer, and Adorno and Horkheimer's student Jürgen Habermas made sophisticated revisions to Marx's original theory, notably through philosophical and psychoanalytical reconstructions of Marxism. They worked in the spirit of defending the Marxist legacy, above all Marx's critique of alienation and his goal of a dis-alienated socialist society. Although they identified themselves as Marxists, by the standards of Marxism-Leninism and orthodox Marxist determinism (see Slater 1977) they betrayed original Marxism by going far afield into aesthetic theory, psychoanalysis, communication theory, and other strains of bourgeois European social and cultural theory. As well, they were indicted (e.g., Colletti 1973) for returning to Hegel (see, e.g., Marcuse's *Reason and Revolution: Hegel and the Rise of Social Theory* [1960]), thus supposedly regressing behind materialism. In the course of this chapter, I respond to these critiques by arguing that the critical theorists *were* correct to understand themselves as Marxists and yet that their lasting significance was their willingness to take intellectual risks in abandoning aspects of Marxism that were no longer relevant and adding to Marxism theoretical ideas from other intellectual traditions (see Agger 1992b: 14–39).

Adorno, Horkheimer, and Marcuse's reformulation of Marxism contained two crucial elements: They offered an analysis of the dialectic of enlightenment (Horkheimer and Adorno 1972: 3–42) to explain how positivism has become mythology, and they offered the concept of the culture industry (Horkheimer and Adorno 1972: 120–167) to explain aspects of ideological and cultural manipulation (which Marcuse [1964] termed "one-dimensional consciousness" and Adorno [1973a] "total administration"). I explore these ideas before I conclude the chapter with a discussion of Habermas's reformulation of the original Frankfurt theorists' reformulation of Marxism. As we shall see, although Habermas builds on Horkheimer, Adorno, and Marcuse, in certain critical respects he diverges from them, addressing both mainstream social theory and social science in ways they did not and reconstructing critical theory in more fundamental terms than did his mentors.

In this section I discuss the political and historical context in which the Frankfurt School's critical theory—which remains the exemplar of what I call critical social theory—developed out of the writings of Marx and early-twentieth-century Marxists. Critical theory belongs to a theoretical movement called Western Marxism (McInnes 1972) mentioned in preceding chapters. Western Marxism was initiated by Georg Lukacs, a Hungarian Marxist intellectual who in 1923 published *History and Class Consciousness*, an important challenge to Marxian and Engelsian orthodoxy at the time. Lukacs attempted to explain why the socialist revolution that Marx had prophesied did not occur: This was not because Marx's critique of the contradictions of capitalist modernity was wrong but because the custodians of capitalism had learned how to manage a variety of social, cultural, and economic crises that Marx in the mid-nineteenth century believed would wreck capitalism through such events as the falling rate of profit and thus prepare the way for the arrival of socialism. In particular, Lukacs argued that Marxists in the First and Second Internationals (international organizations of socialist tacticians in the late nineteenth and early twentieth centuries) placed insufficient emphasis on the role of class consciousness in their revolutionary calculus, stemming from an interpretation of Marx that reduced class consciousness to material conditions that were thought almost causally to produce it. Marx suggested that the economic crises of capitalism would deepen over time. He theorized a tendency of capital to be concentrated in the hands of a few large capitalists, thus throwing small capitalists out of business and workers out of work and hence producing a crisis of "underconsumption" fatal to capitalism. In this context of business failure and rampant unemployment, unsupported by the so-called safety nets of Keynesian welfare-state capitalism that Marx could not foresee, Marx was read to suggest that workers' class consciousness would almost automatically develop and they would thus mobilize to commit the socialist revolution, or "expropriate the expropriators," as Marx expressed it in the first volume of *Capital*.

Lukacs argued that a close reading of Marx suggests that Marx did not regard class consciousness as an automatic response to business failure and unemployment. Lukacs identified places in Marx's writings where Marx suggested that consciousness and material conditions exist in a dialectical, feedback relationship. (In *Western Marxism* I trace the history of this interpretation of Marx; see Agger 1979.) Lukacs further argued that a close examination of Marx indicated the extent of Marx's debt to the German idealist philosopher Hegel, particularly to Hegel's *Phenomenology of Mind* (1967), in which Hegel posited that human consciousness undergoes a historical process of unfolding or coming to rationality, thus suggesting a voluntarist conception of mind and human activity. Marx's early writings, *The Economic and Philosophical Manuscripts of 1844* (1964), support Hegel's interpretation, although it is also fair to say that the later Marx of *Capital* tended to leave the theory of consciousness behind in favor of his concentration on economics. This second reading of Marx, advanced by Althusser in *For Marx* (1970), suggests an "epistemological break" in Marx's body of work between the intellectually immature humanist philosopher and the mature economic scientist. Althusser's reading of Marx counters the tendency of Western Marxists since Lukacs to consider Marx a humanist philosopher of alienation who did not view the socialist revolution as inevitable, given the manipulability and plasticity of class consciousness.

Lukacs, then, attempted to explain the delay in the socialist revolution, which Marx believed was imminent in the late nineteenth century, in terms of class consciousness, which he decoupled from material economic processes in granting consciousness what Althusser calls relative autonomy. As capitalism advanced from its early market form in the 1800s to a global, technologically advanced mode in the 1900s, beginning after World War I, workers lost the immediacy of their formerly dire predicaments and gradually began to accept capitalism as an inevitable if not supremely rational social and economic system. According to Lukacs and the other Western Marxists, capitalists wanted to foster precisely this image in order to divert workers from the possibility of a socialist revolution, elaborated so stirringly by Marx and Engels in *The Communist Manifesto* (1967). Lukacs argued that capitalism increasingly manipulated class consciousness after World War I as ideology—clear-cut but false claims about society made by religion and bourgeois economic theory in order to convince people that radical change was impossible—became what Lukacs called reification, the reduction of social relations and ideas to inert processes that, like nature, appeared frozen and hence unchangeable.

Western Marxists like Lukacs developed a theory of late capitalism. Late capitalism differs from early market capitalism in two senses: In late capitalism the state intervenes directly in the economy as a big spender and a source of social security for the destitute in order to keep them spending and to prevent them from joining radical political causes. Further, ideology ("reification" for Lukacs, "domination" for the Frankfurt School, and "hegemony" for Gramsci) is no longer a clear-cut text that explicitly states that alienation in "this" world can be ameliorated only in the afterlife. Ideology is instead an everyday experience (Althusser: "lived practice") of the world produced and reproduced in various discourses such as popular culture and social science that suffuse the person with a sense of society's inertness and inevitability.

In other words, ideology, in Marx's era, went from being something that could be refuted through ideology critique (counterfactual claims that, for example, there is no afterlife) to a conventional wisdom promoted in everyday life by various sources of hegemony, to use Gramsci's (1971) term. By *hegemony*, Gramsci meant the unquestioned dominance of conformist ideas that reproduce the given society. In late capitalism, everyday life is permeated with discourses and texts that both divert people from their alienation (and suggest certain reliefs, such as shopping and vacations) and portray the world as rational and necessary. But this late capitalist ideology, according to Western Marxists beginning with Lukacs and the Frankfurt School, is inchoate, often concealed, and thus very difficult to refute. The purpose of ideology critique in late capitalism, then, is to uncover and demystify reification, domination, and hegemony found in people's everyday experiences and activities. Ideology in late capitalism is dispersed into culture from texts per se, such as the Bible, and thus requires new conceptualizations and interpretive methods of ideology critique.

In a sense, then, Lukacs was saying that late capitalism became more formidable, less susceptible to radical critiques and political mobilization, as it began to create a middle class that worked in relatively comfortable and safe conditions and could imitate the lifestyles of its managerial counterparts. This economic advance was made possible largely because of the state intervention I noted above, which emerged from Keynesian economic theory as President Franklin Roosevelt responded to the Great Depression in the United States (O'Connor 1973; Habermas 1975). This involved government spending programs, various social welfare measures, and the opening of world markets. Fortuitously for capitalism, World War I also saw all Western countries militarize themselves in girding against big-power conflicts. Only in the 1990s did capitalism begin to move away from a permanent war economy (Melman 1974), the cold war having ended with the arrival of perestroika in the CIS. This economic transition in capitalism made possible an ideological transition from the old-fashioned textual ideology of Marx's era, which propagated falsehoods about the intractability of society and the prospect of salvation in heaven, to the new ideological manifestations of reification, domination, and hegemony.

Although the economic transition from market to late capitalism with the Great Depression and its Keynesian response began to ease the lot of working people, cushioning them against the effects of unemployment, the need for ideological deception at the level of what Marx had called the superstructure was not eliminated. Rather, ideology has become *more* immobilizing now that it is no longer susceptible to ideology-critical counterfactual claims but exists amorphously in the many cultural discourses and practices of everyday life. These cultural discourses and practices "reify" everyday life, in Lukacs's terms, by making human relations appear to be natural or naturelike, much as particles interact in the physical universe. In this sense, Lukacs's critique of reification was strongly tied to his and other Western Marxists' critique of positivism in the social sciences. They argued that positivism helps foster this impression, which is reifying, that social relations resemble relations in the natural world and hence cannot be changed deliberately. This analysis of reification was first proposed by Marx himself when he analyzed the tendency of capitalism to transform human relations into apparent relations between things, not people, a process he termed "commodity fetishism." Marx argued that this tendency of what Lukacs later called reification is inherent in the commodification of human labor power, turning people's labor into a commodity to be bought and sold in the labor market.

Western Marxists such as Lukacs, Gramsci, and the Frankfurt School thought that they were building on Marx, particularly on his theory of alienation, his stress on consciousness (via Hegel), and his concept of commodity fetishism. Lukacs's *History and Class Consciousness* (1971) positioned itself as an extrapolation of Marx: As I just indicated, Lukacs's concept of reification was anticipated by Marx's notion of commodity fetishism, which describes thinglike relations between capitalist and worker. In emphasizing class consciousness as a political factor explaining why capitalism has survived past Marx's expectation of its demise, the Western Marxists thought they were being faithful to Marx's theoretical logic. Western Marxism was viewed as heretical mainly by orthodox Marxists and Marxist-Leninists, who did not stress ideology, alienation, consciousness, and commodity fetishism in their analyses of capitalism. Although I support the Western Marxist reading of Marx, my earlier discussions of deconstruction suggest that there is no single "correct" reading of Marx. My support of the Western Marxist reading of Marx as an alienation theorist and critic of reification who needs updating more than fundamental revision is grounded in my conception of how best to further Marx's political aims in a late or postmodern stage of capitalism. Other readings of Marx stem from different political aims, such as the consolidation of the Communist Party along the lines of the Soviet model of socialist development.

The Western Marxists advanced Marxism from early to late capitalism, which they conceptualized in terms of growing state involvement and more insidious forms of ideology. Although all Western Marxists took Lukacs's

*History and Class Consciousness* and Korsch's *Marxism and Philosophy* (1970) as their theoretical inspiration, the Frankfurt theorists believed they were deepening Lukacs's analysis of reification in their critique of domination (see Lichtheim 1971). They conceptualized domination as an internalized and potent form of reification—the tendency to view society as an immutable piece of nature. Thus, although they certainly preserved Lukacs's analysis of class consciousness developed in the 1920s, they extended his analysis of reification (which they termed "domination") from the "collective subject," or proletariat, to the "subject," or person. By the time they advanced their version of critical theory in the 1940s and 1950s, they were convinced that late capitalism had become even more impervious to social critique and thus consciousness-raising, especially in that capitalism had integrated aspects of fascist control (Adorno: "total administration") in the Allies' victory over the Axis nations in World War II. Thus, the Frankfurt theorists suggested that while Lukacs moved Marxist theory a stage beyond Marx by deepening Marx's analysis of commodity fetishism into the analysis of reification, they were themselves deepening Lukacs in a more evolved stage of capitalism. Thus, the Frankfurt theorists conceived domination as even more intractable than reification.

The Frankfurt theorists came to the United States during World War II (Hughes 1975). Adorno and Horkheimer returned to West Germany following the war, whereas Marcuse remained in the United States and took up successive faculty posts at Brandeis and then the University of California at San Diego. The Frankfurt theorists addressed a "later" late capitalism than did Lukacs. This even later form of capitalism was characterized by the political quiescence and conformity of the years of Dwight Eisenhower's administration in the United States and the Marshall Plan in postwar West Germany. I believe that this "later" late capitalism was still twenty-five years away from becoming what I call postmodern capitalism, which requires a further deepening of the Frankfurt School's concept of domination. Lukacs and the critical theorists argued that ideology has been "routinized," as Weber termed it, in everyday life through various cultural discourses and practices that suggest the inevitability and thus rationality of political conformity. Ideology in postmodern capitalism has become even more dispersed into the semiotics (symbol systems) and discourses of everyday life. Postmodern ideology (Featherstone 1991) is so deeply implanted in everyday popular culture that almost no one, including critical intellectuals, can get a grasp on the difference between truth and falsehood, reality and illusion, which is required by any ideological-critical program that intends to raise political consciousness. Indeed, Foucault, Derrida, and Baudrillard bemoan this loss of epistemological certainty. This "crisis of representation," as postmodern theorists call it, suggests that it is no longer possible clearly to reflect, represent, and know the world in such a way that we can then make distinctions between true and false, reality and illusion. In this context of postmodernity, the critical project of Western Marxism is severely disabled; theorists can no longer attempt to reveal political and cultural illusions in order to raise people's consciousness. Without a handle on truth, postmodern theory becomes an exercise in endless deconstruction.

The interpretive tools of deconstruction, developed by French theorists in postmodernity, are invaluable to critical social theorists who want to detect and then debunk ideologies dispersed into the deep discursive fabric of everyday life itself. Critical theory corrects deconstruction's collapsing of true and false, reality and illusion, by retaining a concept of objective representation, including empirical science. Postmodern theorists talk about "postmodernity," whereas critical theorists talk about "postmodern capitalism," suggesting some of these differences in perspective. In any case, the critical theory of the Frankfurt School, in its stress on ideology, consciousness, and culture, parallels and is enriched by the work of postmodern theorists.

## DOMINATION I:
### THE DIALECTIC OF ENLIGHTENMENT ARGUMENT

Having suggested a relatively smooth evolution of the Western Marxists' concepts of reification, hegemony, and domination out of Marx's own work, I now examine the Frankfurt School's concept of domination in more depth and suggest that seen from a different perspective the Frankfurt theorists sought to make major theoretical transformations in not only Marxism but all theories of modernity. These points are not incompatible in the sense that I am reading their theory both as an extrapolation and deepening of Marx *and* simultaneously as a contribution to postmodern theory, or at least as an anticipation of it.

Horkheimer and Adorno in *Dialectic of Enlightenment* (1972) criticized all previous theories of modernity, including Marx's, for their inattention to issues of what they termed "domination." In this way, they argued that their own critical theory was a much more sweeping critique of civilization than Marx's, which applied only to capitalism. By domination, Horkheimer and Adorno were referring to Western society's penchant for viewing the world, including nature, as an object to be plundered for the uses of humanity. Although Horkheimer and Adorno clearly acknowledged the need for food, farming, and industry—for technology generally—they distinguished between the mastery of nature and its domination. Since the Greeks (and they use Homer's *Odyssey* as a pertinent example), people attempted to overcome their fears by vanquishing various elements in the outside world, including nature, women, members of minority groups, and so-called primitive societies. In achieving control of their social and natural environment, people would not only fill their stomachs but quell their anxieties and realize their identities (see Lenhardt 1976).

Horkheimer and Adorno conceived of positivism as one of the most recent examples of this attempt to dominate. Positivist theories of knowledge suggest that we overcome ignorance and uncertainty through the techniques and procedures of the natural sciences, notably mathematics. The Enlightenment was premised on this Western proclivity for overcoming fear and ignorance with the supposed certainties of science and technology, which were examples of domination. Horkheimer and Adorno did not oppose enlightenment (with a small *e*); as rationalists and Marxists, they thought that enlightenment makes way for liberation. But the eighteenth-century Enlightenment that freed Europe from religion and myth failed to achieve its ultimate purpose by neglecting its own imperfections and disabilities. In positing a science and technology capable of dominating nature, the philosophers of the Enlightenment and subsequent social theorists of modernity who attempted to base social science on the natural sciences turned science itself into a myth.

According to the Frankfurt theorists, the pretensions of the Greeks and then the Enlightenment were too grandiose—to eliminate uncertainty by conquering the world that produces it, to abolish all mystery and myth, to vanquish faith with reason. Although Horkheimer and Adorno, like Marx and Hegel, supported reason and indeed wanted to create a regime of reason, they wanted to humble reason so that it did not engage in intellectual and social domination. The critical theorists opposed hubris, arrogance, in the name of social progress, not in defense of the past. In supposing that reason (here, science) could solve all problems and demystify all myths, earlier thinkers made reason as mythic as the myths, such as religion, that it opposes. This mode of analysis suggests that there is a "dialectic," or alternation, between myth and enlightenment whereby advances in enlightenment always court the return of myth, faith, and belief—under positivism, the faith in science.

Their theory of domination became what they called a critique of identity theory, which Adorno developed further in a later book, *Negative Dialectics* (1973a), a critique of idealist and existentialist philosophies. The Frankfurt School's critique of identity theory closely resembles the postmodern critique of representation, both of which emerge in a critique of positivism. For Adorno, identity theory is another term for a theory of knowledge that suggests that concepts in language can perfectly describe the external world. This is very similar to Derrida's critique of the metaphysics of presence, which suggests that language can come so close to describing the world that we believe we are in the world's presence. Identity theory is not only a theory of knowledge, according to Adorno, but it represents a social theory, even a philosophy of history, which argues that the subject (person) can completely master the object (other people and nature), whether by capturing the object perfectly in scientific concepts or by manipulating the object socially and technologically. This notion of identity lies at the heart of Western civilization's arrogance with respect to the domination of nature, which, according to the Frankfurt theorists, has led to all manner of atrocities, both human and environmental.

Horkheimer and Adorno applied this analysis of the Greeks' and Enlightenment's hubris to their understanding of fascism, which they interpreted as an extreme form of domination. Adolf Hitler dealt with what he took to be threats to the racial purity of Aryanism, going as far as to exterminate whole groups of people, such as Jews, Slavs, and Gypsies, deemed objects in nature to be conquered. These objects were conceived as otherness, challenging subjectivity (people) to master it. In the Nazis' case, the mastery of this racial otherness, viewed as an impurity sullying the dominance of Aryan culture and thus the Third Reich, required the death camps. The death camps not only served the purpose of killing millions in factorylike efficiency. They also symbolically solved the philosophical problem of the nonidentity of subject and object, which, according to Adorno, has haunted Western civilization and called forth "identity theory," leading to the domination of objects by subjects.

It is crucial to point out here that the Frankfurt School theorists were not Luddites; that is, they did not advocate destroying technology and regressing to a primitive, prehistorical state of nature. Marx termed this "primitive communism," a stage to which he did not want to return. Rather, the critical theorists thought that nature could be humanely mastered for human purposes and people who embody "difference" tolerated without giving up the benefits of technological advancement. Indeed, Marcuse argued in *Eros and Civilization* (1955) and later in *An Essay on Liberation* (1969) that the advancement of technology prepares the way for liberation from scarcity, which heretofore had placed objective limits on people's liberation. Similarly, Marx argued that what he called "necessary labor time" must be reduced if people are to taste real liberation.

Scarcity can be "organized" in different ways. Under capitalism, according to the Frankfurt theorists, scarcity is organized irrationally, benefiting only the rich and depriving the working class and the poor. Under a humane form of socialism, they argued, scarcity would be organized differently (such that workers own and control the means of production, as Marx urged) *and* progressively overcome by the reduction of necessary labor time. The Frankfurt theorists believed that work can be humanized and disalienated if capital is owned and controlled by workers, not capitalists, and that the time people need to spend in "necessary labor" in order to reproduce themselves and their families can be reduced through the rational mastery of technology.

What did the rational deployment of technology mean to Marcuse, Horkheimer, and Adorno? Only Marcuse (1969) wrote explicitly on this issue, albeit without providing precise blueprints. He said that science and technology could be reconstructed along the lines of what Freud termed the "life instincts" such that they would express people's desire to play and work creatively with ideas and concepts (science) and tools and machines (technology). This extends Marx's point in *The Economic and Philosophical Manuscripts* (Marx 1964) that people have a positive need to do creative work in order to express their natures as creatures of praxis—the Greek word for self-creative activity. Early Marx argued that we could eventually blur the boundary between necessary labor and self-creating labor by disalienating labor, returning ownership and control of work to members of the working class, who would in effect work for themselves and thus for all of humanity.

Today, a new technology that does not dominate nature but serves human purposes, both material and creative, would need to be set up in harmony with the environment. The Frankfurt School initiated a critique of the domination of nature (see Leiss 1973, 1976), arguing that nature must be conceived as a "subject" and not an "object." The whole environmental movement and its implied or explicit critique of the domination of nature (e.g., the so-called deep ecology and Earth First! movements) were prefigured by the Frankfurt School, who derived the impetus for their critique from Heidegger's critique of technology, which itself derived from Nietzsche. Adorno suggested in *Minima Moralia* (1978), aphoristic musings about a whole range of topics, that social change ought to be assessed by the extent to which it achieves the "redemption of nature," a theme that surfaces repeatedly in the Frankfurt work (e.g., Horkheimer's *Eclipse of Reason* [1974]).

This is a quite romantic strain in the Frankfurt School's work and even in Marx. It suggests that we can both reduce the amount of odious labor people have to do by mastering technology and at the same time remake technology to express human creativity without plundering nature. Although critics of the Frankfurt School's technological utopianism argue that all of this is pie-in-the-sky idealism, the subsequent history of the environmental movement and an environmentally driven critical theory (see Luke 1999) suggest that many of the Frankfurt ideas have been taken a step further and even put into practice by environmentalists and theorists of technology and nature (e.g., see E. F. Schumacher's widely read *Small Is Beautiful: Economics as if People Mattered* [1973], in which he calls for small-scale, "appropriate" technology). Even Habermas in *Knowledge and Human Interests* (1971: 32–33) chides his Frankfurt mentors for their romantic utopianism expressed in the notion of a new science and technology that "redeem" nature. Habermas reconstructs the critical theory of the founders in order to make what he regards as a pragmatic distinction between radical aims that can be met and aims that are simply unattainable and thus should be dropped from the agenda. He achieves this revision of critical theory through elaborate readings of Kant, Hegel, and Marx.

According to Habermas, Marx's collapse of the categories of self-reflection and communication on the one hand and technology on the other led Marx to neglect the possibility that his own theoretical framework would become deterministic. Lacking an epistemological basis for self-reflection, Engels, theorists of the Second International such as Karl Kautsky, and theorists of the Third International such as Lenin developed an economic determinism modeled on the positivist natural sciences (see Bottomore 1978; Blum 1974). Repeating neo-Kantians such as Wilhelm Dilthey and Heinrich Rickert and hermeneutic thinkers such as Heidegger and Gadamer, Habermas suggested that Marx should have separated the logics under which society and nature can be understood in order to prevent Engels from arguing that there is a "dialectic of nature," which allowed Engels to use Marx's dialectical method to understand not only history but also nature. Engels's rather esoteric argument fed into the Bolsheviks' attempt to reconstruct Marxism as "dialectical materialism," in effect a socialist version of positivism.

Marx's failure to separate self-reflection and communication from technology led to economic determinism, which, as Lukacs and other Western Marxists argued, caused theorists of the Second and Third Internationals to ignore class consciousness and thus fail to attack ideological hegemony forcefully. What is more, according to Habermas, Marx's failure caused later theorists such as Adorno, Horkheimer, and Marcuse, who were influenced by Heidegger's critique of technology, to speculate that technology could be transformed into a form of nonalienated labor (creative praxis). Habermas thought that this was foolishly utopian and impractical and hence would divert socialists' attention from more important tactical issues. Although I do not agree with Habermas inasmuch as early Marx lays the foundation for Marcuse's interpretation of Freudian psychoanalysis as the harbinger of a "new science and technology" that express the life instincts, I do agree with Habermas that Marx could have prevented economic determinism by being clearer about the differences between critical social science and positivist natural science. Once left-wing dialectical theorists such as Lenin and Stalin (1973) collapsed social science and natural science into the overarching category of dialectical materialism, the door was open for their argument that Marxism is a natural science of history that seeks to describe social laws in exactly the way that Comte did. Dialectical materialism legitimizes political passivity: If the socialist revolution is inevitable, given certain postulated "dialectical laws" spelled out by Engels and perhaps implied by Marx himself, then tacticians and organizers need not actively plan and agitate.

The original members of the Frankfurt School, unlike Habermas later, argued two things that appear contradictory: First, domination is a deeper and more historical phenomenon than Marx theorized, requiring the critical theorists to develop their critique of civilization as "the dialectic of enlightenment." Second, critical theory anticipates a technologically advanced future society in which domination fades, giving way to a society that does not exploit nature mindlessly and in which people enjoy creative work, both intellectual and technical. In this way, the Frankfurt thinkers were quite pessimistic, suggesting that capitalism was a problem but not *the* problem: The underlying problem, they contended, was the attempt of Western philosophy and culture to dominate the "object," otherness, nature, and other people. Yet they were also profoundly prophetic and hopeful, imagining a society of praxis, creative work and play, in which nature is "pacified" (Marcuse in *One-Dimensional Man*) and "redeemed" (Adorno in *Minima Moralia*).

## DOMINATION II:
### THE CULTURE INDUSTRY ARGUMENT

The Frankfurt School, then, suggested a master principle of Western civilization within which Marx's particular critique of alienation can be situated: Domination in late capitalism can be traced to the early Greek ideas about how the person (subject) can master the world (object). But the critical theorists also addressed cultural sources of domination. In the *Dialectic of Enlightenment*, Horkheimer and Adorno developed the concept of the culture industry, which they elaborated in empirical and theoretical work. By the term *culture industry*, they referred to the ways in which entertainment and mass media became industries in post–World War II capitalism, both circulating cultural commodities and manipulating people's consciousness. Although Adorno devoted a great deal of time to analyzing "high," or mandarin, culture (e.g., his *Aesthetic Theory* [1984] and *Philosophy of Modern Music* [1973b]), his concern with aesthetic theory led him to practice a mode of critique that deployed the most abstract modes of cultural expression, ranging from the novels of Franz Kafka and plays of Samuel Beckett to the music of Arnold Schoenberg.

But the *Dialectic of Enlightenment* as well as numerous empirical articles (e.g., Adorno 1945, 1954) developed the idea that culture, in Marcuse's (1968) terms, has become "affirmative": Popular culture in this sense becomes a late capitalist mode of ideology that does not offer argued doctrines or theses about the necessity and rationality of the present society but rather provides an ephemeral narcotic that diverts people's attention from their real problems and idealizes the present by making the experience of its representation pleasurable. For example, watching television consumes people's time, keeps their minds off other aspects of their lives, and suggests that "people" solve their problems happily within the "real" world as they and we supposedly experience it. By watching these fictive people living happily together, resolving dilemmas within half an hour or an hour of television time, we project our own lives onto the small screen and imagine that we are inhabiting the roles we see depicted. This process of identification as well as diversion allows popular culture to "remedy" our alienation while incidentally producing profit for the television networks, film studios, magazines, and theme parks.

Now Marx understood that ideology such as religion was the opiate of the masses. The culture industry works along the same principle. But there are two differences. First, religion is a structured doctrine, set out in a book or code. As such, it can be studied and criticized. Second, religion promises relief from misery in the afterlife, whereas popular culture offers immediate relief through our identification with the various culture heroes of the moment. In postmodern, or fast (Agger 1989a), capitalism, popular culture inundates our lives, surrounding us with Baudrillardean simulations that coalesce into a thick tissue of representations and images. If religion can be put away on a bookshelf or confined to weekly churchgoing, it is much more difficult to turn off popular culture. In fast capitalism virtually everything becomes advertisement, which is difficult to view critically because it is cloaked in the illusions the culture industry interposes between us and reality.

It is the particular characteristic of late capitalism, according to the critical theorists, that culture is no longer a realm apart, a region of expression and experience in which critical insights can be gained. Marcuse in *One-Dimensional Man* suggested that this "second" dimension of critical insight, offered by novels, painting, and music, for example, has been collapsed into the "first" dimension of everyday experience, which is characterized by hegemony. For Adorno, Horkheimer, and Marcuse, art in the European Romantic tradition as well as in more recent abstract and expressionist forms can provide critical insight, whereas the tomes of critical political and social theory fall on deaf ears or are co-opted. The Frankfurt School suggested that art was a last refuge for critical ideas as well as for the expression and experience of beauty and satisfaction, thus auguring a better society. Through practiced illusion *(Schein)*, culture resists its own commodification, representing expression and experience uncontaminated by the logic of capital and retaining the ability to stand apart and thus think critically.

The post–World War II culture industry, including blockbuster movies, network television, trade books, mainstream newspapers and magazines, and commercial radio, absorbs culture in ways that worried the Frankfurt theorists inasmuch as they contended that culture has historically been independent as a vehicle of critical insight. Adorno in *Aesthetic Theory* (1984) and Marcuse in *The Aesthetic Dimension* (1978) explain the critical functions of art and culture and lament culture's absorption in the cycle of commodification and hegemony. Marcuse uses the example of how Beethoven is reduced from symphonic music to elevator Muzak, thus robbing his music of its ability to stimulate and challenge and turning it into background noise that goes in one ear and out the other. Culture in the nineteenth century meant attending live performances of great orchestral and operatic works and reading serious novels and poetry, requiring the patron to become involved in the work of cultural reception; in contrast, culture today requires merely channel surfing or clicking from Web site to site.

The Frankfurt School's emphasis on the critical potential of noncommodified art and culture, which resists its absorption into the culture industry, has drawn fire from all sides. Cultural conservatives argue that culture is and should be apolitical. Orthodox Marxists argue that culture is not a relevant political battleground, given the primacy of the economy. Proponents of cultural studies indict the Frankfurt preference for "high" culture. And they argue that Adorno missed instances of potentially liberating popular culture by, for example, writing off political rock music from the 1960s and jazz, which he notoriously characterized as fascist. Finally, from the periphery of the Frankfurt School itself, Walter Benjamin (1969) argued that "the mechanical reproduction of culture," its dissemination through printing and the electronic media, has the potential to spread the messages of critique and freedom. He did not accept Adorno's biting critique of "deauratized" art, art that loses the special "aura" of being performed live or hanging in a gallery of original works.

I agree with those who say that the Frankfurt theorists, with the notable exception of Marcuse for a period during the student movement of the 1960s, were too disdainful of popular culture simply because it was popular. They missed the emancipatory potential of certain modes of even commodified popular culture, such as movies that stir anger and spark insight (as Ryan and Kellner examine in their important *Camera Politica* [1988] and as feminist film theorists like Laura Mulvey [1989] note). However, I also agree with Adorno, Horkheimer, and Marcuse that the culture industry has become a crucial political and economic factor in late capitalism, diverting people's attention from their real problems, offering false solutions projected onto the "lives" of fictional characters and encoded in the sweet harmonies of music, and of course making profits for MGM, NBC, and *Time* magazine. The culture industry has helped manipulate consciousness and thus prolong capitalism past Marx's expectation of its demise. Although Marx recognized that culture could function ideologically (e.g., his analysis of religion), he accorded culture relatively little weight in his political-economic analysis of capitalism. Of course, that was neither the product of purposeful omission nor shortsightedness on his part. The movie studios, television networks, and trade publishers were as yet unknown in mid-nineteenth-century Europe. To have prophesied CNN, the "Terminator" movies, or *Penthouse* magazine would have taken a special seer.

Again, the culture industry argument does not undercut Marxism's basic theoretical framework, which links the logic of capital to commodity-fetishized human relationships, making profits through human relationships that are mystified and hence experienced as natural, naturelike arrangements. What Marx called commodity fetishism, which he argued is built into every commodified relationship in which workers exchange their labor power for a living wage, foreshadows cultural hegemony and domination in that it has in common with them *the false representation and hence endorsement of existing social relationships*. These naturelike representations are robbed of their historicity—susceptibility to change. The electronic culture industry of the post–World War II United States greatly accelerates the rate of mystification and deepens it, making it much harder to "unpack" (as postmodernists term it) the cultural representations inundating us from morning to night for their deliberate authorship and hence their political message.

Cultural studies unpacks or deconstructs these cultural artifacts, discourses, and institutions, much as Adorno theorized his experience of listening to radio, watching television, and reading the newspaper. Going to Disney World becomes a book called *Vinyl Leaves* (Fjellman 1992). Watching television and movies becomes *Screens of Power* (Luke 1989) and *Boxed In* (Miller 1988). A road trip across the United States becomes *America* (Baudrillard 1988). Culture becomes "text" for postmodern students of culture, suggesting an integrated series of analytical and theoretical approaches called cultural studies. My point here is that the Frankfurt School initiated cultural studies with their theory of the culture industry, overcoming their own disdain for popular culture with a series of provocative cultural readings. If cultural theory for the Frankfurt theorists was largely an exercise tracing the depths to which domination has sunk in everyday experience, cultural studies for later theorists and critics has focused on ways in which everyday culture affords opportunities for resistance and reconstruction by independent authors, creators, producers, and distributors.

Ultimately, the critical theorists who developed their revisions and extrapolations of Marxism in the context of the Great Depression and later the Holocaust were pessimistic that left-wing social movements could be reinvigorated. What Adorno called "total administration" referred to the way in which all experience is mobilized by system-serving imperatives. After the Holocaust, the Frankfurt theorists became extremely pessimistic, although Marcuse briefly viewed the New Left in the United States as a new "collective subject" to replace the proletariat. He expressed this optimism in his book *An Essay on Liberation* (1969) but recanted it in *Counterrevolution and Revolt* (1973), in which he took the New Left and counterculture to task for abandoning rationality and theory, precisely the charges leveled against many versions of postmodernism today. The concentration camp became a metaphor for Adorno, who argued that democratic capitalism had incorporated the Nazis' penchant for total control while doing away with the appearance of brutal domination and extermination. In Eisenhower's United States, concentration camps were unnecessary as long as television reproduced conformity.

Many, even on the left, have responded that Adorno's apocalyptic Marxism exaggerates and fails to make distinctions, for example between Auschwitz, in which millions of people were exterminated, and the U.S. suburbs, in which people lead stupefied, programmed lives dedicated to shopping and annual vacations. I agree with this critique, although I think there is much to be learned from Adorno, Horkheimer, and Marcuse. In understanding Western civilization as a futile attempt to dominate the "object," Adorno anticipates postmodern theorists' stress on the inevitability of difference, deferral, and undecidability, hence humbling the leftist project. Adorno reminds Marxists to be humble in the face of the imponderability and ambiguity of existence. He teaches irony in the face of the inability of language to convey transparent meaning. Existential Marxists such as Sartre (1976) and Merleau-Ponty (1964a, 1964b) offer many of the same lessons from within their existentialist and phenomenological versions of Western Marxism.

## HABERMAS'S COMMUNICATION THEORY

I already discussed Habermas's neo-Kantian critique of Marx's epistemology, which emerged in his *Knowledge and Human Interests* (1971). As I said, this led Habermas to truncate Adorno, Horkheimer, and Marcuse's emancipatory agenda, abandoning the goals of creating a nonalienated science and technology as well as nonalienated labor. In subsequent work such as *Theory of Communicative Action* (1984, 1987b), Habermas developed a version of critical theory that overcame what he took to be other limitations of the original Frankfurt theorists' critical theory. In particular, Habermas argued that the Frankfurt theorists did not sufficiently differen-

tiate their own critique of domination from the framework within which
the Greeks, German idealists, and even Marx conceptualized the relationship between subjects (people) and objects (other people and nature).
Habermas urged a shift from what he called the "paradigm of consciousness," which accepts the Western duality of subject and object, to the "paradigm of communication." This communicative paradigm conceptualizes
knowledge and social practice not in terms of a duality between subject
and object—which Habermas says can be resolved only through either
pure idealist consciousness (flight from the world) or domination—but
through a reconceptualization of *the subject as inherently intersubjective*.
This intersubjective subject has the primary capacity for communication,
not just labor. If we return to Habermas's earlier epistemological critique
of Marx, we find that he believes that only through self-reflection and
communication can people really control their own destiny and restructure
society in humane ways. Habermas disagrees with Marx that people are
made truly human through labor. Drawing on sections in Hegel's *Phenomenology of Mind* and from communication theory and speech-act theory,
Habermas argues instead that people humanize themselves through interaction.

Only through interaction and communication can people master society,
forming social movements and achieving power. Finally, communication
provides an ethical basis for critical theory, represented in what Habermas
contends is the basic intention of communication to form consensus
through rational discussion between interlocutors (speakers and writers)
who do not browbeat each other, make "of course" statements, use ideology for the purposes of deception, and fail to take turns (Habermas 1979,
1996). Habermas reformulates socialism as the ideal speech situation, in
which chances for dialogue are more or less equal and in which people understand that their interactions are to be governed by the goal of consensus
formation. Habermas first elaborated these notions in terms of what he
calls a "universal pragmatics" of communicative competence, published as
a postscript to his *Knowledge and Human Interests*.

Habermas's theory of communicative action thus both overcomes the
romanticism and utopianism of the original Frankfurt theorists and shifts
critical theory from the paradigm of consciousness to the paradigm of
communication within which theoretical, normative, and ethical problems
can be solved. In developing this reformulation of critical theory, Habermas integrates a wide variety of social and psychological theories, including the work of Durkheim, Parsons, Nicklaus Luhmann (1982), Gadamer,
and speech-act theorists such as Karl Otto Apel (1980) and John Searle
(1979). Habermas also recasts a central theme in Weber when he urges the
reconceptualization of the social system as interacting elements that he
terms "system" and "lifeworld." One of the main problems of late capital-

ism, he says, is that the system "colonizes" the lifeworld in such a way that people are prevented from developing shared cultural meanings—community—from the foundation of everyday experience and language. This is akin to Adorno's concept of total administration, although it is more dynamic in the sense that Habermas argues that we can alter the relationship between system and lifeworld and overcome aspects of the colonization of the lifeworld, notably by developing people's communicative capacities for engaging in rational discussion as a basis of democracy. These efforts can emerge as new social movements, including environmentalism, feminism, and postcolonialism. These social movements, founded on the ethical principles of undistorted rational communication, are our best bets for generating the kind of transformational "collective subject" Marx and Lukacs originally identified as the working class. Indeed, Habermas rejects this notion of collective subjectivity, given his shift from the paradigm of consciousness to that of communication, and instead suggests new modes of democratic intersubjectivity that not only embody rational communication as an ideal form of social life but thereby begin to change society in democratic ways.

There is much to be said for Habermas's communication theory. A close reading reveals that he has not abandoned Marxism but engaged in a reformulation of Marxism more sweeping than any to date. Habermas has been criticized on a number of fronts. Fraser argues that his concept of the lifeworld does not explicitly include women and gender, even though an example of his new social movements is the women's movement. Marxists of a more traditional type claim that his notion of communication ignores power ungrounded in communication. He gives short shrift to economics, notably to Marx's critique of the logic of capital. I think his omission of gender, and especially his inattention to the politics of personal life, is a serious problem. He clearly understands the importance of economics; he is not saying that late capitalism has transcended the contradictory and self-destructive logic of capital identified first by Marx. Indeed, in *Legitimation Crisis* (1975) Habermas argues that the manifestations of the structural crises Marx anticipated as articulations of capital's contradictory logic occur primarily in the political sphere, given the way in which the state now assumes responsibility for managing economic crises. I suspect that Marx, were he alive today, would agree with this extension of his argument.

Other critics contend that Habermas inflates communication into a grand metaphor of social life that not only constitutes the medium in which people are oppressed but also serves as a moral standard (e.g., undistorted communication; the ideal speech situation) by which social reform should be judged. But all social theories work metaphorically, reducing the complexities of social life to a few structural linchpins. For Marx, this structural linchpin was the commodification of labor in capitalism.

This structure both exploited workers (the labor contract being only a *fictio juris,* or legal fiction, masking the theft of "value" imparted by labor to the commodity) and was to lead to the downfall of the system, given the tendency of the rate of profit to fall. For Parsons, society could be understood in terms of four variables constituting both personality systems' and social systems' self-regulating, pattern-maintaining tendencies. For Adorno, "identity" was a societal logic expressing the dominating tendencies of Western civilization, including capitalism. For Derrida, the metaphysics of presence concealed the undecidability of all language and writing. To indict Habermas for inflating communication into a metaphor, especially given the elaborate detail with which he has developed his communication theory, is somewhat unfair.

However, the concept of communication itself, as it exists in Habermas's work, tends to exclude what postmodern theorists call discourse, which is a broader category than interpersonal communication. Although discourse can take place between two people, it also includes other cultural expressions all the way from advertising to the journal page of science. Discourse includes the representation of women in literary and visual culture. Discourse includes writing in academic disciplines. To understand these discourses as contested sites of power, as Foucault does, is very important for critical social theorists who want to make sense of the insidious, often almost invisible nature of ideology today. The central contribution of postmodern theory to critical theory is precisely this conceptualization of discourse, which both broadens Habermas's concept of communication and provides interpretive tools and techniques (e.g., deconstruction) with which to "authorize" these discourses in bringing their hidden assumptions and arguments to light, thus contesting them. Habermas misses discourse theory and its deconstructive mode of ideology critique because he dismisses postmodernism as a form of neoconservatism. Habermas believes that postmodern theory abandons the project of modernity, which all rationalist and modernist theorists, especially Marxists, must embrace. Although I agree with him that many postmodern theorists, especially in the United States, celebrate postmodernity and thus cannot offer radical social criticism, postmodern theory itself affords critical theory vital insights and interpretive techniques for making sense of popular culture's current hegemony.

This leads to a second problem with Habermas's concept of communication. He does not take seriously enough the concept of the culture industry and thus does not offer a version of cultural studies appropriate to understanding various cultural discourses and practices today. Habermas is certainly concerned to protect various everyday cultures springing from the lifeworld against their colonization by what he calls the system (thus reformulating the original Frankfurt theorists' critique of cultural domination). But his conception of colonization suggests that people's attempts to produce genuine civic cultures that help reconstitute the public sphere are simply thwarted by what he terms the "colonization" of everyday life from without and above. His solution to this colonization is communication—consensus formation through ideal speech. I think this falls far short of an adequate conception of culture and of cultural hegemony. How can people create cultural meaning from the ground of everyday life if the production and distribution of culture take place through the massive central institutions of television, movies, publishing, recording, and journalism and are then disseminated in ways that make these texts difficult to "read" as the political discourses they really are? Habermas does not offer an adequate conception of cultural resistance and reconstruction apart from the vague notion of ideal speech.

The other problem with Habermas involves his reception as a social theorist. In the preface to the first volume of *Theory of Communicative Action* (1984), Habermas indicates that he wants his elaborate reformulation of critical theory to be taken seriously in the university. He realizes that Adorno and Horkheimer were marginal intellectual figures and lost potential influence because they disdained and were disdained by the bourgeois university and its organization into narrow academic disciplines. By engaging with existing non-Marxist social theorists, including Durkheim, Weber, and Parsons, Habermas hopes to convince non-Marxist social theorists to take his own theory seriously, thus legitimizing critical theory in the university and increasing its potential political influence. Although I in no way disagree with Habermas's project, there has been a tendency for Habermas to get swallowed by the traditions from which he draws in order to create dialogue with bourgeois social theorists. In other words, the very "communication" Habermas lauds as a form of free human association has required him laboriously to borrow ideas from opposing traditions, for example Parsons's structural functionalism, in order to impress their partisans with his seriousness and theoretical legitimacy. But the influence of these opposing theories on his own critical theory has tended to transform it into yet another elaborate, densely argued but politically irrelevant edifice that best resembles a lengthy and erudite doctoral dissertation. In displaying his intellectual respect for these opposing traditions not only by citing them but by engaging with them at length—in order to win respect for his theory—Habermas has made too many accommodations to them. Thus, his *Theory of Communicative Action* is as scholastic as Parsons's work, earning Habermas points for scholarship but robbing his work of political vitality.

Unlike some leftist theorists, I do not "blame" Habermas for this. Blame is beside the point. He decided he had to make concessions in order to be taken seriously and get his points across. He is correct that Horkheimer and Adorno were fugitive intellectuals who produced huge bodies of highly

erudite work and wrote biting social criticism that was largely ignored in
the American and German university. Habermas rightly wants to avoid this
fate. The marginalization of critical theory defeats its own intent to raise
consciousness and change minds. The issue of critical theory's lack of accessibility is an important one, as Jacoby argues in *The Last Intellectuals*
(1987). By writing scholarly books aimed at a few similarly expert readers,
critical theorists ensure their own isolation. Does Habermas solve this
problem? Although he writes for other social theorists who have strong
disciplinary identities, he does not write particularly accessibly, nor does he
engage broad public issues in a way that would have addressed not only
other academics but members of the reading public at large. Jacoby argues
that few critical theorists under the age of forty-five write "big" public
books of the kind that used to dominate the American intellectual scene,
such as the works of Irving Howe, Lewis Mumford, and C. Wright Mills.
Although Habermas does partly achieve his desire to be taken seriously by
disciplinary social theorists, for example by scholars such as Jeffrey
Alexander and Richard Münch (Alexander et al. 1987) who address the
so-called micro-macro problem from within sociology, he does not overcome critical theory's isolation or increase its audience in a meaningful
way. If anything, given his own enormous erudition and breadth of scholarship, his work requires a readership as well educated as he is.

Has the price of theoretical accommodation to the likes of Parsons
greatly enhanced the public positioning of Habermas's critical theory? Although it has given Habermas a somewhat bigger academic audience share
than either Adorno or Horkheimer enjoyed as well as greater academic legitimacy in light of his engagement with some standard disciplinary literatures, thus mainstreaming critical theory, Habermas has not engaged the
public, as I just noted, nor has he addressed social problems in a vivid way.
His works read like standard academic theoretical fare. This stands in
sharp contrast to Marcuse, who from the mid-1950s to the mid-1970s
wrote many accessible works such as *One-Dimensional Man* (1964) and
*Essay on Liberation* (1969). Alone among the first generation of the
Frankfurt School who fled fascism, Marcuse remained in the United States
after the war. This allowed or perhaps required him to write "to" Americans, encouraging stylistic accessibility and more direct address to pressing
social problems and social movements than Horkheimer, Adorno, or
Habermas achieved. But the work of Marcuse has largely fallen into obscurity (see Agger 1994b). In this light, Habermas enjoys the higher academic
profile, even if he has had to make compromises in the way he has engaged
and incorporated bourgeois theoretical literatures in order to be taken seriously as a social theorist.

# CHAPTER 5

# Feminist Theory

## PATRIARCHY: ENGENDERING THEORY

Feminist theory has contributed a great deal to the development of critical social theory. Like Betty Friedan, who in *The Feminine Mystique* (1963) argues that the problems of middle-class women go largely unspoken, feminist theorists give voice to issues neglected by most male theorists. Indeed, to treat feminist theory in a book on almost exclusively male theories is itself controversial, given feminist theorists' often unsparing critiques of "malestream" knowledge and theory. However, I believe that this strategy is defensible in light of the growing body of work (e.g., Fraser 1989; Benhabib 1992) dedicated to demonstrating connections between Marxism and feminism. Indeed, the Marxism-feminism relationship informs much of this chapter. I treat feminist theory as a legitimate variety of critical social theory. Many of the tenets of critical social theory outlined in Chapter 1 form the foundation of feminist theories that explain domination in social-structural terms.

Although I address the diversity of feminist theories, for they do range widely (see Donovan 1985; Jaggar 1983; Walby 1990), I discuss the generic contributions of most versions of feminist theory to critical social theory. I also address distinct parallels between certain feminist themes and themes found in other male critical theories. What I mean by a "male" critical theory is not necessarily a theory developed by a man but a theory that ignores issues of the politics of gender. Thus, the first distinctive achievement of feminist theory is in making the politics of sexuality central to understanding oppression. Heretofore, gender politics were invisible to male social theorists, who regarded issues of sexual politics as nonissues because they were located in the so-called private sphere of domestic life. Feminist theorists located the politics of sexuality in the household, notably in the household division of labor as well as in prevailing conceptions of femininity and masculinity. They then connected these household political dynamics, such as who does the childcare and cooks the meals, to political and economic dynamics outside the home, notably in the realm of paid work.

Their argument is that patriarchy, or male supremacy, arises from the sexual division of labor, which exists in both the so-called private and public spheres. Feminist theory not only politicizes sexuality and domesticity but connects domestic gender politics to gender politics in the paid work force and public life. There are in effect two sexual divisions of labor or two levels of the sexual division of labor that are tightly connected: That women are largely responsible for domestic labor is reflected and reproduced in the fact that they are also relegated to poorly paid and nonunionized "pink-collar" sectors of the work force. Feminists conceive of patriarchy as a structural problem for women that has generally been ignored by male social theorists, who locate domination in political and economic issues from which women have been largely excluded. An interesting point of contention between feminists and Marxists (e.g., see Hartmann 1979; Shelton and Agger 1992) has been the issue of the relationship between patriarchy and capitalism.

Feminists argue that male theorists have disregarded the oppression of women in the household, labor market, polity, and culture because they see women essentially as noncitizens. Indeed, women won the vote only relatively recently in the United States and even later in other Western countries. (In 1869 Wyoming was the first state to grant women the franchise; the federal government did not follow suit until 1920.) The view that women are not citizens stemmed from classical Greek political philosophy, which reserved the polis, or polity, only for men; women and slaves were considered noncitizens or subcitizens (see Elshtain 1981) who could not participate in public life and thus could be ignored by political and social theorists. The devaluation of women took the form not only of denying them citizenship but also of denigrating or devaluing their work, including domestic labor and various service and support jobs in the paid labor market (Eisenstein 1979). Male social theory thus did not make thematic either women or the work they do, and hence their social problems, until very recently.

This is true even of Marxism. Although Engels (1972) wrote a book after Marx's death on *The Origin of the Family, Private Property and the State*, attempting to explain how socialism would solve the problems of women in that it would free them to enter the labor market, neither he nor Marx dealt with male supremacy as a theoretical topic in its own right. It is probably true that all of these male social theorists since the Greeks were personally sexist, but what is more important here is that their theories were sexist in that they ignored women's oppression as a legitimate topic.

That is, even if the theorists had not been sexist, their theories were, inasmuch as they did not deal with women except as an afterthought.

This discussion recalls my earlier examination of multiculturalism. Feminists, like proponents of multiculturalism, argue that it is wrong to identify class as the only relevant dimension along which people are exploited. They argue that gender and race are structuring dimensions of inequality in their own right. Hence, multicultural theorists argue that class, race, and gender form a theoretical trinity that should guide all theorizing and research. Implicit is the assumption that class, race, and gender are separate, separable dimensions of oppression and should not be collapsed together. I believe that it is possible to theorize class, race, and gender as part of the same overarching system of domination, but I agree with feminists who contend that women's exploitation cannot simply be reduced to their class position. Rather, although women's typically disadvantaged class positions contribute to their overall oppression, it is also their gender that disadvantages them inasmuch as they are oppressed *as women*. By now, after extensive social and economic research on women's inequality, it is very difficult to deny this. Similarly, it is difficult to deny that people of color are disadvantaged not only because they are members of a certain class or underclass but also because they have been victims of racial discrimination per se.

My argument against postmodern multiculturalism is that class, race, and gender are typically treated not only as analytically separate but that this analytical separation underlies an identity politics necessarily fragmenting the working class, people of color, and women into separate and even competing interest groups. This produces a neoliberal political agenda that leaves the large structures of our society intact but simply attempts to improve the lots of individuals within these various multicultural fractions. Although these are "good" efforts (e.g., affirmative action programs) in the sense that they improve the everyday lives of people, they are not inconsistent with the structural agenda of critical social theory, which is to change "everything" while also changing particular things. But multiculturalism is quite tempting in light of male social theorists' typical neglect of issues of gender and race.

Marxism arose from Marx's writings, which helped inform various socialist workers' movements in his wake; in contrast, feminist theory arose directly from the 1960s women's movement, which split off from the male-dominated New Left (see Breines 1982; Evans 1979). In this sense, Marxism has always been more interested in issues of doctrine and theory than has feminism. Although academic bookstores and college courses are bursting with interest in feminist theory, much of this work followed upon and is continually informed by pragmatic issues of feminist struggle. The original American suffragettes argued that women must win the franchise, setting off the first wave of the U.S. women's movement. The second wave of the women's movement, which began in the 1960s, attempted to win abortion rights, pay equity, and protection against sex discrimination and sexual harassment. Although there have been feminist classics such as de Beauvoir's *Second Sex* (1953), Greer's *Female Eunuch* (1971), and Friedan's *Feminine Mystique* (1963), these books derived from the ongoing struggles of women as well as from women authors' personal struggles to win equality both in the household and labor force. As such, they do not lay out doctrine in the way that Marx's works did, which liberates feminism from issues of canonical interpretation and affords feminists a flexibility not enjoyed by Marxists. Once Marx set forth his exhaustive and rather technical analysis of the logic of capital in his many books, he set the stage for future Marxist disputation. Deviation from Marx's canon was deemed apostasy by true believers. As well, Marx's inconsistencies and ambiguities occasioned decades of Marxist scholarship dedicated to establishing what Marx "really" said.

For these reasons, feminists have developed their theories in a more grounded way than have most Marxists. Their theoretical work reflects and affects their personal and public struggles to achieve feminist progress. This raises the second important contribution of feminist theory to an understanding of patriarchy. In addition to developing the notion of the politics of sexuality framed by the sexual division of labor, feminist theorists have argued that the personal is political, refusing the traditional Greek separation of private and public spheres. That women were excluded from public life helps explain their insistence that politics for women unfolds in venues not traditionally deemed important by male theory. This has caused feminists to pay theoretical attention to the politics of sexuality and domestic labor, addressed above. It has also importantly reflected the contention of feminists that the process of social change begins and ends with the ways in which we conduct our intimate lives, involving sexuality, childcare, housework, and authority relations. If social change does not bring about these qualitative personal changes, including changes in fundamental values, it is not worth achieving. Similarly, feminists argue that the only way to produce permanent change is to begin to live better lives in the here and now, not postponing liberation.

Here feminist theories parallel a central theme in the Frankfurt School's critical theory. Marcuse (1969) made much the same argument for what he called "the new sensibility," a proponent of which would initiate social change in his or her own everyday life, recognizing that the long road to socialism, littered with privations and sacrifices as well as an expedient authoritarianism, never ends. As Korsch said, the dictatorship "of" the proletariat became a dictatorship "over" the proletariat as Soviet state power was entrenched. The history of socialism has proven Marcuse and Korsch correct: Short-term authoritarianism, justified theoretically by various notions of revolutionary exigency, only reproduces and intensifies authoritarianism.

Like the Frankfurt School theorists, feminists have deeply understood that personal and interpersonal changes must underlie structural changes. Although various feminist theories differ on the priority they place on personal change, with liberal feminists arguing that most long-term goals can be achieved solely through the efforts of individual women, all feminists link personal and public change both for practical and moral reasons. One must live a "feminist" life and act like a feminist if one hopes to convert everyone else to feminism and bring about a feminist society. Of course, differences remain about what exactly constitutes a feminist life, for example, around the issue of whether women should oppose pornography as an expression of patriarchy or whether they can accommodate feminist erotica, as sexual-agency feminists do.

Feminists thus address the politics of sexuality and domesticity on both personal and public levels, arguing, through the concept of the sexual division of labor, that women's subordination to men in each sphere is in fact linked. The third main contribution of feminist theory to the gendering of male social theory, then, is the notion of the sexual division of labor, which helps explain how women's subordination in the labor market, polity, and culture mimics and accentuates their subordination in the household. Feminists oppose male-anthropological defenses of the sexual division of labor as a rational way of dealing with the original economic and domestic requirements of hunting-gathering societies. They also oppose the Victorian idea of the family as a happy haven grounded in romantic love. In the Victorian family, which remains the contemporary model of the so-called nuclear family, women were to nurture men and children in return for their share of the alleged family wage (the wage paid husbands by employers in order to support not only themselves but also their wives and children).

Feminists oppose the sexual division of labor because there is no biologically necessary reason why women should raise children and do housework while men work outside the home for wages, thus making wives dependent on the goodwill of their husbands for sustenance. Feminists also oppose the sexual division of labor because it provides a model for the devaluation of women's activities in all spheres—household, politics, economics, culture. That women are denied a wage for their domestic labor, which is economically necessary for the perpetuation of capitalism inasmuch as it reproduces both husbands and children, sets a precedent for denying women money, power, influence, and personhood.

The sexual division of labor makes way for the objectification of women by men, which is the fourth important contribution of feminist theory to male social theory. As objects for men in the family, acting as both helpmates and sexual partners, women are objectified in the public sphere. The long history of misogyny (men's hatred of women) stems from men's treatment of women as in effect objects of their sexual desire and economic and emotional needs. Although this is not to deny that heterosexual women may need and want men, too, as sexual-agency feminists persuasively argue, women's objectification by men prevents women from realizing their own authentic needs for love, sex, and nurturance. A paradigm of women's objectification, according to feminists, is women's physical and cultural degradation by a society in which it is permissible to turn women into a spectacle and receptacle for male pleasure. Thus, the sexual division of labor not only disempowers women politically and economically; it also degrades women sexually and culturally.

The fifth contribution of feminist theory to male social theory is its critique of compulsory heterosexuality, which is a central precept of the Victorian concept of femininity and derives from its assumption that women acquire value in terms of their emotional and sexual value to men. At issue here is not simply the obvious fact that some women are lesbian (perhaps "by nature") but, even more important, that femininity/masculinity is not a dichotomous variable but is better seen as a continuum, as sex researchers and psychoanalytic theorists have been arguing for years. Masters and Johnson (1966), for example, have shown the empirical "normalcy" of same-sex encounters for the majority of both women and men in the United States. Although these may be one-time-only encounters, these data and much of the rest of their research demonstrate convincingly that people do not come neatly packaged as either (and only) "man" or "woman," either masculine or feminine. Feminist theory challenges the notions that femininity is derived from male perception and pleasure and that femininity and masculinity exist as dichotomous categories or variables into which people can be easily sorted. Indeed, one implication of this approach to feminist theory is to suggest that many people are really bisexual by orientation, even if they do not act on these impulses. This is especially true for women who view having sex with men as necessarily fraught with power dynamics that rob their sexual encounters of both pleasure and meaning.

This aspect of feminist theory is receiving increasing attention from feminist theorists who question the very norm of heterosexuality. A rapidly burgeoning offshoot of feminist theory and feminist studies, gay and lesbian studies is coalescing into a body of work known as queer theory, which assails heterosexual culture theoretically and politically (Butler 1990; Fuss 1991). Queer theorists argue that to be a lesbian is to occupy a certain subject position from which one does not allow oneself to become an object of male desire and thus rejects prevailing sharp cultural distinctions between femininity and masculinity. Straight women as well fall under the purview of this approach to gay and lesbian feminist theory when they, too, reject their subject positions as objects "for" men and clear distinctions between femininity and masculinity (Kitzinger 1987). Indeed, psychoanalytically inclined feminists (e.g., Chodorow 1978; Benjamin 1988), queer theorists (e.g., Di Stefano 1991), and feminist social constructionists (e.g., Connell 1987) argue that the traditionally bifurcated categories of "man" and "woman" are in fact much more blurred, given people's bisexual tendencies and given that people actually "produce" their genders in ways that they perceive to be socially and culturally relevant. Thus, what it means to "have" or "be of" a particular gender is quite variable, suggesting modes of masculinity and femininity that closely resemble each other and perhaps even blur to the point of indistinguishability. A February 1994 survey by *Esquire* suggests that many American women between the ages of eighteen and twenty-five deny being feminist (inasmuch as they identify feminism with a certain didactic and anti-male doctrine that has been surpassed in our supposedly "postfeminist" era), *but* they are also quite tolerant of women with lesbian and bisexual identities. Upon closer examination, most of these women are essentially feminist in that they support significant economic, political, and cultural goals of feminism. Indeed, their feminism even extends to queer theory inasmuch as they deem lesbianism an acceptable subject position.

Here, being a lesbian does not only mean that a woman has sex with women (see Hoagland and Penelope 1988). (After all, many women have sex with both women and men. And even if they have sex only with men, they may want to have sex with women, too, or exclusively.) Feminist theory raises important questions about the nature of sexual orientation, beginning with Rita Mae Brown's concept of women who are "women identified" as opposed to defining their identities and orientations, including sexual, in terms of their subordinate relations with men. To be a lesbian, for queer theory, means that one does not accept the objectification of women, which defines women's value in terms of male perception and pleasure. Rather, one embraces one's own subjectivity as "queer"—that is, as neither masculine nor feminine as traditionally defined in Victorian culture, in terms of differentiated sex roles that derive from a rigid sexual division of labor. If femininity has historically meant that women were not-men—did not earn money, vote, or maintain emotional stoicism—queer theory constructs femininity in terms of women's own identification of their subject positions as people not defined in relation to men or in relation to their difference from men. In this sense, gay men—and even straight women and men—can be "queer" when they shed traditional sex roles, identities, and orientations framed in terms of the polarity of masculinity versus femininity (Sedgwick 1990). Although queer theory is a recent variety of feminist theory that is far from widely accepted, given its challenge to heterosexual norms that depend on the sharp bifurcation of the masculine and feminine, its argument about the relativity and social production of gender is important. It challenges Victorian assumptions about the clarity of gender categories and in particular interrogates femininity as a subject position largely defined for women by men.

These five contributions of feminist theory to male theory do not exhaust the richness of feminism's particular implications both for theory and empirical research (e.g., see England 1993). Feminist theorists have attempted to correct male theorists' blind spots with respect to issues of gender as well as their unexamined assumptions about patriarchy. Feminist theorists who favor postmodernism tend to argue that feminist theory can no more solve all problems or address all issues than can any "male" social theory (Flax 1990). Instead, feminists must appreciate "difference," including differences among various feminist approaches (e.g., Africana, lesbian, socialist, postcolonial). Feminist theory, especially when conceived under the influence of postmodernism, shies away from being a "totalizing" theory that addresses "everything" (Weedon 1987). This is a significant difference from male social theories, most of which, at least until French theory, intended a universality of explanation. Even now most male social theories, apart from postmodernism, view themselves as total frameworks for social understanding. Feminist theorists argue that this is yet another conceit of men who project their own gender perspectives, as well as race, class, and national origin, onto everybody else.

## VARIETIES OF FEMINIST THEORY

Alison Jaggar offers a useful overview of the types of feminist theory in *Feminist Politics and Human Nature* (1983). Since that book was published, Africana feminism, queer theory, and postmodern feminism have come into their own. In this section I survey the species of feminist theory, attending to overlap as well as differences. As I said above, feminist theory proliferates difference, which feminists do not regard as a bad thing but as an appreciation of the world's heterogeneity as well as a reflection of the different subject positions feminists occupy and thus the different ways in which they theorize their circumstances. Most typologies of feminist theory begin with a discussion of liberal feminism, radical or cultural feminism, and socialist feminism. My account proceeds the same way, although, as I just noted, I also address Africana feminism, queer theory, and postmodern feminist theories, which now supplement the original trio.

*Liberal feminism* (e.g., Friedan 1963) argues that women can improve their positions in the family and society through a combination of individual initiative and attainment (e.g., higher education), rational discussion with men, especially husbands, who can be convinced to modify their gender roles, the passage of legislation regarding daycare, which will allow women to pursue careers, and the defense of laws granting the right to legal abortions and protecting women against sex discrimination (e.g., Title VII of the Civil Rights Act). This combination of reforms and persuasion, including political lobbying, has been the tried-and-true approach of the mainstream women's movement, characterized by the National Organization of Women (NOW). Liberal feminists are probably in the numerical majority of American feminists. As I noted above, many self-styled postfeminist younger women embrace liberal feminist values and political methods even though they eschew the feminist label either because they think it is old-fashioned or because they think its connotation is too militant and anti-male. So-called postfeminism is an interesting topic in its own right, to which I return in a later section.

Liberal feminists (e.g., Wolf 1993) accept the idea that it is normal, even natural, for people to want to form families composed of a heterosexual adult couple with biological and/or adoptive offspring. That is, they do not assail the family, as many radical feminists and queer theorists do, as the source of women's oppression. Increasingly, younger feminists and more radical liberal feminists accept lesbian families as legitimate. This is not to say that liberal feminists do not find fault with aspects of many families today but simply that they accept that family is here to stay and, indeed, that people need to build families in order to fulfill themselves. (Many liberal feminists accept singlehood-by-choice as a legitimate lifestyle alternative.)

The problems of the family, according to liberal feminists, include an unfair sexual division of labor, such that women do more than their share of childcare, household labor, and emotional work. The solution to this is largely an interpersonal one, with wives negotiating a "better deal" with their husbands, who should be encouraged to take part in parenting, housework, and emotional nurturance. This is not simply designed to benefit the mother, who can then embark on a fulfilling career. Nancy Chodorow's important *Reproduction of Mothering* (1978) argues persuasively that boys suffer when they are brought up in "father absent" families, families in which fathers are distant role models uninvolved in the everyday process of nurturance. Boys raised this way do not sufficiently work through their ambivalence about women and thus learn to be sexist in their adult lives, according to Chodorow.

Liberal feminists maintain that men can be reasoned with—convinced to shoulder more of the burden of childcare and domestic labor in the interest of greater marital equity. But studies (e.g., Blumstein and Schwartz 1983) show that husbands become resentful when their wives expect them to do more around the house. That is, husbands have a vested political interest in maintaining an unbalanced household division of labor. Indeed, there is *more* conflict in couples with greater marital equity in this respect than in couples with traditional household divisions of labor. Of course, that in itself is no reason for wives not to urge their husbands to do more; change is often hard-won. But liberal feminists assume that women's rational negotiations with their husbands in the context of the nuclear family will win important gains for women, neglecting the possibility that men have a structural interest in oppressing women and denying more radical alternatives such as the avoidance of marriage altogether (see Ehrenreich 1983; Shelton 1992). Liberal feminists do not challenge the norm in this society that women are meant to couple heterosexually with men and have their babies.

Liberal feminists' belief in the power of reason extends to their political postures, which are reformist and generally nonadversarial, utilizing established political and legal institutions where possible. Although one should not diminish electoral gains made by women candidates or successful legal challenges to existing sexist laws, these routes certainly constitute a "long road" to overall change for women. These strategies neglect the economic basis of sexism (e.g., women earning 70 percent of what men earn in paid work) as well as the cultural representations of women as objects for male pleasure. Although critical social theorists do not in principle reject "working within the system," they do not restrict such efforts to the political and legal superstructure, as Marx called it, but also attack central economic and cultural institutions that promote domination.

One of the main reasons why liberal feminist women shy away from questioning the family more radically is their heterosexism, the belief that heterosexuality is the normal state, with homosexuality constituting deviation. Inasmuch as "family" in Western society has always meant a domestic unit with one woman and one man, coupled legally, radical feminists' argument that lesbians should be seen both culturally and legally to constitute a family is threatening to liberal feminists who view homosexuality as unnatural and wrong. This is certainly not to say that all liberal feminists, who negotiate gender roles rationally with their husbands and work within established political and legal institutions for gradual change, are homophobic (hate homosexuals). Many are not. By and large, women in this society are more accepting of homosexuality than are men. But rarely do liberal feminists question the very institution of marriage that unites husband and wife legally and plays a particular economic and cultural role. The heterosexual family is a given. Indeed, most liberal feminists strongly defend "family" and "family values," even though they also argue for a more "companionate" and egalitarian marital unit. (For a discussion of the textbook representation of this version of family, see Agger 1989c: 229–300.) Family is seen to constitute a haven somehow unsullied by the heartless political concerns of the public world.

One of the main reasons liberal feminists take a "mainstream," reformist posture of working through dominant political and legal institutions is that they accept or assume the fundamental goodness and permanence of capitalism. Only socialist feminists (e.g., Eisenstein 1979) challenge this assumption. In this sense, liberal feminists accept the capitalist rules of the game and formulate reform strategies both in terms of slightly modifying those rules (e.g., legalizing abortion; mandating universal daycare; preserving Title VII) and in terms of individual women's career advancement. This is the yuppie feminism of *Ms.* magazine, NOW, and the Democratic Party (Steinem 1986). Again, one hesitates to condemn this approach to feminism inasmuch as feminism rightly stresses that social change can be deemed successful only if it improves the lives of actual women. But Marcuse and more radical and socialist feminists argue that the gains of individual women, whether achieved through rational negotiation with husbands or earned by extra initiative in the labor market, must be "dialectically" connected to larger structural changes that benefit everyone, regardless of class, race, and gender. One reason liberal feminism has been attacked by Africana feminists (see hooks 1984; Collins 1991) is that it only speaks to white, middle-class women and not to poor women of color, who do not formulate their survival strategies or develop their expectations in terms of mainstream middle-class careers. Again, liberal feminists assume the capitalist framework, which structures people's work lives into individualistic competitions in which "winners" prosper at the expense of "losers."

*Radical or cultural feminism* refers to a rather different version of feminist theory, with roots in the late 1960s and early 1970s (e.g., Firestone 1979; Atkinson 1974). This approach (e.g., see Dworkin 1974) argues that the oppression of women occurs mainly or even solely because of patriarchy, which operates both on the level of the family and its expectations of compulsory heterosexuality and on the level of culture, in which sexist images of women serve to objectify and hence oppress them. Radical feminism is similar to lesbian feminism or lesbian separatism in its critique of the heterosexist family as the main source of women's oppression. It also anticipates various themes in queer theory, discussed earlier, such as the cultural hegemony of heterosexism, which produces sharply bifurcated notions of masculinity and femininity.

Radical feminists argue that feminists need to abolish or radically modify the family and to create a nonmisogynist culture in which women are not objectified. Radical feminism includes but is not limited to a trenchant critique of heterosexism, which not only argues that all people are by nature heterosexual but in addition suggests that women derive their identities from being coupled (especially married) to men and having their children. Lesbian feminism is radical feminist, even though not all radical feminisms are lesbian separatist in the sense that they advise women to couple only with women. That is, radical feminism does not require personal denial of heterosexuality. It does, however, require a radical rethinking of the family, including the notion of compulsory heterosexuality. It also requires a commitment to create a culture in which women do not define their identities and worth in terms of their relations to men.

Radical feminism tends to place relatively little weight on economic inequalities between women and men. Like liberal feminism, radical feminism either assumes or embraces capitalism as the framework within which radical feminists do their political work and live their lives. Radical feminists blame women's predicaments on patriarchy, which they believe originates from the family and the way in which women are in effect trapped in roles of subservience and obligation. Radical feminists argue that women and men occupy separate spheres (e.g., Rubin 1983; Bernard 1972, 1981) and use different types of reasoning, political logic, and moral concepts with which to understand the world. Hence, rather than reforming the family, changing laws and joining social movements designed to benefit women in a heterosexual society in which it is assumed that women remain coupled to men not only to have children but to obtain money and even acquire identity, radical feminists want to create spaces in which women can thrive on their own (even if, as I just said, they are heterosexual). Women are to be women-identified, that is, to cultivate relations with other women, who are viewed as sisters, mothers, and sometimes lovers.

Radical feminists do not necessarily interrogate assumptions about the clear bifurcation of sexual orientation, as queer theorists and feminist social constructionists do. Rather, radical feminism is an explicit or closet essentialism that argues that women and men are fundamentally different in the ways they approach, talk about, and act in the world. Carol Gilligan (1982) suggested that women and men engage in quite different kinds of moral reasoning (see Hekman 1995). Although radical feminists do not necessarily argue that women and men are "destined" by their biological natures to be different (in the sense in which Freud said that "anatomy is destiny"), they usually adopt positions on gender difference that are de facto essentialist in the way they accept that men and women occupy separate spheres and then conclude that real liberation for women will happen only in a largely women's world.

Although radical feminists can well converge with queer theorists and feminist social constructionists who argue that sexual orientation is a nondichotomous and shifting category and that women can have sex with men but derive their emotional sustenance (and also possibly sexual gratification) from relations with other women, radical feminism diverges from queer theory and feminist social constructionism on this issue of essentialism. Radical feminists tend to argue that femininity and masculinity are quite stable categories, allowing us to posit the existence of separate spheres occupied by men and women: They do not view men and women simply as temporary occupants of subject positions that they "produce" by way of certain normatively assigned gender behaviors but as more or less permanent placeholders on a topographical map of gender that has only two locations, male and female. Radical feminists, like queer theorists, can well endorse lesbian sexuality and bisexuality, but unlike queer theorists and feminist social constructionists, they do not view sex and gender as fluctuating, reversible, even ephemeral categories within which women and men occupy multiple subject positions throughout the course of a life. Or to put this somewhat differently, queer theorists believe that bisexuality is a more typical subject position than do radical feminists.

Radical feminism today increasingly takes the form of postmodern feminism. The French feminists such as Irigaray, Kristeva, and Cixous extend the radical feminist theoretical logic by arguing that women and men use language differently, thus expressing fundamental unconscious differences between the feminine and masculine. The French feminist reconstruction of radical feminism through Lacan's postmodern psychoanalytic theory is increasingly persuasive among radical feminists influenced by postmodern theory and interested in developing a cultural feminism, which stresses the ways in which women can and do create distinctive feminine/feminist cultures and discourses.

*Socialist feminists* such as Zillah Eisenstein and Heidi Hartmann argue that women cannot achieve social justice without abolishing both capitalism and patriarchy. Although there are debates among socialist feminists (e.g., see Walby 1990; Delphy 1984) about how best to conceptualize the capitalism-patriarchy relationship and thus what "weight" to give capitalism and patriarchy as sources of women's oppression, they generally agree that Marxism and feminism must combine in order to address the present circumstance of women successfully. Socialist feminists stress both economic and gender aspects of women's oppression, arguing that women can be seen as occupants of economic classes in Marx's sense and "sex classes," as Shulamith Firestone termed them. That is, women perform valuable services for capitalism both as workers and as wives who receive no wage for performing their domestic labor.

Much of the impetus for socialist feminism came out of the Wages for Housework movement in the early 1970s in the United Kingdom and Italy. Theorists such as Mariarosa Dalla Costa and Selma James (1973) argued that feminists must recognize the economic value that their unwaged domestic labor contributes to capitalism, hence opening the way theoretically for socialist feminist understandings of the capitalism-patriarchy relationship. Although orthodox male Marxists reject this argument, instead contending that domestic labor does not produce value in Marx's strict sense of the term, socialist feminists respond by saying that labor does not need to be commodified (remunerated by wages in the labor market) in order for it to produce value, in the case of housework the value represented by having children and thus replenishing the work force, doing housework and preparing meals, and keeping male workers relatively content through emotional support and sex. Socialist feminists persuasively argue that capitalism requires this hidden unwaged labor in order to function. Indeed, the Wages for Housework leaders called capitalism's bluff by demanding wages for women who do unpaid domestic labor, recognizing, of course, that capitalism was not about to come up with sufficient wages to "valorize" women's domestic labor. But they made the telling theoretical point that capitalism creates profit not only on the backs of waged male workers but also on the backs of their wives and children, who perform all manner of domestic chores in return for nothing other than the mythic family wage.

In this sense, socialist feminists view women as oppressed by both capital, which denies them wages for their domestic labor, and husbands and boyfriends, who in effect treat them as indentured servants. The Victorians conceived the family-wage notion precisely to induce women to withdraw from the paid work force in order to reduce male competition for jobs, provide an unwaged source of domestic labor, and create the ideological notion of romantic love and domesticity that ameliorated workers' alienation in the happy haven of family life. Today more than 75 percent of American women under age fifty-five work outside the home for wages, reducing wives' dependence on their husbands but not significantly diminishing their responsibility for domestic labor (see Hochschild 1989). Women do a "second shift" as homemakers and paid workers. For all the talk about a revolution in gender values, men do little more domestic labor in the early twenty-first century than they did in the mid-1970s. The only measurable change in the household division of labor is that women employed outside the home do a bit less domestic labor, given their time crunch. For the most part, men do not pick up the slack by sharing domestic labor.

Perhaps more than anything else, the reality of the second shift demonstrates that women are oppressed both by capital and by their husbands and boyfriends, who, even if they are themselves alienated laborers under capitalism, benefit by having their wives and girlfriends do the lion's share of the childcare, cooking, and cleaning. An interesting pattern of the gendered division of household labor emerges upon close inspection: Women are primarily responsible for nondiscretionary tasks, tasks that have to get done daily and on schedule, such as cooking and childcare. Men are primarily responsible for discretionary tasks, such as mowing the lawn and auto maintenance. When men are involved in childcare, it is usually in the "fun" activities, such as play. Although the women's movement, coupled with sheer economic necessity, has since World War II liberated women to work, it has failed to convince men to do their fair share of domestic labor. After all, if husbands and boyfriends have been able to convince their partners to do "something for nothing," why change now?

Why, then, do women put up with this? Why, especially, do women with jobs and careers tolerate male indolence on the home front? There are at least two reasons. First, sometimes it is perceived to be more trouble than it is worth to goad husbands and boyfriends to do their fair share and, if they do, to get them to do their tasks competently and on time. The price of overcoming male resistance to doing domestic labor may be higher than even "liberated" women are willing to pay. Second, even "liberated" women have been acculturated to accept the notion that housework is women's work and, moreover, that women are *better* at such things as childcare and cooking, given their allegedly nurturant and caring nature. Patriarchal culture has worked hard to convince women that "femininity" makes women more loving, nurturant, sensitive, and intuitive than men. These lessons die hard, even among women who intellectually "know" them not to be true or at least recognize that they are not good for women or for men, who are thus removed from the sphere of parenting and emotional support, nonparticipant in the lives of their children and spouses.

One of the central themes of socialist feminism is the relationship between domestic labor and paid labor, or, as sociologists prefer to call it, between family and work. As I explained above, the concept of the sexual division of labor helps tie together family and work in the sense that the sexual division of labor positions women in the dual hierarchies of domestic labor and paid labor. Expected to do the bulk of the childcare and housework at home, women are also channeled into lower-paying jobs in the pink-collar sector of the labor force. These two aspects of women's positioning reinforce each other, with the hours women expend in domestic labor reducing their earning power directly, by consuming hours they could otherwise spend in paid labor, and indirectly, by preventing them from acquiring further education and skills, which can be converted into future income. And where women are stuck in dead-end, low-paying jobs, they do not have the marital or relational power to insist that their male partners share domestic labor.

## AFRICANA FEMINISM

Africana feminism arose because African American feminist theorists did not believe that liberal feminism, radical feminism, or socialist feminism sufficiently addressed the African American experience. Feminists such as Alice Walker, Toni Morrison, Patricia Hill Collins, and bell hooks argue that black women experience unique aspects of domination that require feminist articulation in a theoretical voice somewhat different from the voices adopted by white women. There are two issues here: First, Africana feminists say that women of color experience a kind of superexploitation,

exploitation above and beyond the exploitation experienced by white women, thus requiring new theoretical concepts and categories. Second, Africana feminists maintain that there are important experiential and narrative issues involved in "telling" the Africana feminist story that necessarily distinguish Africana from white feminisms. Like many multiculturalists, most Africana feminists argue that only African American women can really know and thus theorize about what it means to be a woman of color (see hooks 1989, 1992, 1996).

Most critical social theorists accept the notion of superexploitation (or of a synonym) as theoretically useful and important. Although I argue that class, race, and gender are often artificially separated, especially by postmodern multicultural theorists who derive identity politics from difference theory, it is clear that poor women of color face obstacles simply unimaginable by people who do not experience the world in terms of these triple aspects of subordination. It is not clear that poor women of color require special theoretical treatment, as Africana feminists argue. For them to receive special treatment is heuristically useful inasmuch as it draws attention to aspects of superexploited experience that are rarely addressed by male and even white feminist critical social theories.

Marx reserved discussion for the lumpenproletariat, the underclass, as sociologists now call it. He recognized that some members of the working class, especially those who are chronically unemployed, slip even further beneath the level of gritty subsistence experienced by the working class and even the working poor. His discussion of the lumpenproletariat is extremely apt today in light of what William Wilson (1987) calls the truly disadvantaged, for example the homeless, who seem to fit few of the categories of critical theory. Similarly, it is undeniable that people of color are enormously overrepresented in the total group of people who experience abject poverty. Race and gender deepen people's exploitation, often pushing them underneath the line separating the working class, who harbor at least modest expectations of the future, from those below, who view life as an unending hell characterized by dire poverty, crime, drugs, illness, broken families, and utter hopelessness.

I believe that race has not received enough attention from critical social theorists, who are just beginning to appreciate the importance of gender as a basis of oppression. Joe Feagin (Feagin and Sikes 1994; Feagin and Vera 1995) has done important work on the enduring salience of racism even for the black middle class in the United States. This type of empirical research converges with the theoretical work of Africana feminists, who argue that critical theory needs to address the distinctive experiences of women of color. The benefit of this type of work is that it sensitizes critical social theorists to race and the interaction between race and gender. The risk of this work is that it repeats the traditional neo-Weberian assumption that class, race, and gender are not only analytically separable but describe quite separate realities or variables that defy overarching ("totalizing") theoretical understanding.

## POSTMODERN FEMINISM AND QUEER THEORY: SEPARATION VERSUS HISTORICITY

Postmodern feminist theory (see, e.g., Flax 1990; Hekman 1990; Lather 1991; Brodribb 1992) has received widespread recent attention and deserves a section of its own here. In many respects, postmodern feminists derive their framework from the postmodern theory discussed in Chapters 2 and 3. They apply difference theory and French theorists' critique of modernity to women's problems. Indeed, postmodern feminist theory was first given voice by French feminists such as Irigaray, Kristeva, and Cixous, who, as I mentioned above, derive their work from Lacan's postmodern interpretation of psychoanalysis. These French feminists have not produced much in the way of systematic social theory. Rather, they have written essays on literary interpretation, philosophy, culture, and psychoanalysis that defy many of the stylistic conventions of critical social theory in the sense that they attempt to exemplify what they call *l'écriture féminine*, or womanly writing (see Meese 1992). Following Lacan, these feminist theorists argue that women have a different relationship to their unconscious (which, as Lacan argues, is structured like a language) than do men. Men occupy the realm of the symbolic and technological, whereas women occupy the realm of the imaginary. This is akin to the radical feminist argument that women and men occupy separate spheres within which they conduct their everyday lives quite differently. Although radical feminists do not necessarily derive their contentions about separate spheres from Lacanian psychoanalysis, as the French feminists do, their argument about how women should cultivate their distinctive identities as women and create a women-identified culture is very similar to the French feminists' argument for *l'écriture féminine*.

The first key theme of postmodern feminism is the contention that liberation is achieved largely through narrativity, storytelling, which both forms feminist identity and creates feminist culture. This is the reason the French feminists spend so much time theorizing writing as a gendered activity. They view women and men as "narrating" (talking and writing about) the world differently, reflecting their different natures, relationships to their unconscious, and subject positions. Inasmuch as postmodernists argue that people are positioned for the most part by their languages and discourses, it is easy to see why the French feminists place so much stress on feminist narrativity as a means of liberation, identity, and cultural creation.

Much like Lyotard, postmodern feminists reject the notion that there are singular grand narratives such as Marxism that summarize history and people's experience. These feminists oppose not only grand narratives in general but male narratives in particular inasmuch as men's stories about society tend to ignore or obscure women's experiences. Just as Africana feminists argue that white feminism misses their experiences as women of color, so postmodern feminists suggest that men's "stories" are in their nature different from women's "stories." The second key theme of postmodern feminism is difference, which, as with Lyotard and Derrida, is more characteristic of people's subject positions and the narratives they produce than is sameness or similarity. In deciding "for" difference and "against" sameness, postmodern narrativists exclude the possibility of common narratives, notably theoretical ones, which generalize about people's oppression. Postmodern feminists reject the possibility that generalizing ("grand") narratives can emphasize *both* sameness and difference, for example theorizing everyone's oppression and at the same time theorizing women's oppression in particular.

Queer theorists and feminist social constructionists view gendered subject positions (identities) as inherently fluid. They call into question the whole notion that to-be-men or to-be-women is somehow fixed, allowing us to derive Lacanian notions about feminine writing and masculine writing. French feminists introduce an essentialism, albeit a postmodern one, into the theory of gender, although it is not derived from Freud's version of psychoanalysis. Queer theorists would argue that men, essentially gay men, can "become" women in the sense that they identify with women's subordinate subject positions and have experiences that are womenlike in their degradation. Postmodern feminists appear to deny this possibility because, like radical feminists, they want to simplify the world into two separate spheres, arguing that women will find liberation only in their own sphere. This ontological and existential separatism stands opposed to all critical social theories that emphasize the contrary notion of historicity.

Feminist theories that emphasize women and men's separation tend to endorse radical feminist strategies of feminist identity and culture formation. Feminist theories that emphasize the historicity and fluidity of gendering tend to endorse strategies enlisting women and men in common cause. This is especially true of the emerging gay and lesbian movements, galvanized in their opposition to homophobia and to lagging federal commitment to eradicating AIDS. Although it would appear that feminist difference theorists could easily accommodate strategies that combine occupants of subject positions characterized by difference (e.g., women and men), theorists who stress the historicity and fluidity of gender not only combine differences strategically but *reconceptualize apparent differences as in fact similar*, which is the more powerful strategy. It is more powerful because it demonstrates a commonality of experience and interest that underlies apparent differences and demonstrates that our assumed gender distinctions are historical artifacts themselves contributing to domination.

Queer theory bests French feminism where it historicizes the category of gender to the point that to-be-gendered is a matter of one's positioning with respect to power, notably a heterosexual mainstream ("malestream") that produces gender as a set of political categories. To be feminine means to be submissive and nurturant. To be masculine means to dominate. To be either means to be straight. Queer theory defends our bisexuality not in the sense that it argues that people should have sex with members of both sexes but in the sense that it shows our potential for producing behavior characteristic of each so-called gender, thus overcoming our positioning as either men or women. Queer theory wants people to be both men and women, to work at both ends of the sexual division of labor, to write evocatively and systematically, to be bisexual as a way of defying our culture's sexist and heterosexist positioning of women and men into singular, stable subject positions.

It could be argued that in emphasizing the historicity, fluidity, and bisexuality of gender queer theory is more genuinely postmodern in subverting arbitrary modernist distinctions than is French feminism, which retreats to modernist dualities of gender. This returns to my earlier discussions about the meaning of postmodernism. Some interpret postmodernism as a critical theory that subverts dualities by revealing them to be hierarchies—in this case of men over women. Although Parsons and Robert Bales (1955) suggest that men and women perform complementary roles best suited to their skills and personalities, with men earning bread and women nurturing children, thus justifying the sexual division of labor, they really intend to justify male supremacy by suggesting the reasonableness of this arrangement, which, according to feminists, is unfair to women in that they do not obtain either power or money. A postmodern critical theory "deconstructs" this apparent duality of femininity and masculinity and their attendant roles by revealing that duality to conceal male-supremacist hierarchy.

A different postmodern reading of Parsons's duality of masculinity and femininity, owed to the French feminists, would perhaps accept his duality but argue that women can liberate themselves within their realm of privacy, domesticity, intuition, and nonlinear thought and expression. For example, housewives can engage in *l'écriture féminine* by writing while their children nap or play. This version of postmodern feminism accepts the separation of the allegedly masculine and feminine worlds, although the French feminists would not fall back on Parsons's role theory, which assigns husbands and wives different roles based on their different vocational aptitudes. Neither would they endorse the explanation of Gary Becker (1980) that husbands, who command greater amounts of human capital (e.g., occupational skills, educational degrees, likelihood of maintaining continuous careers unhindered by childbirth and childrearing) than their wives should play the roles that will prove to be better investments of that human capital, such as developing careers, while their wives stay home and perform domestic labor. French feminists do not entertain these sociological and economic justifications of separate spheres but rather ground their own defense of the masculinity-femininity duality in Lacan's postmodern psychoanalysis and his notion that men do better with linear thinking and women with their nonlinear imaginations. Of course, these sociological, economic, and psychoanalytic justifications of separate spheres are not at all incompatible but simply address the duality of the masculine and feminine on different levels.

Parsons and Becker are not feminists. They endorse the sexual division of labor as sociologically and economically rational. They would disagree with me and other feminists that the sexual division of labor exploits women in all private and public realms. Am I saying that French feminism is in effect nonfeminist? Yes, if feminism requires the rejection of the sexual division of labor and the separate-spheres concept. In other words, I am "for" the notion of the historicity of gender (with queer theory and feminist social constructionism) and "against" the separation of genders on sociological, economic, psychoanalytic, or other essentialist grounds.

At issue, then, is the very idea of gender (see Lorber 1994). Some liberal feminists simply accept the categorical separation of two genders as a given. Others, such as French feminists and many radical feminists, endorse separation as a way for women to find their own "space" within the realm of feminist imagination and culture building. Although I accept the blurring of genders that derives from the notion of gender's historicity, there is something to be said for the strategy of separate spheres, at least as a defensive maneuver in a world increasingly hostile to the feminist project. If Susan Faludi (1991) is correct that there is a backlash against the women's movement—and evidence such as the mounting attacks on abortion clinics and political celebration of "family values" suggests she is—it makes sense to protect women's sphere against misogynist attacks.

Queer theory attempts to create precisely this space for women by validating women-with-women relationships. The gay and lesbian movement is one of the most active parts of the women's movement today, gaining both self-confidence and numbers as it becomes more socially legitimate to be gay. (The administration of Bill Clinton in the United States began with President Clinton's attempt to make it permissible for gays and lesbians to serve in the U.S. military.) Misogyny is resisted by creating relationships, families, and whole communities of women-identified women, notably including lesbians. But queer theorists go about this family building and community building differently than do French feminists. Queer theorists ground lesbian community not in an essentialist notion of womanhood, as French feminists do, but rather in the strategic defense of sexual difference conceptualized fluidly and historically. Thus, one can be a lesbian feminist queer theorist and protect women's right to live their lives largely unencumbered by misogynist men (as, for example, women do in Northampton, Massachusetts, a noted site of lesbian community building) *without* endorsing an essentialist concept of sexual orientation and gender. Indeed, one of the main political, cultural, and sexual themes of lesbian feminism today is that lesbians—dykes, proudly proclaimed—are not captive of the traditional bifurcation of masculinity and femininity, which sorts gender and gendered activities into two neat categories.

The Canadian musician k. d. lang is a lesbian feminist culture hero who refuses gender bifurcation in her whole presentation of self and music. One might say that she is both masculine and feminine or, perhaps better, *neither*. She and others like her who live "queer" lives interrogate the very meaning of gender as a social construction that is, in Derrida's terms, inherently undecidable. A *Vanity Fair* cover featured a photo of lang reposing in a barber's chair while she was being shaved by the model Cindy Crawford, who was clad in black lingerie and boots. They both appear to be enjoying what is going on. This kind of gender bending is central to queer theory, which does not decide in favor of lang over Crawford or suggest that Crawford is coming out of the closet. Although many male theorists would not consider *Vanity Fair* a reputable theoretical venue, I believe that this magazine cover contributes to a feminist social theory that interrogates the very bifurcation of gender, which is conceived as a more or less immutable category.

## BEYOND GENDER: FEMINISM OR POSTFEMINISM?

The February 1994 issue of *Esquire* contained a series of related articles on the new feminism, or postfeminism, as it was called. The main article argued that there is a new feminism afoot that the author termed "do-me" feminism. Part of postfeminism, which supposedly began in 1983 and allegedly bears some relationship to postmodernism, this "do-me," or sexual-agency, feminism turns the table on men by suggesting that women should not shun sex with men, thus problematizing date rape and pornography, as Andrea Dworkin (1974) and Catharine MacKinnon (1987, 1993) do, but instead use sex as a type of empowering. The article quotes such feminists as Naomi Wolf and bell hooks. Self-confident and unintimidated, do-me feminists assert their sexual rights as a way of asserting all of their rights. They reject the passive, fragile notion of femininity without necessarily rejecting their heterosexuality. Indeed, the author argues that sexual-agency feminism and postfeminism heterosexualize gay and lesbian attitudes toward sexuality as empowering, thus refusing abstinence and man-hating as capitulations to fragile femininity.

Barbara Ehrenreich terms this growing movement "beyond-bitch feminism," suggesting that feminist intellectuals have misunderstood American women's rejection of feminism as doctrine even though they embrace many of the social goals of the women's movement, such as equal pay for equal work and the protection of reproductive rights. ("Beyond Bitch" is from a bumper sticker, which, a postmodernist might conclude, is where the most interesting social theorizing is going on.) "Beyond bitch" connotes a mode of postfeminism (but not antifeminism) in which women reject the whole masculinity-femininity duality and, by implication, their role as victims. Ehrenreich argues that this is why women in record numbers are purchasing guns for self-defense and why women vigorously supported Lorena Bobbitt, the woman who cut off her sleeping husband's penis for allegedly raping her.

Postfeminism might be seen to include both sexual-agency (do-me) feminism and beyond-bitch feminism, which are the sexual and self-defense modes of postfeminism, respectively. Postfeminism refers to a theoretical understanding of gender that does not tie feminism tightly to the women's movement and to feminist doctrine, both of which are seen to be somewhat antiquated by post-baby-boom women, but that retains many feminist social values. Indeed, postfeminists are somewhat impatient with the pro-victim stances of some baby-boom feminists and theorists such as Dworkin and MacKinnon and historians such as Susan Brownmiller (1975), who portray women as victims of men. Although women can be victims, postfeminists want to narrow the range of victimhood in a way that represents women as powerful agents. For example, postfeminism would decriminalize the crime of rape without, of course, licensing rape-like behaviors. Rather, they would recategorize rape as assault, thus removing all connotations of rape as a crime of passion, insisting that it is nothing more or less than a crime of violence.

Also, postfeminists, especially sexual-agency ones, reject MacKinnon and Dworkin's well-known arguments that pornography constitutes as well as promotes violence against women. Sexual-agency postfeminists argue that pornography is a valid source of pleasure as long as it does not depict women as subordinated or victims of violence. Some sexual-agency feminists even argue that depictions and representations of S-and-M (sadomasochistic sexual practices) are acceptable. Their point is that women should not abdicate the right to enjoy sex simply because men often translate sex into power over women. Some feminists such as Gloria Steinem (1994) have tried to distinguish between erotica and pornography, where the former is a valid form of sexual stimulation for feminists and the latter a representation of the objectification of women for the pleasure of men. Although this makes theoretical sense to me, it is difficult to define the distinction between erotica and porn.

Postfeminism is seen to appeal largely to post-baby-boom women who were not politically and culturally formed in the 1960s. Postfeminists may reject the feminist label but support many feminists causes such as Title VII, affirmative action, pro-choice, and various progressive stances on such issues as the government's responsibility to address AIDS and tolerance of gays and lesbians. It is clear from these and other similar data that post-baby-boom women unformed by and unattached to the 1960s-era women's movement disavow feminism either as unnecessarily ideological and doctrinal or as superfluous, having already successfully established careers alongside men and having begun to establish relatively egalitarian gender roles in their households. Whether feminism is ideology or anachronism, postfeminists disavow it even as they support its aims. One might conclude that the women's movement has been metabolized into the mainstream of domestic life, in a sense making it superfluous in the eyes of post-baby-boomers.

# CHAPTER 6

# Cultural Studies

## MARXIST CULTURAL THEORY AND THE CONCEPT OF IDEOLOGY

In the preceding chapter, I "read" a bumper sticker as a telling theoretical text. I also discussed the magazine *Esquire* as a relevant feminist source. I took these examples from popular culture, not from erudite feminist theoretical texts. In this chapter I discuss one of the most important contemporary theoretical movements, cultural studies (see Grossberg et al. 1992; Agger 1992a). One of the most rapidly growing interdisciplinary academic movements, proliferating in courses, conferences, articles, and books, cultural studies draws on a variety of interrelated sources, including the work of Marxist sociologists of culture, the Frankfurt School, feminist theorists, and postmodernists. In this respect, cultural studies is one of the best examples of an interdisciplinary critical theory that genuinely spans disciplines and theoretical sources. In the sections below, I take up each of these theoretical contributions to cultural studies, identifying both similarities and differences.

I distinguish between cultural studies as a theoretical movement and cultural studies as a largely atheoretical mode of cultural analysis and critique that does not derive from or contribute to the project of critical social theory. Although it is certainly possible to defend the second, more atheoretical mode of cultural studies as a legitimate intellectual project, as many in humanities departments would do, I am more interested in the mode of cultural studies that contributes to critical social theorizing and particularly to the critique of ideology outlined by Marx. That is why I begin here with Marxist cultural theory, extending from Marx to Lukacs, Goldmann, Gramsci, and then the Frankfurt School. My appreciation of cultural studies as a mode of critical social theory derives from the Marxist and neo-Marxist frameworks for analyzing culture, both elite and popular, as a mode of ideology. This is not to say that I accept the mechanistic reduction of cultural ideology to the economic "base" of capitalism such that culture becomes merely a reflection and extension of the base. Marx and Engels (1947) themselves suggested this type of cultural critique; in *The German Ideology* they noted that "the ruling ideas are the ideas of the ruling class." Although few Marxists would disagree with the general sentiment expressed here, namely that ideology protects the capitalist status quo, Marxist cultural theory, especially the Frankfurt School's analysis of the culture industry, views culture as a more independent phenomenon than Marx and Engels's comment suggests. Culture is not simply a reflection or representation of the economic system but necessarily appears to operate independently of the economy. This appearance is necessary, according to Marxist cultural theorists, precisely for culture to have a dampening effect on people's behavior and imaginations. If culture were seen simply to preach the values of the system as doctrine, it would not be as effectively "hegemonic" (pervasive and yet apparently independent of the economy) as Gramsci suggested. Rather, culture plays a more subtle role in late capitalism, as the Frankfurt School argued in developing their analysis of what they called the culture industry.

Thus, on the one hand, Marxist cultural theorists work within Marx's framework for analyzing and criticizing ideologies such as religion and bourgeois economic theory, agreeing with him that such belief systems help reproduce the present social and economic system by suggesting that freedom awaits people in an afterlife and that the capitalist economic system is rational and equitable. On the other hand, Marxist cultural theorists reject the notion that ideology is simply a reflex, reflection, and representation of the economy, thrown up by the economy simply as a symbolic system of deception. In this sense, Marxist cultural theory, which initiated the cultural studies movement, reformulates the Marxist concept of ideology. Marx understood ideology to be a system of mystifications that "invert" and thus distort reality, propagating falsehoods such as claims that when people die they go to heaven; Marxist cultural theorists, in contrast, argue that ideology has become a more complex and irrefutable system of ideas, concepts, and representations that at once close the door on radical social change and open the door on individual self-betterment, including such diverse "promises" as personal occupational mobility, vacations, weight loss, entertainment, sexual and chemical gratification, and participation in sports.

Of course, the list is much longer than that, including all of the releases that Marcuse in *Eros and Civilization* (1955) characterized as "repressive desublimation." By this term Marcuse meant that people in late capitalism are "allowed" to ease the constraints that have been self-imposed and imposed on them during early industrial capitalism since the Victorian era.

He used Freudian theory to explain that people no longer have to so severely constrain themselves and renounce gratifications denied them during an earlier stage of capitalism. Indeed, he theorizes, people must be released from renunciation in order for them to continue to perform their various economic, social, and domestic "duties" willingly. But there is a catch: The easing of renunciation does not really liberate people, according to him, because people pursue cultural and recreational activities that are still "repressive" in the sense that these activities only harmlessly divert people from recognizing their own alienation. Furthermore, these activities are commodified, thus benefiting capitalism by creating new, "false" needs at a time when many people's basic needs can be met.

Marxist cultural theorists treat culture, such as television, journalism, movies, and advertising, as both an ideological and economic realm, involving consciousness, discourse, and consumption. They agree with Marx that capitalism requires ideologies to create false consciousness so that people do not recognize the true injustices of capitalism. But they argue that ideology can no longer postpone liberation to an afterlife and simply deny people this-worldly gratifications but must "allow" people room for individual betterment, both occupational and recreational. That is, ideology must not only proscribe or prevent behavior such as radical social change; it must also promise people modest relaxation of many constraints formerly governing their personal and public lives, allowing them what Marcuse called desublimation.

Marxist cultural theorists explore culture as a realm of ideology much more vast and complicated than in Marx's era, when people worried mainly about putting food on the table. Going to the mall (Kowinski 1985), let alone a theme park, were not issues for people in early industrial capitalism. Hence, ideology, purveyed by cultural doctrines and discourses such as religion and economic theory, did not need to pervade their lives but could exist as "superstructure" in the tomes and treatises of the "good book" and other such sources of false consciousness. Although it is crucial to note that capitalism today does not dispense with false consciousness, which, as ever, is required in order to convince people that utopia is impossible and that "this" is the best of all possible worlds in spite of its many imperfections, ideology has become more total, more pervasive than when Marx wrote.

Today people must experience ideology, not simply read it or receive it through active ideological indoctrination. Ideology must permeate people's everyday lives, disguising itself in order to convey its subtle, even subliminal message. Ideology is not harsh, nor is it even discursive, carefully argued, and systematic. Instead, ideology is so bound up with cultural discourses, practices, representations, and experiences that people lose the distinction between what is real and what is illusory. It is not even clear anymore what is *text*, which has been the traditional form of ideological representation since the beginning of doctrinal religion. The distinction between text and world blurs in postmodernity to such an extent that people do not recognize advertisements as the ideological enjoinders and arguments they really are, celebrating consumerism as a way of ameliorating alienation. Nor are television, movies, newspapers, even academic textbooks "read" as sources of political argument. They are so entangled with "reality" that we forget the distinction between *Everybody Loves Raymond* and real families or the movie *JFK* and what happened in Dallas n November 22, 1963.

This is not to say that "reality," as I am calling it, is easily accessible to readings, either by experts or amateurs. Deconstruction suggests otherwise (Culler 1982). Reality is accessible only through various texts, which necessarily distort and simplify. But it is the peculiar character of ideology in late capitalism, recognized even in the 1920s and 1930s by the first Western Marxists, that *ideology today conceals its representation of the world in order to increase its efficacy as silent argument.* Ideologies that appear "ideological"—polemical, doctrinal, adversarial, advisory—are viewed as old-fashioned at a time when people do not read or consider arguments carefully in the stage of what I have called fast capitalism.

Marxist students of culture theorize fast capitalism, promotional culture (Wernick 1991), or media culture (Kellner 1995) because both the rate and intensity of ideology have increased greatly since Marx. The electronic media dramatically quicken and intensify the production and distribution of ideologies, which cannot be considered carefully, line by line, but zip by, segueing from show to ad to show and thus conveying the impression that what is being televised is not text but world, represented without bias or perspective through the camera's lens. Of course, cultural theorists and television critics alike recognize that the electronic media present what used to be called arguments: They are selective; they reveal the world through the use of perspective; they elaborately construct character, plot, and mood.

As such, cultural theorists and media critics necessarily engage in social theorizing when they "unpack" or deconstruct the media and advertising, revealing them to be texts that present arguments. This sort of cultural reading reveals that cultural discourses and practices such as the media *make assumptions, advance arguments without inviting rejoinders* and *conceal their own text-making* in order to appear "realistic" and convincing. Critical cultural analysis *authorizes* these cultural discourses and practices, which appear not to be texts at all but simply objects occupying the postmodern landscape. Marxist cultural theorists, especially those who deploy postmodern interpretive techniques, turn ideology into a text, hence making it susceptible to readings, refutations, and new texts.

Although the ultimate interest of Marxist cultural theory today is still the elevation of consciousness, the truth or falsehood of consciousness is

not the immediate issue for these cultural theorists. First, they want to put
ideology into words, to deconstruct the everyday environments and experiences of people into ideological discourses with which they can then contend. What Marxists call ideology critique takes a backseat to the identification of ideology as a discernible text, which necessarily precedes it today.
Although ideology still reinforces people's views that "society cannot be
changed" in that ideology affords people certain limited opportunities for
self-betterment, the critique of ideology cannot be conducted in the way
that Marx criticized capitalist economic theory in his book *Capital* as a
way of preparing for revolutionary change. Today, such books have no
meaning for most people, who do not read lengthy, challenging books nor
particularly care how economic theory and the economic system work. By
comparison to the mid-nineteenth century, when people were desperate to
improve their miserable lives by forming unions and joining social movements of fellow workers, today's society is characterized by depoliticization, the erosion of the public sphere as a venue of meaningful human activity (Sennett 1977). In this context, ideology critique falls on deaf ears.

People are fed up with traditional politics and politicians, who have been
revealed as venal, self-serving, and even corrupt. As well, ideology has been
effective in diverting people's attention from politics and the public sphere.
People's troubles are increasingly personalized and psychologized, treated by
various twelve-step programs, diets, and religion, both traditional and
evangelical, as well as by shopping and spending. The depoliticization of
public life is a hallmark of late capitalism, shrinking the public sphere vener-
ated by the Greeks into the coaxial cables carrying electronic traffic, Gore's
information superhighway. Indeed, the shrinkage of the public sphere,
discussed in Chapter 4 with reference to Habermas, is a primary topic of critical social theory, requiring theoretical revision of the concept of ideology.

The decline of public ideologies such as religion has been met by the increasing importance of popular culture in people's lives, diverting their attention, fulfilling their fantasies, allaying their anxieties, and causing them
to shop. Ideology has not gone away; it is now found in venues unanticipated by Marx, who could not have foreseen the culture industry, let alone
the World Wide Web. Although Marxist cultural theory in Lukacs (1962,
1963, 1964), Gramsci, Goldmann (1964, 1972, 1975, 1976, 1981), and
the first generation of the Frankfurt School (Horkheimer and Adorno
1972: 120–167) concentrated on "high" culture as a relevant theoretical
topic, Marxist cultural theory developed by these Western Marxists
quickly gravitated to topics and themes in popular culture (see Ross 1988,
1989; Huyssen 1986). Horkheimer and Adorno's World War II exodus to
Los Angeles and New York City made them aware of the new ideological
importance of radio, television, and journalism. Marcuse continued this
line of analysis into the 1960s.

As I discussed in Chapter 4, the Frankfurt theorists identified "high" culture as a haven from the co-opting, commodifying tendencies of popular culture, which, they argued, was riddled with banality. As I said there, the Frankfurt theorists hoped that ideals of freedom and beauty as well as critical ideas could find refuge in high-cultural expressions. Their cultural theory took two directions: Following the lead of Lukacs and Goldmann, they explored "high" culture through close analyses of music and art; they also increasingly focused on the depoliticizing effects of popular culture, a theme addressed in their theory of the culture industry. They viewed high culture as relatively invulnerable to ideology, even though Lukacs took a different tack when he argued that products of high culture should be examined for what they reveal about the class position and worldview of their authors.

In this sense, Lukacs's Marxist cultural theory suggested that art and culture should be read for their ideological investment, which Lukacs understood in class terms. When the Frankfurt theorists applied this format to comparisons of works of high culture (e.g., Adorno's discussion of Stravinsky and Schoenberg in *Philosophy of Modern Music* [1973b]), the issue was not the class outlook of the work under analysis but whether the work was "affirmative" or critical. By "affirmative culture" the Frankfurt theorists meant culture that did not challenge the existing society, either by suggesting unfulfilled dreams and hopes of liberation or by echoing the "dissonance" of the existing society. For them, popular culture was almost completely "affirmative," reproducing the existing social order by celebrating its values, discourses, and experiences and thus producing conformity. Later agendas of cultural studies have not been as dismissive of popular culture, either because they detect critical threads in popular culture and everyday life or because they do not reject "affirmative culture" out of hand.

Western Marxists all focus on ideological issues in their analyses of culture, whereas the Frankfurt theorists added a concern with *cultural political economy* (see Goldman and Papson 1994) to the ideology-critical interests of Lukacs and Goldmann. Their concept of the culture industry stressed both culture's opportunities for challenging or reproducing hegemony and the extent to which culture has become a commodity in late capitalism. The Frankfurt theorists opposed the "commodification" of culture in the same way they as Marxists opposed the commodification of labor power, which Marx argued was the root cause of workers' alienation. Once culture became a commodity like every other, they argued, it lost its potential to stand apart from everyday life in order to enlighten people buried in the grind of making a living and raising families. Turning culture into yet another commodity robbed it of its aloofness, its apartness, which the Frankfurt theorists argued was necessary for culture to convey ideology-critical messages and thus to reverse false consciousness.

Their focus on the culture industry thus attacked both cultural domination (e.g., the content of television) and cultural institutions (e.g., network television) that profit by selling culture. These aspects of the culture industry are inseparable, according to the Frankfurt theorists. Their "solution" to the culture industry in both of these respects was not simply to change the content of television shows or to support nonprofit public television but to decommodify culture in total, which, presumably, could happen only in a qualitatively different society. Until this society was created, culture was to resist its own commodification and eschew popularity, both of which would suck cultural products and practices into the maw of the culture industry, preventing culture from gaining distance from everyday life. Thus, the Frankfurt theorists did not intend to translate esoteric works of culture, including their own theorizing, into pedestrian terms but to cultivate *otherness* as a way of preserving culture's autonomy.

This posture invited the charge that they were too elitist, too mandarin, and, ultimately, conservative in the sense that they disdained ordinary people who did not share their own sophisticated intellectual and cultural backgrounds. These people watch network television and go to blockbuster movies. They do not attend the symphony, let alone read aesthetic theory. The Frankfurt solution to cultural domination seemed to be cultural decommodification, thus reversing what Walter Benjamin had called the mechanical reproduction of culture, which at least had the advantage of making culture available to many people unable to afford art and symphony tickets. Both sides of this debate are illuminating: The Frankfurt theorists were correct that culture needs to be decommodified and demonopolized, thus empowering cultural producers and consumers outside the cultural mainstream. Although the Frankfurt theorists want artists and other cultural creators to be able to make a living, the logic of their argument about the culture industry suggests that it is very difficult to subsist outside of the gigantic cultural institutions such as CBS and MGM that dominate the landscape. Benjamin and later cultural studies proponents argued for a nonmandarin, nonelitist cultural studies that addresses popular culture not only as a venue of domination and false consciousness but also as a possible site of critical resistance and intelligence. The Frankfurt theorists tended to inflate their legitimate disdain for the mass culture produced (for profit) in New York City and Hollywood into a condemnation of the popular per se.

## THE BIRMINGHAM SCHOOL

The approaches of Marxist cultural theorists set the stage for later varieties of cultural studies. The Western Marxists in particular found both false consciousness (ideology) and true consciousness (critique) embedded in culture. For the Frankfurt theorists, "truth" was to be found "higher" in culture than for later leftist students of culture such as members of the Birmingham School. Whatever their particular emphasis, the Western Marxists drew serious attention to culture and cultural politics, legitimizing later approaches to cultural studies. Although the sociology of culture has been a venerable pursuit since Weber, cultural studies as it emerged from Marxist cultural theory and later branched out into the Birmingham School's work, feminist cultural theory, and the postmodern cultural theory of Baudrillard diverged from Weberian and Durkheimian approaches to culture in the sense that issues of culture were essentially political and oriented toward issues of radical social change. The versions of cultural studies under discussion all focus on the ways in which culture involves both ideology and political economy, both "domination" and "commodification," as the Frankfurt theorists termed them.

Although Marxist cultural theory in general and the Frankfurt School's cultural and aesthetic theory in particular initially articulated the agenda of cultural studies, the term *cultural studies* began to be used only with reference to the work of members of the Birmingham School, clustered in the Centre for Contemporary Cultural Studies (CCCS) at the University of Birmingham. Scholars such as Stuart Hall (1978, 1980a, 1980b), Paul Willis (1977, 1978), and Dick Hebdige (1979) developed a highly original body of scholarship indebted to Marxist theory but going beyond existing Marxist approaches to culture with the aid of a creative synthesis of rather diverse intellectual and political influences, including Gramsci, Foucault, and feminism. That the Birmingham scholars did not produce much in the way of systematic doctrine could be seen as both a strength and a weakness. It was definitely a strength inasmuch as their lack of preoccupation with theory liberated them to do highly original analyses of particular cultural and political topics, all the way from critical studies of representations of women in culture to studies of working-class culture. The work of the CCCS scholars was particularly inflected by their engagement with Thatcherism, the policies of Prime Minister Margaret Thatcher, which, even more than Reagan's eight-year presidency in the United States, profoundly affected British intellectual culture, both giving it a target of critique and crippling British higher education through draconian budget cuts.

Birmingham cultural studies has been conducted much closer to everyday politics and social movements than was the work of the Frankfurt School, which deployed aloofness as a political necessity. The British intellectuals who contributed to the cultural studies movement did not have that luxury; because they were forced to combat Thatcher's attacks on the working class, intellectuals, and the left, their work had an engaged, ground-level quality. For example, Hall's (1988) book on Thatcherism is

less theory or metatheory than a critical empirical engagement with
Thatcherite policies and outcomes. Although such work has always been
theoretically driven, the Birmingham scholars produced few statements of
doctrine or explications of their theoretical logic that are not heavily
freighted with political context. Even R. Johnson's (1986–1987) "What Is
Cultural Studies Anyway?" and Hall's (1980b) "Cultural Studies: Two
Paradigms" ground cultural studies directly in political critique.

Arising out of the tradition established by Richard Hoggart's *Uses of
Literacy* (1957) and Raymond Williams's *Culture and Society* (1958), two
important works of British cultural sociology, the Birmingham approach to
cultural studies borrowed European concepts and deployed them in a
British historical, cultural, and political context. Energized by Gramsci's
notion of cultural hegemony, Birmingham cultural studies analyzed hegemony at the level of everyday cultural works and practices. With Gramsci,
the Birmingham scholars hoped the result of these critiques of hegemony
would be counterhegemony, alternative formulations of culture and everyday life that counter their dominant formulations. In this way, they intended cultural studies as a direct political intervention and not simply as
an academic activity designed to build curriculum vitae and careers.
Unashamedly leftist and feminist, the Birmingham scholars rejected both
the Frankfurt School's mandarinism and orthodox Marxism's economism,
neither of which took issues of cultural hegemony and counterhegemony
seriously enough. Much of the Birmingham work was developed in dialogue with Althusserian structuralism, which had a more important presence in the UK than in either Germany or the United States.

The Birmingham people take Althusser seriously, especially his notion
that culture is "relatively autonomous" in late capitalism, but they view his
structuralism as overly deterministic and oriented to the Bolshevik model
of the vanguard party. Like the German, French, and Hungarian Western
Marxists, the members of the CCCS group reject the Soviet model of socialism as irrelevant to Western societies, which have liberal democratic
political cultures. Although theorists such as Hall are Marxists and socialists, they acknowledged the welfare state capitalist framework of Britain as
a framework within which they conceive their own intellectual project.

Originally a loose collection of relatively nondoctrinal and unsystematic
works springing from the culture-and-society tradition in Britain as it was
informed by Continental influences, cultural studies has become an organizing label for both British and American scholars intent on turning it into
both a legitimate academic pursuit and a distinctive theoretical logic. A
number of conferences in the United States, bringing together cultural studies proponents from the University of Massachusetts at Amherst and the
University of Illinois at Urbana (see Nelson and Grossberg 1988), have
stimulated interest in developing a full-blown intellectual agenda under the

rubric of cultural studies. A lengthy collection of essays entitled *Cultural Studies* (Grossberg et al. 1992) disseminates this ongoing work and makes way for further theoretical interventions. My *Cultural Studies as Critical Theory* (Agger 1992a) discusses the various frameworks of left-wing cultural studies, including feminist theory. Other work (e.g., Luke's *Screens of Power* [1989] and *Shows of Force* [1992], Fiske's *Television Culture* [1987], and Walters's *Material Girls* [1995]) further the project of cultural studies in the U.S. context, even if these works do not derive directly from the influence of the CCCS. (Walters [1992] acknowledges time spent at the Birmingham center as having been intellectually formative.)

The American reception of British cultural studies has been recognized as politically threatening by Weberian and Durkheimian sociologists of culture in the United States, who seek to stake out the field of cultural sociology without reference to European Marxism, feminism, and postmodernism. American cultural sociologists such as Robert Wuthnow (1987, 1989), Wendy Griswold (1986, 1994), and Jeffrey Alexander (Alexander and Seidman 1990) do cultural analysis within disciplinary sociology, refusing the critical political implications of the Birmingham project as a sullying of value-free sociology. By and large, the U.S. cultural studies movement has had a much more positive reception in departments of English, comparative literature, and media studies, where the politicization of the literary and cultural canon has been widely accepted by scholars influenced by postmodernism.

In these humanities departments, cultural studies has become a significant movement, challenging traditional literary methods and cultural values. The cultural studies movement in the humanities has been influenced heavily by the Birmingham School, postmodern approaches to literary and cultural deconstruction, and feminist cultural theory, especially film theory. It is taken for granted in the humanities that what I earlier called the "new scholarship" is a valuable way to update traditional approaches to criticism and the canon in light of challenges posed by the Birmingham scholars, postmodernists, feminists, and multiculturalists. Although certain die-hard humanists reject the new scholarship and cultural studies for politicizing the allegedly apolitical study of humanistic literature, culture, and values, these are increasingly minority voices in the most prestigious and trend-setting humanities departments (such as the English department at Duke, formerly including Stanley Fish, Fredric Jameson, and Frank Lentricchia) in which the new scholarship and cultural studies have become firmly entrenched.

Cultural studies has made two contributions to the humanities. First, it has challenged the canon, the pieces of literature (e.g., Shakespeare) thought to convey indispensable Western values (see Eagleton 1983). Like the Birmingham scholars' insistence that working-class cultures should receive attention, humanistic purveyors of cultural studies argue that the canon needs to be broadened to include work done by women, minorities, and non-Western writers and artists. The cultural studies movement in the humanities rejects the values conveyed by the white male, Eurocentric canon, notably capitalism, Christianity, and male supremacy. In this respect, cultural studies has drawn much fire from neoconservatives such as Allan Bloom and Dinesh D'Souza for enforcing a narrowly leftist agenda of political correctness from which intellectual and curricular deviation is punished. These critics of the new scholarship and cultural studies blame cultural studies for arguing that "other voices," such as the fiction of Alice Walker, belong next to the "greats" such as John Milton and Mark Twain, diminishing the greats and hence weakening cultural values.

The broadening of the canon not only involves the inclusion of women's and minorities' voices; it also broadens the definition of culture to include popular culture as a legitimate venue for cultural analysis and criticism. In his introduction to *Boxed In*, Mark Crispin Miller (1988) recounts how his faculty mentors chastened him for addressing television rather than traditional literature in his dissertation. Andrew Ross's work, especially *No Respect* (1989), argues for the broadening of traditional literary studies to include cultural discourses and practices all the way from movies to music. (For a variety of cultural studies approaches to rock and other forms of contemporary music, see Frith [1983], Grossberg [1992], and Aronowitz [1993, 1994].) The Birmingham School legitimated this broadening of the "culture" concept to include many aspects of popular culture that could be "read" (analyzed) by people in cultural studies, hence enriching the traditional oeuvre treated in literature programs.

The new scholarship in humanities departments informs critical social science in that it reads cultural discourses and practices as ideological and commodified and helps formulate more general theoretical understandings of society. For example, the work of Jameson, the author of numerous important books on cultural and social theory from *Marxism and Form* (1971) to *Postmodernism, or, the Cultural Logic of Late Capitalism* (1991), clearly contributes to the project of critical social theory. Jameson is in dialogue with critical theorists and postmodern theorists. He develops a postmodern Marxism that learns from but does not succumb to the detotalizing implications of postmodern theory. Although many of Jameson's references are from culture and literature—whereas Habermas's, for example, are from social theory and communication theory—Jameson in effect "does" postmodern critical theory in his readings of works of literature, architecture, music, painting, and philosophy, presenting not only close textual analysis but extending his readings into generalizations quite similar to those of postmodern social theorists (e.g., Aronowitz, Luke) in social science disciplines.

This returns to my earlier discussion of interdisciplinarity, which is a hallmark of the Birmingham School's cultural studies and indeed of cultural studies generally. Cultural studies is inherently a pandisciplinary project in the sense that culture, as the Birmingham theorists conceptualized it, is not only found in everyday life as well as in museums and concert halls but also concerns a wide range of disciplines in the human sciences or human studies, broadly conceived. Virtually no social science or humanities discipline falls outside of the possible purview of cultural studies, which could be seen as a theoretical perspective, a discipline, a corpus of writing, and even an analytical methodology. Like the Unit for Criticism at the University of Illinois, in which Cary Nelson, Lawrence Grossberg, and Norman Denzin had part-time faculty appointments, the CCCS at the University of Birmingham has brought together scholars from a variety of disciplines. Like interdisciplinary projects such as cognitive science, cultural studies is a visible interdisciplinary project collecting scholars who believe they cannot pursue their interests in cultural studies within their home disciplines or who want to claim an identity somewhat different from their disciplinary identities. By and large, scholars in humanities departments have been better able to do and teach cultural studies within their home disciplines, especially where their home disciplines have embraced the new postcanonical, postcolonial, feminist scholarship. Social scientists have had a greater tendency to define their interest in cultural studies outside of their disciplines proper (for instance, at the Bowling Green popular culture group [e.g., Browne 1989]), many of which have been reluctant to abandon their relatively narrow concepts of culture in favor of a more inclusive one or do not acknowledge the need to pursue the study of culture outside of a discipline for which the study of culture has always been central, such as sociology and anthropology.

This difference between the ways that humanists and social scientists configure their identities, affiliations, and academic practices as cultural studies scholars is also reflected in their respective attitudes toward the issue of politicization. Although most scholars around the campus who do cultural studies are leftist and feminist, social scientists tend to position cultural studies as an empirical and theoretical contribution without close ties to politics, hence legitimizing their work within basically empiricist and objectivist disciplines. Humanists tend to embrace their close ties to politics, as the Birmingham scholars did, even arguing that curricular politics, including the politics of the canon and the struggle to define and implement multiculturalism, is an important venue for social change today (see Watkins's [1989] discussion of English departments' production and circulation of cultural capital; also see Bourdieu's *Homo Academicus* [1988]).

Cultural studies increasingly splits into politicized and apolitical camps, with the former group deriving from Marxist cultural theory and combining the influences of the Birmingham School, feminism, and Baudrillard. The latter group includes scholars who do not view cultural studies as a political project but rather as an occasion for deepening their own disciplines or working across disciplines. Much work on popular culture, such as that of the Bowling Green group mentioned above, comes from this second group. Humanists are more likely than social scientists to belong to the first group. This is ironic in that left-wing and feminist cultural studies grew out of Marxist social and cultural theory and only later was adapted by humanists such as Jameson to their own projects. In this sense, critical social theorists interested in culture tend to cluster in humanities programs, or if they work in social science departments, they are usually isolated among their colleagues. It is much more common to find clusters of culturally oriented critical social theorists *outside* the social sciences, for example, in English and comparative literature departments and programs. At my former university, I held my main faculty appointment in a sociology department, in which most of my colleagues were quantitative positivists. I also held a cross appointment in a comparative literature program in which there were many faculty and graduate students interested in critical social and cultural theory.

Although these comparative literature students and faculty are more overtly and unashamedly politicized than most of my erstwhile colleagues and students, they approach society through the text, whereas people like me approach the text through society. This distinction is far from absolute. Nevertheless, much of the best critical social science and social theory is being done in humanities disciplines. Why are social science disciplines such as sociology relatively inured to the new scholarship, cultural studies, and critical theory? The answer largely involves the organizational politics of the university: Sociology, for example, sought greater institutional legitimacy by attempting to imitate and incorporate the methods of the natural sciences, as I discussed in Chapter 1 (see Lemert 1995; Seidman 1991a). Disciplines such as English, comparative literature, women's studies, and media studies were concerned with culture as well as politics and thus were natural gathering points for faculty and students interested in the politics of culture.

## FEMINIST CULTURAL STUDIES

Although cultural studies grew out of Marxist cultural theory, as I argued above, it also springs from Marxism's neglect of women and women's issues, which helped create feminist theory. Feminist cultural studies (see Walters 1995), especially its branch devoted to feminist film theory, elaborates the agendas of Lukacs, Goldmann, the Frankfurt School, and the

Birmingham School by making women focal in ways that women have never been for male social theory. Feminist cultural studies has three main themes. First, *it makes the invisible visible*, drawing critical and theoretical attention to cultural works by and about women, thus adding them to the venerable white male canon. Second, *it unmasks and opposes the sexist objectification of women in culture*, notably but not exclusively through the critique of pornography (Dworkin 1974; MacKinnon 1987, 1993) and feminist film theory (Lauretis 1984, 1987; Mulvey 1989), challenging conventional representations of women that falsify women's real existences. Third, *it raises the question of the "engendering" of cultural works and interpretation* (Kolodny 1975, 1980, 1984), thus addressing issues of how femininity and masculinity are constructed through culture.

In these senses, it is somewhat artificial to distinguish between feminist theory, which I treated in Chapter 5, and feminist cultural studies. Feminist concerns with the cultural representation of women as well as their invisibility have been central to contemporary feminism, which has thoroughly merged political and cultural concerns. Like the work of the Birmingham School and much more than the Frankfurt School's cultural and aesthetic theory, feminist cultural studies has interrogated the experiences and lives of everyday women who struggle to create feminist identities and thus engage in feminist practice in a culture in which women are either invisible or sexually objectified.

For the earliest feminists in the 1960s, the women's movement sought to empower women to speak in their own voices about their own experiences and imaginations, leading naturally to a feminist cultural politics. Movies such as *Thelma and Louise*, books such as *The Color Purple*, and television shows such as *Kate and Allie* represented women in ways in which they had never been seen before, not only making them "real" but also depicting them as powerful, both authors and agents. The 1960s feminist founders recognized that women's images in culture helped them form their own images of themselves, which, later, became a key theme of postmodern feminism (e.g., see Benjamin 1988; Flax 1990). Misogynist culture not only legitimized rape as routine male behavior (Brownmiller 1975) but taught women that they were to be victims.

Women fought back by creating their own culture, starting magazines (like Steinem's *Ms.*) and making films. Feminist film theorists argued that the camera is too often captive of and thus reproduces the male gaze, which objectifies women for both women and men viewers. The "male" camera, like male culture generally, ignored women, distorted them, lusted after them, and thereby helped create images of femininity and masculinity that trap women in subordinate roles. As I discussed briefly in Chapter 5, radical feminists and cultural feminists stress the creation of a feminist, nonmisogynist culture as one of the most important aims (and, for some, *the* most important aim) of the women's movement. Radical feminists and cultural feminists are cousins. Radical feminists stress the dual importance of overthrowing the patriarchal family and creating a feminist culture. Cultural feminists, although certainly sympathetic to the problems of male supremacy in the family, tend to place less emphasis on changing the family (and some, like liberal feminists, even accept the heterosexual family, with its traditional sexual division of labor) than on cultural issues.

By now, feminist cultural studies has become so important, both intellectually and politically, that liberal, radical, cultural, socialist, and Africana feminists all emphasize issues of feminist cultural politics. Although each feminism conceptualizes these issues somewhat differently and places different explanatory weight on cultural issues, very few feminists dispute that representations of women in culture, issues of the gendering of cultural creation and expression and access to canonical status matter greatly. Multicultural feminists make feminist cultural politics explicit, beginning the long march toward gender equality in the university, particularly with respect to curriculum and canon, as I discussed in the previous chapter.

As feminist cultural studies gathers momentum and cuts across the various feminisms, it is being incorporated into male cultural studies, which can ill afford to ignore gender themes. After all, the representation of women by men certainly involves or implies the representation of men. Queer theorists and feminist social constructionists aptly argue that gender is a relational concept: There can be no concept of femininity without a related concept of masculinity, which in Derrida's terms is marked by their "difference" from each other. Feminists are increasingly revisioning what feminism means for men, both gay and straight (e.g., see Kann 1991; Schwalbe 1996). Indeed, a key theme of postfeminism is that men belong to the feminist solution, too, thus avoiding their demonization and expecting intellectual, cultural, and behavioral changes of them. This postfeminist theme is apparent in attempts to address the gender biases of the "male gaze" not only by replacing male directors with female directors but by changing the male gaze itself such that men represent themselves and women differently in their cultural work.

Postfeminism seems to imply that "men are back," as one recent advertisement proclaims. Although this campaign only wants to sell products to men and the women who buy for them, men *are* back for feminist theory and especially for feminist cultural studies. Feminist cultural creators, theorists, and critics wonder how feminists, both male and female, should represent men (in relation to women)—and thus how they should represent women. This issue of the gendered politics of representation definitely involves both men and women on both sides of the camera and desk, thus fortuitously bringing men back into feminist concerns and developing a more complete concept of gender and thus a more complete feminist movement. Queer theorists are at the forefront of this bisexual strategy, including its cultural politics, in the way that they have forged political and theoretical alliances between gays and lesbians around issues of homophobia and AIDS (see Adam 1995). Predictably, queer theory has been heavily devoted to cultural issues.

This bisexual orientation to feminist cultural studies and cultural politics contrasts with another, particularly radical-feminist tendency in feminist cultural studies to split the male and female gazes in irreversible ways. This is precisely the posture of postmodern feminists who derive from the French feminists' Lacanian splitting of women's imagination and men's intellect into ontologically or, as I call it, bio(onto)logically, separate spheres. Thus, a separate-spheres feminist cultural studies and cultural politics contrasts with the bisexual themes of queer theory and feminist social constructionism. Separate-spheres feminists respond to the hegemony of the male gaze in cultural production by arguing that women must develop a female gaze, which they view as categorically different from men's cultural representation of femininity and masculinity. Bisexual feminists agree with separate-spheres feminists that women should make films, write scripts, and run newspapers, but they reject the duality of male and female gazes because they believe that we can blend gender perspectives once we liberate men and women from masculinity and femininity as bio(onto)logical, ahistorical constructs.

Although these two versions of feminist cultural studies begin at the same point, with women empowered to create culture, separate-spheres feminists believe that the cultures created by women and men will be fundamentally different, reflecting their different Lacanian and Gilliganian proclivities. Bisexual feminists suggest that there would be one culture, full of diversity, in which we would gradually lose the ability to distinguish between films and novels done by women and films and novels done by men, through their respective gender filters. This second version of feminist cultural politics is the more radical in the way that it interrogates the very notions and practices of femininity and masculinity as falsely bipolar concepts and practices.

Feminists who place heavy weight on the importance of cultural politics confront some of the same problems encountered by culturally oriented Marxists such as the Frankfurt School theorists. They tend to supplant "real" politics with aesthetic politics, consuming themselves with a politics of representation in which objectifying images of and narratives about women are replaced by feminist images and narratives. To be sure, these are very important issues inasmuch as feminism links the personal and political, thus connecting domestic patriarchy with public patriarchy via the concept of the sexual division of labor. A key contention of radical, cultural, and socialist feminists is that the objectification of women in cultural representations both reflects and reproduces their sexual, economic, and political objectification, with images of degradation both following from and leading to social degradation. This critique of women's inferiorization through culture is an important contribution of cultural feminists.

But there has been a tendency for culturally oriented feminists to abandon the sexual, political, and economic battleground for the purely cultural one. Although films matter to the way we view ourselves and thus conduct our everyday lives, gender is produced not only through culture but also in social relationships, both household and market, in which women and men deal with each other through various divisions of labor. Of course, the bipolar construction of gender really conceals a hierarchy—masculinity "over" femininity—that is heavily affected by culture, from childhood play in which girls are mommies and boys daddies, to the color of their clothes, to the dreams about adulthood implanted in them by parents, teachers, and television. Yet gender is a practice that includes but extends beyond culture. For example, that women and men duplicate the household division of labor in workplaces in which women serve male managers as secretaries requires an economic analysis that assesses the relative aggregate compensation of women and men as well as the culture in which girls are taught to aim low while boys aim high. Thus, liberal and socialist feminists have tended to concentrate on the income gap between men and women in the United States.

The cultural representation of women is intimately linked to the economic and political exploitation of women. Both are realms in which the currency of "gender" is exchanged, thus adding value to the bipolar construction of masculinity and femininity. People are called "women" when they do housework and childcare, wear makeup, and earn less than men in jobs that mimic women's place in the domestic division of labor. The cultural construction of women and men takes place not only through popular culture but through occupational positioning that frequently makes women subordinate to and pays them less than men. Feminist theorists need not choose between cultural emphases and economic emphases when in fact the cultural and occupational positionings of women take place through bipolar constructs of gender and thus reinforce those constructs.

Socialist feminists have always taken these economic concerns seriously, thus linking what happens to women in the household and family and what happens to them in their jobs. Cultural feminism and socialist feminism need not work at cross-purposes, as they have a convergent concern with the construction of gender (which returns us to issues I raised in Chapter 5). The bipolar construction of gender necessarily implies gender hierarchy, "difference" that actually signals subordination. Cultural and socialist feminists oppose gender bipolarity when such bipolarity disadvantages women as the putatively weaker, needier sex. Separate-spheres cultural feminists do not reject gender bipolarity but argue that women can liberate themselves from men only by taking refuge in the women's sphere, which is largely a cultural sphere. But bisexual cultural feminists, especially queer theorists and feminist social constructionists, join socialist feminists in drawing attention to the ways in which gender bipolarity is constructed to the disadvantage of women. One of the most important points here is that the "construction of gender" takes place not only through cultural definitions and representations, such as movies and fiction, but through behaviors and discourses of femininity, both in the private and public spheres. "Gender" is not only a set of directives, conveyed ideologically and culturally, but also an ensemble of behaviors and roles that mark us differentially as "men" and "women."

Thus, women can be seen to produce themselves as occupants of subordinate gender positions where they enact what it supposedly means to be a woman, both at work and in the home. This broadening of the concept of gender helps unify cultural and economic aspects of feminist theory, drawing attention to their linkages and thus overcoming the dualism of culture and economics. Feminist cultural studies that rejects the separate-spheres concept helps us understand gender as an ensemble of experiences, discourses, and behaviors constructed in all venues in which women lead their lives. It also suggests that feminists must not only empower women to produce culture and earn wages equal to men's but destroy the bipolarity of gender that sorts people into separate and unequal subject positions via the experiences, discourses, and practices that make up what we take to be femininity and masculinity. (Again, this returns to many of the themes of queer theory, discussed in Chapter 5.)

## BAUDRILLARD AND FOUCAULT

Postmodern theory has had great influence on cultural studies through Baudrillard, who in *For a Critique of the Political Economy of the Sign* (1981), *Simulations* (1983), and *America* (1988) developed a perspective on postmodernity that blends aspects of French postmodern theory and German critical theory. His notions of the "simulation society" and "hyperreality" provide a foundation for a postmodern cultural studies that segues nicely into critical social theory. Postmodern theory has also contributed significantly to cultural studies through Foucault, who has astutely analyzed the connection between power and discourse in the "disciplinary society" (see O'Neill 1986). Both Baudrillard and Foucault help us analyze cultural texts, discourses, and representations as sources of power and discipline in postmodernity, suggesting a critical cultural studies that

both evaluates these texts, discourses, and representations for their encoded ideologies and helps reformulate them from the ground of everyday
life. For example, Foucault in *Discipline and Punish* (1977) analyzes the
discourse/practices of criminality and sexuality as sources of social control
that construct marginal subject positions for criminals and sexual deviants.
Foucault sought both to understand how power works and to deploy it for
purposes of liberation. He thought that Marx's implication that power is a
thing (like capital) possessed by people fell short because it did not comprehend sufficiently that power is also a process involving agency, discourse, and practice flowing from the ground up. This is similar to the notion of gender as a social construction accomplished through discourses
and practices that assume a bipolar construct of gendered subject positions. Queer theorists and feminist social constructionists, like Foucault,
do not believe that women are simply "forced" by men into their subordinate subject positions, although force is sometimes applied. Rather, certain
women reproduce a culture in which femininity and masculinity are "signifiers," in Derrida's terms, channeling women and men into different activities and hence power positions.

Foucault's understanding of the connection between power and discourse initiates a mode of discourse analysis resembling but going beyond
the Marxist study of ideology. This Foucaultdian analysis locates ideology
both in doctrinal texts and in discursive practices that transform ideological admonitions and recommendations into lived experience, for example
women "producing" their gender by wearing lipstick and pantyhose discursively positioned for them by advertising and other social texts of gender. Both Foucault and Baudrillard suggest the concept of the "social text,"
which comprises old-fashioned doctrinal texts and various discursive practices from advertising to academia. Cultural studies addresses these social
texts of power and control, revealing them as politically positioning and in
the process suggesting reformulations of such discursive practices as gender
and criminality.

Baudrillard goes further than Foucault in that he argues that postmodernity moves beyond what Marx called the mode of production into a mode
of simulation and information displacing the process of power from production per se to information and entertainment. Luke's *Screens of Power*
(1989) attempts to blend this aspect of Baudrillard's analysis with cultural
themes from the Frankfurt School. Baudrillard argues that in postmodernity, or what he calls "hyperreality," we lose all distinctions between reality
and the "simulations" of reality such as advertising, journalism, and science
that litter our posturban landscape. I make much the same argument in *Fast
Capitalism* (Agger 1989a), where I contend that the traditional distinction
between textuality and reality is rapidly fading, thus "dispersing" discourses of power and control directly into people's sentient environments.

This moves the critique of ideology into a new realm, as Baudrillard tries to do. Marx patiently worked through bourgeois economic theory in the many hours he spent in the British Museum in London, piercing its false representations of economic reality in order to produce a truer version of the dynamics of capitalism. In fast capitalism or hyperreality we can no longer assume that texts such as Marx's *Capital* can persuasively remove themselves from reality in order to reveal it. Texts (e.g., trade books for general audiences and mainstream magazines) are sucked into the whirlpool of everyday experience, becoming disposable cultural commodities read quickly on the beach or in the dentist's office and thus losing their ability to anger and educate. Texts lose distance from reality in a stage of hyperreality, and thus "discourse," as Baudrillard and Foucault term it, becomes a secret text, found everywhere but in libraries and bookstores.

The efficacious social texts of our time are *People* magazine, advertisements for Guess jeans, *Entertainment Tonight,* the movie *Pretty Woman.* As discourses dispersed in everyday life, they help "simulate" reality and thus in a sense become "realer" than reality "itself." That is, they have more social influence than traditional texts written to be read slowly and considered critically. Although books as such still exist, few publishers publish challenging, critical books for a general audience. (See Jacoby's *Last Intellectuals* [1987] and Herbert Schiller's *Culture, Inc.* [1989] for discussions of the commodification of writing and publishing in late capitalism.) Even academic publishers such as university presses publish books for profit (trade books), on baseball and first ladies. Textuality loses the character of considered argument, to be perused in a sense outside of reality, and becomes simulation, representation, reproduction, photograph, and figure, thus subtly presenting itself to readers as reality itself (and not an authored text promoting one version of reality among many possible versions).

Postmodern cultural studies becomes, then, a critical practice that *restores the author and hence the argument* to simulations and social texts in postmodernity. Advertising, for example, is "unpacked" as the argument it is for certain commodities and for the world in which people lead lives defined by campaigns in which people are positioned in certain determinate ways (Harms and Kellner 1991). Thus, the campaign for Dockers pants is not only an argument for buying Dockers but also an argument for a Dockers world in which yuppies commune to play volleyball, go sailing, and take walks with their dogs after having earned their keep in the world of work (Goldman and Papson 1991). Similarly, McDonald's campaigns sell not only burgers but family and community.

During his first presidential campaign, Clinton, who brilliantly understands the social texts of the United States in the 1990s, made it a point to be photographed in McDonald's franchises across the country, achieving populist contact with people who do not live on either coast and who drink restaurant-chain coffee instead of café au lait. Baudrillard would say that it is quite immaterial that Clinton may actually "like" McDonald's coffee. More important is that he understands McDonald's to be a text, a discursive practice positioning him in middle America. Similarly, Clinton reached out to generation X voters (post-baby-boomers) by blowing his saxophone and wearing shades on MTV and Arsenio Hall's talk show, allowing himself to be "read" as a youth-oriented presidential candidate. The sax and the shades perhaps more than any other text positioned Clinton for post-boomer voters who in previous elections had voted overwhelmingly for Ronald Reagan and then George Bush.

An issue dividing critical social theorists is whether Baudrillard is indeed correct that simulations replace representations of reality that distinguish between true and false. If "everything" is simulated, cultural studies subverts more materialist social and economic analyses. The Frankfurt School's cultural studies stopped short of this, although I would add that the Frankfurt theorists did not sufficiently understand that power and discourse are connected and hence ignored the ground of discourse (e.g., mass culture) in everyday life, viewing it as irremediably pedestrian and commodified. This prevented them from reformulating everyday discourses at the level of popular culture and everyday life, instead concentrating on the preservation of elite culture that conveyed the "truth" about domination.

Also at issue (as I mention in Chapter 2) is whether Baudrillard and Foucault "end" the social or so differentiate it into incommensurable subject positions that they also end social theorizing (e.g., see Seidman 1991a), which formulates society in big-picture terms. Postmodern cultural studies quickly becomes close readings of particular texts and discourses, without any overarching social-theoretical understandings linking the powerful simulations to large-scale structures of capital, patriarchy, and racism on a national and even global scale. Luke (1989, 1992) demonstrates convincingly that one can do close deconstructive readings of cultural texts and discourses without renouncing the "metanarratives" of social-theoretical analysis that help provide the big picture. Of course, Baudrillard ends both the sociological and the social (e.g., see Game 1991) when he argues that it is no longer possible to analyze hyperreality in traditional metanarrative terms, given that we no longer possess epistemological criteria or guidelines for differentiating between "reality" and reality's simulation. In this sense, cultural theory and analysis become simulation themselves, producing anti-metanarrative texts such as his *America* (1988), which builds an understanding of American locales on top of a road trip he took across the United States. Although this sort of ethnography provides rich vignettes and insights, it offers little in the way of structural analysis and political strategy. In hyperreality the end of the social is matched by the end of the political.

In spite of cultural studies' rich metadisciplinary perspective, there are "boundaries" to cultural studies, such as Baudrillard's aversion to meta-narratives that inflate particular readings of cultural simulations into social theory and social science. Postmodern theory usefully provokes critical social theory to take discursive politics seriously, providing a much richer perspective on the culture industry and thus domination than was achieved by the Frankfurt School, which wrote off popular culture as politically hopeless. In doing so, though, postmodern theory tends to lose the coordinates of reality that allow one to generalize, analyze, and criticize. Again, this issue turns on how one theorizes the break between modernity and postmodernity. Baudrillard views the break as qualitative, requiring whole new analytical discourses for grasping the posited end of the social. I disagree with him that postmodernity is something entirely novel. I prefer to view it as the latest stage of capitalism, requiring theoretical innovations such as discourse-oriented cultural studies but not obviating the need for big-picture social and cultural theory that attempts to resolve "difference" into a comprehensible mosaic—theory, by another name.

CHAPTER 7

# Critiques of
# Critical Social Theory

## MIDWESTERN EMPIRICISM AND
## THE REAL-SOCIOLOGY CRITIQUE

Here, I consider arguments against critical social theory made by sociologists and social scientists. After all, many researchers and theorists are unpersuaded by critical theory, postmodernism, feminist theory, and cultural studies. Although these perspectives continue to attract adherents in both the social sciences and humanities, there are many who reject them out of hand, if not the whole project of social theory. In this first section, I examine the case some social scientists, especially sociologists, make against all theorizing. Following this, I consider the contention that Marxism, the foundation of critical social theory, is "wrong" (e.g., obsolete). Finally, I further explore the arguments of rational choice theory, which is rapidly gaining ascendance in sociology as sociologists incorporate an economic logic into their work (e.g., Becker's human-capital theory and Coleman's social-capital theory) in order to discredit leftist structural explanations.

Since Comte (1975) coined the neologism *sociology* and modeled it on physics ("social physics," revising and strengthening the Marquis de Condorcet's notion that social science should be "social arithmetic"), sociologists have attempted to legitimate sociology on the basis of its claimed affinity to the "hard" physical and natural sciences, seeking cause-and-effect explanations of social phenomena and utilizing quantitative methodologies (see Mills 1959; Gouldner 1970). In the wake of Reagan-era budget cuts in U.S. higher education, many sociology departments have put distance between the political engagements of 1960s sociologists and the highly technical, policy-oriented, and grant-supported sociology of the 1990s. Within universities, buttressing sociology departments in this man-

144

ner has been an attempt to convince skeptical and cost-conscious administrators that sociology can not only pay its own way but contribute useful
understandings of social issues, all the way from health care to families.

I have chaired a sociology department in an American research university and attempted to justify the department's existence, thus claiming a
greater share of resources from the administration. We made our case by
emphasizing the utility of sociology for students, scholars in other disciplines, the university budget (through grants), and society at large (through
policy-oriented research). This project of self-justification has been neoliberal at best and neoconservative at worst. That is, for sociologists to accept
the grant-driven model of the university, especially the public university,
and thus to do "useful," fundable research necessarily supports the existing society by helping iron out its social problems, conceptualized not as
major structural flaws, such as capitalism, racism, and patriarchy, but as
remediable interruptions en route to the postindustrial promised land. Indeed, this model of sociological fine-tuning, contributing to what is called
"policy," which is necessarily carried out by the state or government on behalf of capital, dates back to Comte, Durkheim, and Weber. Marx said that
the social and human problems of capitalism could not be solved with mi-
nor reforms, given that the state is the "executive committee of the bourgeoisie," but only through a thoroughgoing socialist revolution (see Rule
1978; Diesing 1982). Although Marx's prophecy and program of socialist
change is now outdated because of the expanded roles of the state, which
intervenes in the economy to protect it, and of culture ("culture industry"),
which intervenes in everyday life and people's psyches in order to amelio-
rate psychic crises, critical social theorists accept Marx's idea that social
problems cannot be solved piecemeal. Instead, all social institutions must
be transformed, albeit in a "dialectical" way that recognizes the inseparable relationship between microlevel changes in everyday life, a key theme
of both the Frankfurt School and feminism, and macrolevel changes in major social institutions, to be achieved through what Habermas calls new social movements such as the women's movement and environmentalism.

This is not mainly a commentary on the institutional survival strategies
that sociology chairpeople adopt. After all, in an era of increasing academic accountability and attacks on tenure, academics seek to protect their
jobs by justifying their departments' existences. Typically, this requires the
policy-oriented, grant-supported, high-science strategy I just outlined.
However, there is a certain obvious tension between a critical theorist's
chairing a sociology department and arguing for his discipline's significance to policymaking, grant-getting, and science, which necessarily
frames the work of his positivist colleagues who defend the status quo by
postulating social laws, and the critical theorist's own investment in radical
social change, albeit of a kind that departs from the program Marx formu-

lated in the nineteenth century. And in fact many mainstream sociologists
have not flocked to critical social theory either because they think it is bad
institutional strategy reminiscent of the 1960s, thus delegitimating sociology in the eyes of administrators, tuition payers, and taxpayers, or because
they genuinely believe that critical social theory is not "real sociology" or
indeed is bad sociology.

In this section I explore what I call the "real sociology" critique of critical
social theory. After all, one can argue about which institutional survival
strategies sociology chairs should adopt, especially given a relatively high
degree of institutional variability. For example, what works at a public research university such as Wisconsin or Buffalo might be less successful at
Princeton. Lacking a doctoral program, Texas-Arlington sociologists attempt to demonstrate that their graduates contribute productively to the
Dallas–Fort Worth metroplex and region. Although I think a convincing
case can be made that sociology departments need to demonstrate that they
pay their way in the overall organization of the university and that this is
sometimes best done by emphasizing policy, grants, and high science—and
indeed I as chair have used that very strategy in my former university, with
mixed success—it is not clear that critical social theory *necessarily* fails to
help sociology departments justify themselves. In elite liberal arts colleges
such as Oberlin, for example, sociology may be expected to raise students'
consciousness and lead them to ask questions about their privileged class,
gender, and race positions rather than produce grants and mainstream journal publications. At some institutions, nonquantitative and even theoretical
sociologists are the norm, especially where there is not a high premium
placed on grants and methodological technique. There is much variance in
the expectations university administrators have of sociology departments,
which reflects the overall variation in the structural positions of colleges
and universities, ranging from four-year schools and liberal arts colleges to
land-grant public institutions and Ivy League universities.

The real-sociology critique takes critical social theory to task for three
interrelated shortcomings. First, critical theory is nonquantitative, failing
to achieve the methodological standards of science. Second, critical theory
is avowedly political, refusing to adopt the allegedly value-free stance of
positivists. Third, critical theory does not have "data," remaining purely
speculative. It is armchair sociology. This third criticism is not the same as
the first criticism inasmuch as mainstream sociologists embrace a methodological hierarchy that puts quantitative work at the top but places qualitative work involving such methods as in-depth interviews, ethnography, and
participant observation above theory. At least qualitative sociologists such
as symbolic interactionists and ethnomethodologists have data collected
from the "real world," if not data gathered from large surveys that are susceptible to quantitative analysis.

This is not to exaggerate the disciplinary legitimacy of qualitative data: Sociologists who mount the real-sociology critique of critical social theory also tend to value only quantitative methods. Qualitative methods are a poor relation in the eyes of these positivists and neopositivists, who dominate sociology departments at most major midwestern public research universities such as Wisconsin, Michigan, and Ohio State, constituting a neopositivist sociological genre I have called "midwestern empiricism" (Agger 1989b: 6–13). Midwestern empiricists (some of whom work outside of the Midwest but who share these values) valorize grants, policy work, quantitative methods, and publication in a handful of refereed sociology journals such as *American Sociological Review* and *Social Forces*. Nevertheless, when midwestern empiricists are faced with a choice between non-Marxist qualitative sociology (e.g., in the social-problem-oriented tradition of the venerable Chicago School, which produced symbolic interactionism [Fine 1995]) and postmodern-feminist critical theory, there is no contest.

Midwestern empiricists view most theorizing—liberal, conservative, and radical—as illegitimate inasmuch as it does not address what they take to be the "real" world. The only acceptable kinds of theory are what Robert Merton called "middle-range sociology," or "middle-range theory"—theory that does not attempt macro or global explanations but contents itself conceptually to organize the findings of low-level empirical investigations, for example explaining how people migrate in "steps," or stages, or how punishment deters certain kinds of crimes but not others. This middle-range theory is abundant in mainstream sociology, finding its way into virtually every empirical subspecialty, all the way from demography to criminology. This is not theory in the sense of the traditional grand narratives provided by Durkheim, Weber, Marx, Parsons, and Habermas, who tried to explain society comprehensively at a certain level of abstraction. It is more akin to the empirical literature reviews that are supposed to open sociological journal articles, carving out a niche for the research contribution at hand by building on and yet differentiating itself from past research. (The "past" here is usually no longer than ten years and sometimes much less.) Middle-range sociology frames empirical research by explaining its significance according to its contribution to an extant research literature, often expressed in terms of its middle-range conceptual contribution to a set of issues at hand. Calling an empirical literature a "theory" actually legitimizes the particular research. For example, a mundane empirical article on social movements gains significance if it is said to contribute to group-mobilization theory, which represents an oeuvre of articles and books organized loosely around the conceptual theme of group mobilization.

In talking about middle-range theory, Merton not only intended to characterize a certain level of explanation, above the picayune but below grand theory. As a positivist, he was also trying to urge that theory actually "test" propositions with reference to empirical data. Group-mobilization "theorists" would go out in the field and collect data or analyze the data of others in order either to improve their own explanatory framework or perhaps to discard it in favor of another. Thus, critical social theorists are said to engage in armchair speculation without empirical referents, which is bad both because sociology is supposed to address the real world and because it is supposed to do so using the methodological techniques of science. For midwestern empiricists, theory is tolerable only if it tests propositions or hypotheses (if-then statements) that, taken together, constitute theories (e.g., group-mobilization theory) allegedly accumulating into laws, thus arriving at the social physics defined by Comte as the mission of sociology. Another term for this approach to the verification or falsification (Popper 1959) of empirical propositions (hypotheses) is positivism, which is bound up with a representational theory of knowledge rejected by critical social theorists.

Here the issue is what sort of theorizing sociological positivists will tolerate, since they will not tolerate the politicized theorizing of critical theorists. They will tolerate and sometimes engage in the middle-range theorizing that organizes testable and tested propositions into coherent shape, thus giving their empirical research much-needed context. Without these middle-range framings (e.g., work on household labor being organized into the relative-resources perspective as against other midlevel perspectives), empirical sociological research, typically published in refereed journal articles, would be aimless, claiming no derivation from prior research (which Kuhn called "normal science") and having no implications for further research, which, as sociology matures, should cumulate into laws. Although that day appears distant, sociologists who accept the status of sociology as a normal science that accumulates evidence in order to arrive at physics-like understandings of social cause and effect need to frame their everyday research as significant steps toward this eventual outcome. All sociological journal articles, which open with "theoretical" sections that review the literature, are supposed to end with discussions of the reported research's implications for policy and for future research, which necessarily proceeds within the same frame. Although sociologists do not usually follow up on these programmatic suggestions, it is essential that articles close with a reckoning of their contributions to normal science and an augur of their relevance to future normal science, thus creating the impression that scientific progress is being made.

Positivist articles tend *not* to produce linear connections to future articles simply because sociologists busily produce careers (see Lewis 1975, 1996), not scientific continuity, which, most critics of positivism are convinced, is a myth. One produces one's career (see Bourdieu 1984; Knorr-

Cetina 1977, 1979; Mulkay 1979, 1985) by carving out a research niche within which one can proliferate a series of articles, often funded by grants, that establish one's expertise as a person who deals with a small set of specific empirical problems—for example, juveniles who murder, the living patterns of the Hispanic elderly, the delivery of health care by teams. In most research-oriented sociology departments, especially those that use the midwestern empiricist model, sociologists typically need ten or fifteen well-placed journal articles clustering on a narrow theme to receive tenure and promotion to associate professor and another ten or fifteen articles for promotion to professor. It is clear that career building is one of the main reasons quantitative empiricists deploy what they call theory to justify a string of narrow interrelated articles that build on existing empirical literatures and make way for new ones. These are not the grand metanarratives of critical social theory but at best Mertonian framings of data-driven journal articles.

Even though midwestern empiricists claim to be theoretical in the way they frame their data analyses, thus giving their own narrow research significance in its relationship to the body of normal science (the "literature"), they reject the metanarratives of grand theory (see Mills 1959) that do not "test" theoretical propositions but embrace midlevel propositions whose falsification and verification supposedly advance knowledge within particular disciplinary subfields. But critical theory comes in for even harsher criticism than Parsonian theory or the theoretical classics by the real-sociology people, who contend that critical theory is not only absent data but nonquantitative and political. Durkheim and Weber supported the capitalist project of modernity. Indeed, mainstream empirical sociology journals occasionally publish interpretive articles on the classics (e.g., Camic 1987) not because they are "real sociology" but because they perform a certain canonizing function, establishing that the narrow empirical articles published in the same volume of *American Sociological Review* or *Social Forces* derive from a founding sociological canon and are not simply technical forays designed to enhance sociology's science aura. (I make this argument through close textual readings in Agger 1989b.) In this sense, most major sociology departments have a person who can teach "the classics," thus grounding students in the history of the discipline and canonizing their empirical dissertation work. A leading sociology department recently advertised for a tenure-track faculty member who could teach and publish in the sociological classics. One of my former students interviewed for this job and before the interview was told by a prospective supporter in the hiring department not to stray from the classics in her job talk, avoiding postmodernism, critical theory, and French feminism. It was clear that the department did not want a politicized theorist but one who could competently explicate Durkheim. Another major department recently sought to hire a sociological theorist who could publish in the *American Sociological Review*, thus giving the department luster and helping serve the canonizing function I just discussed.

In these senses, midwestern empiricists who mount the real-sociology critique of critical social theory can *say* that they are not antitheory. In the same way, they can say that they are not opposed to qualitative methods (as long as qualitative faculty and students do not achieve hegemony in their own departments). Theory has a place in mainstream sociology within journal articles as literature reviews and off the beaten path as canonizing interpretation of classical theory. But the unashamedly politicized theory of postmodernists, critical theorists, and feminists is strictly off-limits to mainstream sociologists, who demonize such work as flaky, irrelevant, subversive, and not real sociology. Stories abound about how mainstream sociology departments attempt to extirpate this sort of work, making it taboo for graduate students and blocking the advancement of faculty who espouse it. A leftish theorist in a high-profile mainstream department told me that his case for promotion to full professor was challenged by some of his colleagues on the ground that his work was destructive of sociology. He has published three reputable books with good publishers, but still his colleagues reject his work not on grounds of quality but because they contend it is not real sociology. As I have tried to argue here, this does not constitute a reasoned case against critical social theory but rather reflects the territorial imperative of mainstream sociologists, who define nonmainstream work as illegitimate. In effect, the real-sociology argument against critical social theory is a political argument designed to promote one intellectual and methodological style over another.

## "MARX WAS WRONG"

Midwestern empiricists' critique of critical social theory as political and hence unscientific belongs to a larger neoliberal (and of course neoconservative) appraisal of Marxism that deems leftism of all kinds obsolete in light of the Soviet Union's demise. As I discussed in Chapter 1, Marxism inaugurates critical social theory both theoretically and politically. Although most contemporary versions of critical social theory differ with Marx and with later Marxists on many points of substance, these versions are all in dialogue with Marx and Marxism on a whole host of issues. If Marxism is no longer valid, as many in the West now contend in light of perestroika and the dismantling of the Soviet "empire," critical social theory would appear to lose much of its theoretical and political purchase. If Marx was wrong, surely critical theory's reason for being as a sympathetic revision and extrapolation of Marxism dissolves.

To make a clear picture somewhat muddier, one *can* be a "real" number-crunching sociologist and also harbor Marxist politics, as the example of the notable Wisconsin sociologist Erik Olin Wright (1985, 1987) indicates. Although most real sociologists who disdain critical theory do so on the aforementioned ground of critical theory's politicization, Wright demonstrates that one can conduct large-scale survey research in a quantitative mode and address questions of class and class structure. There are positivist Marxists, just as there are many more positivist non-Marxists. Here the Marx-was-wrong dismissal of critical social theory pertains to those number-crunching positivists who combine or conflate being a Marxist with rejecting the aims of mainstream sociology, which real sociologists regard as antithetical. Although Wright can do real sociology and hold Marxist values and even intrude some of his values into his sociological research, most mainstreamers believe that "real sociology" *by definition* excludes Marxist political aims and thus disqualifies critical social theory. Real sociology excludes Marxism not only because Marxism is not value free but also because Marxism prophesies a historical outcome most real sociologists deem undesirable. These sociologists would probably contend that Wright can do "good" sociology even though he is a political Marxist, as long as he clearly compartmentalizes his research and his political values. (In the same way, a real sociologist could belong to an offbeat religious sect and still have a successful sociological career.)

This is not to suggest that Wright has won over the sociological masses. Although he has a high-profile position in Wisconsin's sociology department, arguably the most visible sociology department in the United States, Wright does not edit a major journal and is not a power broker in the discipline. He has published in the *American Sociological Review*, which in itself legitimizes him. But Wright has won legitimacy in spite of his Marxism, which reduces his mobility in the discipline. Although midwestern empiricists dislike critical social theory because it is nonquantitative and lacks data, what bothers them most about critical theory is its Marxist derivation. To be sure, most of the versions of critical social theory discussed in this book are in critical dialogue with Marxism and build on Marxism's failures as well as successes. The real-sociology critique of critical social theories rests on a simplification and demonization of their allegedly Marxist loyalties, which allows real-sociology critics of critical social theories to dismiss them now that the Soviet Union has collapsed.

This strategy combines guilt by association, notably critical theories' affiliation to the Marxist paradigm, and sloppy political and intellectual history, notably the conflation of the Stalinist version of Marxism-Leninism and the "evil empire" it legitimized with Marx and Marxism. Like U.S. journalists and politicians, many mainstream sociologists blame Marxism for both Soviet political terror and economic and social irrationality. This is an extremely dubious strategy for two reasons: In the first place, critical social theorists are critical of Marxism, even though they are more critical of non-Marxist social theories. In the second place, Stalinism was not intended or authored by Marx but rather emerged out of Stalin's revision of Lenin's own revision of Marxism, which Lenin conducted in the political heat of the moment. Lenin revised Marx in order to explain and expedite a socialist revolution in agrarian czarist Russia, a country that Marx deemed unlikely to foster the capitalist economic crisis and incipient class struggle of the kind he expected in mature capitalist societies. Lenin argued that tight political discipline exacted by the Communist Party of the Soviet Union coupled with the New Economic Policies designed to industrialize a backward agricultural society could accelerate capital accumulation ("state capital") in the Soviet Union and create an appropriate socialist political superstructure, thus preparing the way for the transition from socialism to full communism via the withering away of the state and the Party.

The Marxism-is-wrong critique of critical social theory not only lays the responsibility for the failure of the Soviet experiment at Marx's feet; it also suggests that the whole Marxist theoretical logic produces both an expedient authoritarianism and utopianism. These go hand in hand: Had Marx not aimed so high, hoping to reconstruct both society and human nature, he would not have sanctioned the deployment of draconian strategies such as the dictatorship of the proletariat and forced labor in order to rid socialism of counterrevolutionary elements. Whether Marx actually sanctioned such strategies is doubtful. In fact, the whole Western Marxist reconstruction of Marx and Marxism argues (with the support of the *Economic and Philosophical Manuscripts of 1844*) that Marx was a humanist and democrat who did not advocate a reign of terror but rather quite the opposite. The Marxism-is-wrong critique simply dismisses this reading of Marx, instead taking Lenin and Stalin at their word when they allege authentic filiation with "what Marx really meant."

But the claim that Marxism is wrong is not peculiar to neoliberals and neoconservatives, including mainstream sociologists. The claim is also made by many postmodernists, who argue that Marxism's alleged authoritarianism derived from Marx's intention to write a Eurocentric, androcentric master narrative (Lyotard) that homogenized the heterogeneous experiences and discourses of people who occupy numerous different subject positions. Thus, whereas Marx emphasized the universality of the alienation of labor, many postmodernists emphasize its aspects of "difference," which, they argue, require situation-specific narratives of liberation that acknowledge diversities of gender, race, culture, and religion. What earlier I termed "post-Marxism" arises from a version of postmodern theory that puts distance between its polyvocal narrativity and Marx's metanarrativity. Many of these postmodern post-Marxists contend that the demise of the

Soviet Union demonstrates that Marx's metanarrativity was wrongheaded, especially given the ethnic conflicts that tore apart the USSR and as such demonstrate Marx, Lenin, and Stalin's insensitivity to "difference." The difference between this postmodern Marx-was-wrong claim and the Marx-was-wrong claim made by real sociologists is that the French theorists were sympathetic to Marx's nonauthoritarian political program but thought that it was undermined by Marx's deafness to polyvocality. Lyotard, Derrida, Foucault, and Baudrillard intended their critique of metanarrativity to be framed within the coordinates of emancipatory theory, much as Sartre, Merleau-Ponty, and de Beauvoir blended existential-phenomenological themes with their humanistic, Hegelian version of Marxism. Although I think that the postmodern French theorists jettison more Marxism than is necessary and more than did the French existential Marxists clustered around Sartre's journal *Les Temps modernes*, Lyotard and his colleagues did not gloat when the Soviet Union disintegrated, trumpeting not only the end of communism but also the end of Marxism. Their post-Marxism was neither neoliberal nor neoconservative in the sense that they did not reject Marx's aims but only his approach to narrativity, which they found too sweeping.

Now, to return to an earlier issue, there are many postmodernisms. By and large, the American reception of postmodern theory has transformed postmodernism from a serious critique of civilization based on notions of difference and polyvocality, which were leftist and feminist in sympathy, into a celebration of posturban global capitalism. The American reduction of postmodern theory to an essentially apolitical literary method of deconstruction suppresses the political origins of postmodern theory in antiauthoritarian French New Left politics formulated specifically as an attack on French Marxist structuralism (e.g., Althusser) and the authoritarian politics of the French Communist Party. A great deal of what transpires under the banner of "deconstruction" in American humanities departments, all the way from "deconstructions" of Mark Twain to "deconstructions" of rap music, lose political touch with the leftist and feminist polyvocal narrativity of the original French theorists, who intended what later came to be called deconstruction as a way of reading that sought the silent authorship animating writing. This excavation (Foucault called it "archaeology") of silent authorship would overturn the subordination of reading to writing, empowering readings to join public debate and thus to create precisely the sort of democratic public sphere urged by Habermas, albeit from within rationalist communication theory. "Deconstruction," as Americans associated with the Yale School, such as Paul de Man, termed it, was a political project of post-Marxists sympathetic to new social movements (see Eagleton 1990). These post-Marxists argued that Marx's Eurocentric, androcentric master narrative of radical social change had to be imploded into the plural, polyvocal "small" narratives of women, people of color, postcolonialists, and environmentalists, all of whom speak different languages but have the common aim of overturning hierarchy. The most important overturning of hierarchy for the postmodern theorists was the "deconstruction" of distinctions between narrator and narrated, empowering the alienated to recount and theorize about their own predicaments in their own voices, untranslated by Western male theorists into a single discourse of liberation.

Thus, there are different varieties of the Marx-was-wrong thesis. Real sociologists, neoliberals, and neoconservatives contend that Marx was wrong about "everything," notably including his political ideals of a disalienated, classless society. French postmodern theorists by and large accepted Marx's political ideals and rejected only his metanarrativity, which, they argued, had something to do with the overly "totalized" model of Soviet socialism that doomed the architects of Bolshevism. These postmodernists contended that Marx was wrong mainly about discourse, the possibility of a universal vocabulary of liberation, which made Marxist-Leninists wrong about a centralized Soviet state impervious to ethnic differences. This is not to suggest that Lyotard clearly disentangled the critique of metanarrativity from the denunciation of Soviet socialism. His blurring of these issues, at least by omission, allowed later postmodernists who celebrate capitalism to celebrate as well the end of communism as the end of Marxism. Postmodern post-Marxists have, in my opinion, implied that in surpassing Marxism they are embracing capitalism. These are quite separate issues, especially in that Western Marxists have convincingly demonstrated the possibility of a nonauthoritarian, democratic, humanist Marxism specifically opposed to Soviet Marxism (see Marcuse 1958).

### RATIONAL CHOICE THEORY AND THE ECONOMIZATION OF SOCIOLOGY

Ralf Dahrendorf (1968) argued for the distinctiveness of sociology by proposing a concept called *Homo sociologicus*, thus drawing attention to people's social identities. Many others (e.g., Berger 1963; Mills 1959; Friedrichs 1970; O'Neill 1972; Lemert 1995; Bourdieu and Wacquant 1992) have elaborated the distinctive identity of sociology. Real-sociology critics of Marxism sometimes fault Marx for being an economic determinist, thus ignoring sociological explanations of human behavior. Even if they do not call Marx an economic reductionist, they argue that Marx placed too much weight on economic factors, especially by comparison to Weber, who considered economics to be an important "variable" but who did not reduce behavior to economic determinants. The Weber renaissance (e.g.,

Giddens 1972, 1984) positions itself in opposition to Marxism partly by claiming territory traditionally held by Marxists, such as the analysis of economic correlates of social behavior.

A subtext of the concern with Marx's alleged economic reductionism, which supports a critique of critical social theory, is the notion that he was overly collectivist in his economic theories. Those sociologists who view economics as important tend to reject Marxian economics for its collectivism, which is seen to issue in illiberal nonmarket societies such as the Soviet Union. Thus, an important critique of Marxism has been mounted from within mainstream sociology that acknowledges the importance of economic behavior but challenges certain key Marxian assumptions about collectivity, the market, and the logic of capital. Of course, bourgeois economists have always been opposed to Marxism because they believe that a free-enterprise economy, based on the right of people to hold private productive capital and thus to make profit, is the most rational and desirable social system. They defend the right of individuals to invest their private funds in potentially profit-making enterprises, accepting the desperate risk of insolvency and thus having a right to profits, sometimes enormous, if their business ventures succeed. Although Parsons, like Weber, defended capitalism in *The Social System* (1951), the canon of structural functionalism, he did not really blend a sociological with an economic rationality in the way that later theorists have done, notably including Gary Becker, the founder of human-capital theory, discussed earlier, and James Coleman, the author of social-capital theory.

Coleman's work develops and defends rational choice theory, which borrows many concepts from economic theory and thus rebuts Marxism. Rational choice theorists oppose Marxism both at the level of explanation and in terms of basic social, political, and economic values. Rational choice theory emerges from human-capital theory, extending from economics to sociology. It has influenced a wide range of sociological subspecialties, from theory to demography. It is a friendly neighbor of exchange theory, which begins with the works of George Homans (e.g., see his *Human Group* [1950]). Rational choice theory is not so much a set of empirical propositions as an explanatory framework within which individual-level behavior is linked to macrolevel behavior, much the way that economists bridge microeconomics and macroeconomics. Coleman's lengthy treatise *Foundations of Social Theory* (1990), summarizing the rational choice agenda, twists Becker's (1980, 1981, 1996) human-capital theory, which extends economic theory to the explanation of the household division of labor, into a more explicitly sociological framework, with human capital termed "social capital."

Rational choice theory is relevant here for three reasons. First, its constructs, discussed below, oppose the constructs of Marxism at the basic level of their understanding of human behavior. Second, by *economizing* sociology, Becker and Coleman usurp Marxism's stress on the importance of economics. Third, this incorporation of economic theory into sociology upgrades sociology's disciplinary status by adopting concepts from the more prestigious and "harder" discipline of economics. This is thought to be a good survival strategy at a time when sociology departments suffer because administrators consider them throwbacks to the 1960s, when sociologists participated in social movements and did advocacy research. Increasingly, rational choice theory is becoming the latest attack on the left in sociology.

Rational choice theorists argue that social behavior can be explained in terms of the "rational" calculations that individuals make about the options available to them. This is the basic logic of capitalist economic theory, which describes what happens when people with limited resources are placed in the economic marketplace. Economists theorize that individuals attempt to maximize their benefits through strategies of investment and consumption. Becker argues that families, which behave like rational economic actors, maximize their overall benefits by having the spouse with the most marketable job skills (e.g., credentials, experience) shoulder the burden of market labor, while the spouse with fewer marketable job skills stays home to raise children and do housework. It would be irrational to have the more market-worthy spouse stay home and perform household labor inasmuch as this would cause the family to forgo income. According to Becker, this aspect of the sexual division of labor is not caused by sexism, which feminists conceptualize as both ideology and discriminatory behavior, but by spouses' rational choices about how best to maximize their overall economic utilities.

In this way, Becker exemplifies the rational choice agenda, which is to reduce social behavior to individual-level rational choices and thus to dispel the notion that people act with what Marxists call false consciousness or in response to domination. For rational choice theorists, phenomena such as economic exploitation, racism, and sexism do not exist; that is, they are not meaningful sociological concepts, given their premise that behavior can be explained satisfactorily simply with reference to people's "rational" choices.

In undercutting notions of exploitation and domination, rational choice theorists undercut critical social theory. Notions of sexism and racism become mere political slogans, which do not have empirical referents so dear to the real-sociology crowd. This is not to say that there cannot be an agenda of feminist rational choice theory; after all, simply because one explains gender inequality in terms of individual-level rationality does not mean that one cannot advocate social policies that on an aggregate level benefit women by helping them upgrade their skills and credentials. Rational choice theory does not simply ignore social problems but traces these problems either to people's rational choices or to aspects of irrationality that may result from people having less than perfect information about the choices available to them or being insensitive to the long-term consequences of short-term decisions. For example, an alcoholic who takes a drink may well behave rationally if he or she is at a cocktail party thrown by his or her boss, at which it is normative for all of the employees to drink. But in the long term the alcoholic's job may be at risk if he or she falls off the wagon, even if there are certain short-term benefits to be derived from accepting a drink proffered by the boss.

Not only do rational choice theorists reject notions of exploitation and domination; they also scrap the whole concept of social structure, which exists apart from or over the heads of individuals, because they explain individual behavior in terms of rational choices. This eliminates the need for theories such as Marxism and heals the so-called micro-macro problem (see Alexander et al. 1987; Agger 1992b: 56–72), which has been paramount since Parsons. In effect, macrolevel explanations can be reduced to the aggregate of microlevel decisionmaking, conceptualized as having been conducted rationally. For example, that women earn only 70 percent of what men earn in the United States reflects not an explicit program or doctrine of male sexism but rather the aggregated effects of individual couples' rational choices about how the more market-worthy spouse should be absolved of all or most domestic labor.

This abandonment of structural analysis, using concepts such as exploitation and domination, vanquishes leftist social theories. It also makes sociology more "elegant" and rigorous in mathematical terms, enabling sociologists to mimic the economic modeling of social behavior, thus strengthening its science aura. Mathematical modeling, which is premised on rational choice constructs of individual-level behavior, is becoming a common approach in a host of social science disciplines such as sociology, economics, and political science. Mathematical modelers do high-status work inasmuch as it resembles the work done by scientists, who replace discourse with figure, and thus approach the "scientificity" of the hard physical sciences. This fulfills the original positivist vision of knowledge as mathematics, which is as old as the Enlightenment.

## "FRIENDLY" CRITIQUES

In this chapter I have outlined the central hostile arguments against critical social theory, including the real-sociology critique, the Marxism-is-wrong critique, and rational choice theory's critique. In this concluding section, I outline sympathetic critiques of critical social theory that indicate problems with some or all of the perspectives covered so far in the book. These "friendly" critiques include the critique of obscurantism and the critique of groundedness. I do not necessarily accept these arguments; indeed, I think that they can be turned on themselves so that what they criticize about critical social theory can be seen as a virtue. Opponents of critical theory mount either or both of these critiques as well, albeit in ways that deny critical theorists the possibility of making corrections to their theories without abandoning their entire theoretical frameworks.

The critique of obscurantism is directed at the Frankfurt School, postmodernists, and the French feminists. Some of the appeal of French feminists lies precisely in their inaccessibility, thus giving women opportunity to master an esoteric code and exclude patriarchs, much as men often exclude laywomen from their totemic codes. It is clear that Wolf does not want to condemn her French feminist sisters; indeed, her "power feminism" is ecumenical and nonjudgmental. And yet as a lucid writer herself, she is miffed by the practiced obscurity of French feminism. By the same token, virtually everyone who reads contemporary social theory despairs at the stylistic difficulty of Adorno. Although Habermas is not an easy read, his writing is fluent compared to Adorno's dialectical allusions in books such as *Negative Dialectics* (1973a). Many sympathetic to the Frankfurt School's work reasonably ask why critical theorists cannot compose in a more accessible language, making themselves available to readers who lack the philosophical, cultural, and theoretical erudition of Adorno and Horkheimer and the encyclopedic breadth of Habermas.

This *is* a powerful critique when one considers the democratic aspirations of critical social theories. These theories want to overturn a number of hierarchies, especially ones based on differential access to knowledge and discourse. There is abundant irony in critical theories that preach democracy, equality, and what Habermas calls ideal speech but frustrate most people's understanding. This is not to take a plain-language view that all sentences should be short and simple, sacrificing complexity to ratings. Some issues are difficult and must be addressed complexly. Other issues require prior acquaintance, such as writings about Hegel or Freud. Although exposition is a valuable and economical tool—as shown in this book, I hope!—exegesis does not substitute for more sophisticated treatments, which transcend exposition and aim for analysis, critique, and synthesis. Nor should every theoretical writing have to be cut from a standard mold, which does not reflect or acknowledge differences in topic and readership.

The critique of obscurantism has been most powerfully advanced by postmodern thinkers who question assumptions about modernity, notably about the role of intellectuals. This is no accident inasmuch as postmodern theorists take the politics of discourse seriously. As I have argued in *Decline of Discourse* (Agger 1990), postmodernism suggests an archetype of public intellectuality deriving from Derrida's empowering notion that readings are necessarily writings in the sense that they complete texts by reckoning with their inherent "undecidability" (inconsistencies, deferrals of meaning, internal tensions). Although his empowering of readers may appear to run counter to his *dis*empowering of his own readers, who struggle with his devilishly challenging prose, Foucault, Baudrillard, and Lyotard compose themselves in relatively accessible ways. And even if they present stylistic difficulties, the implication of postmodernism is that the postmodern intellectual will deploy a variety of "polyvocal" discourses that address different audiences and engage different texts and cultural practices. This versatility reflects the postmodern acknowledgment that there is no single expert language or literary style but rather plural narratives reflecting the heterogeneity of people's subject positions.

Thus, the postmodern intellectual will be able to deal with narrative "difference" constructively, ranging from the everyday to the erudite, depending on the contextual requirements of the moment. The only member of the Frankfurt School who approached this polyvocal versatility was Marcuse, who, as I discussed earlier, successfully wrote for the American ear during his post–World War II career in the United States. Much less obscurantist than Adorno but equally philosophically and culturally sophisticated, Marcuse tried hard to avoid obscurantism without compromising the depth and breadth of his social and cultural criticism. Even then, ordinary-language philosophers from the Anglo-American tradition attacked Marcuse, accusing him of obscurantism, elitism, mandarinism, and a sheer inability to write clear prose. For his part, Ernest Gellner (1959) in turn criticizes Anglo-American analytic philosophers' penchant for what they take to be plain language, which, Gellner and others argue, necessarily excludes difficult, dialectical, and troubling argumentation, all of which the Anglo-Americans reject as obscurantist.

There is no clear standard of lucidity independent of context. Reading theory, especially polyvocal postmodern theory, is like learning a new language; after a while it begins to make sense and one can even learn to use the new language. One of Derrida's most powerful insights is that textual "undecidability" blocks the development of a master discourse into which one can translate all local discourses and thus reduce their muddying "difference." There is no language outside of language with which to conduct this translation exercise, which is why translating books and articles into a different language is necessarily a political exercise requiring selective emphasis, omission, and nuance. By the same token, Jameson (1981) argues that all narratives can be "transcoded" into all others, acknowledging that these transcodings cannot be evaluated according to a transcendental, ahistorical, context-free criterion of representation such that certain translations are judged to be objectively better than other translations. Jameson calls for theoretical transcoding because he wants to resist the postmodern tendency to celebrate polyvocality to the point that one refuses to make sense of theories framed within different narrative parameters. For example, he wants Marxism to learn from postmodernism and vice versa. This does not reduce postmodernism to Marxism but sets up dialogue at once acknowledging the inescapability of polyvocal difference and the possibility of what Habermas calls rational communication.

Thus, the issue here should not be whether theorists write clearly or not, for clarity is not an objective criterion that exists outside of language. The issue should rather be whether theorists compose themselves in polyvocal ways, moving back, forth, and across different discourses (or what Wittgenstein called language games) without being entrapped permanently in any single discourse. Theorists should write in ways that acknowledge their theories' transcodability, their transformation into different frameworks; indeed, they should do this transcoding themselves, wherever possible clarifying complicated concepts without refraining from using complicated concepts in the first place. At the same time, theorists should not defend stylistic difficulty, as Adorno sometimes did, because clear writing inevitably will be co-opted and reduced to affirmative banalities. This is not inevitable, as Jacoby demonstrates in *The Last Intellectuals* (1987), where he offers numerous examples of "public" books combining intellectual challenge with accessibility. Although Jacoby does not say this, his archetype of public intellectuality seems very much consistent with the postmodern stress on polyvocality, which includes the ability to write prose comprehensible to nonspecialist readers who, in reading, become writers in the sense that they competently confront the ambiguity, inconsistencies, and muddiness of all writing and thus "give sense" to what they read (see Bourdieu et al. 1994).

The criticism of critical social theory's groundedness is the opposite of the critique of obscurantism. Sympathetic critics claim that the Birmingham School and many feminist theorists are too close to the ground of everyday life, culture, and politics, thus reducing their theoretical work to the exigencies of organized political and social movements. Members of the Frankfurt School mounted precisely this critique of what they called orthodox Marxism, which, they contended, was too bound up with working-class politics, missing aspects of the "big picture" in late capitalism that combine to frustrate organized left politics and thus require new theoretical constructs. They argued that theory is not simply to reflect the political exigencies of the moment, whether framed in terms of orthodox Marxism or other emancipatory agendas, but to gain a certain critical distance from society so that theory can serve as both guide and conscience.

Without this critical distance, as they call it, theory is sucked into the dominant political consensus, or what Gramsci called hegemony. The Frankfurt theorists argued that Marxist theorists had for the most part

failed to achieve this critical distance, especially once Soviet ideologists began to dominate the Third, or Communist, International, after the Russian
Revolution. Theory, in effect, became doctrine, losing its distance from the
revolutionary practice of the Communist Party of the Soviet Union, which
above all required intellectual oversight and even criticism. Theory was not
supposed to act as a political cheerleader, losing its autonomy. The Frankfurt theorists would have opposed what we today call "political correctness" as an abandonment of intellectual autonomy on grounds of facile
doctrine. They opposed not only doctrine but also the essentially liberal
notion, now embraced by many multiculturalists, that people who are exploited enjoy a certain epistemological and narrative privilege. As such, not
every "narrative" is as good, true, or rational as any other.

One problem with the abandonment of metanarrativity is the concomitant abandonment of rationality, which is necessarily a universalistic notion. This represents a central difference between Habermas and postmodern theorists who reject Habermas's preservation of the "project of
modernity," which enshrines the notion of a universal rationality grounded
in unfettered communicative action. It is wrong to suppress this rather fundamental difference between the Frankfurt theorists, especially Habermas,
who remain committed to the possibility of a single narrative of global social change, and postmodern theorists, who reject the possibility and desir-
ability of a single narrative (metanarrativity) and who thus ground theory
in the particular narratives and struggles of people framed by their local
concerns of gender, race, nation, and religion.

The critique of grounding admonishes critical social theorists to extrapolate the universalistic implications of their particular engagements with the
local. Although this applies mainly to postmodern multiculturalists, who argue against such metanarrativity, it also applies to non-postmodern critical
theories such as cultural studies and aspects of feminist theory that tie their
theorizing to particular people and groups. Although the grand abstractions
of Adorno's theory err in the opposite direction, sacrificing the local to the
global, grounded critical theories risk ignoring the global altogether and thus
fail to build theoretical and political bridges between occupants of different
subject positions who, together, possess greater political efficacy.

Luke articulates this critique and argues for balance between the local
and the global, which he dialectically reformulates as the "glocal." A critical theory born of both German and French influences refuses to accept as
exhaustive the dichotomies of global versus local or metanarrativity versus
small narrativity, arguing instead for various middle positions combining
respect for people's particular struggles and discourses with sensitivity to
consensus building among occupants of these various subject positions.
The notion of the glocal positions itself against neoliberal multiculturalism,
which assumes that exploited people and groups necessarily differentiate

into irreconcilable subject positions, and against Eurocentric and androcentric male Marxism, which conveniently ignores all sorts of "difference,"
including women, people of color, and non-Western cultures.

In Hegelian-Marxist terms, the critique of groundedness is much like the
critique of what Hegel called "immediacy." By immediacy he referred to the
way in which positivists believe that the world can be known and represented without the "mediation" of certain categories, such as what Kant
called "the categories of the understanding." Hegel's stress on mediation
expressed his conviction that people have the capacity to reason and that
rationality cannot be replaced by sheer sense perception (or, later, mathematics), as positivists contend. Critical theory's groundedness is an example
of "bad immediacy," collapsing critical-theoretical categories into the din of
people's everyday struggles to survive and even thrive. Although critical theory argues emphatically that emancipatory theories cannot afford to ignore
the everyday and local, without which there is no impetus or rationale for
change, Hegelian-oriented critical theorists argue for what Adorno (1973a)
called the "nonidentity of concepts and experience" as a way of differentiating (as well as dialectically connecting) theory and practice. All Hegel-influ-
enced critical theorists argue for the merging of theory and practice, agreeing with Marx's contention in the eleventh thesis on Feuerbach that the
point of philosophy is not only to understand the world but also to change
it. But this merger does not blend theory and practice so completely that
these categories blur to the point of indistinguishability. Theory and practice are "mediated" categories, connected and autonomous.

Critical social theories appear to divide between those that prize "mediation" as a way of differentiating theory and practice and thus preserve the
autonomy of theory (the Frankfurt School) and those that prize "immediacy" as a way of making theory relevant and productive (postmodernism,
feminist theory, cultural studies). The Frankfurt theorists were more strongly
influenced by Hegel, who first defended mediation, than were postmodernists, feminists, and cultural studies scholars, who are more politically engaged than were the German critical theorists. Hegel's rationalism is particularly distasteful to postmodernists, who "deconstruct" rationalism as a
framework that excludes non-European, nonmale versions of rationality.
This critique of rationalism is well taken, although metanarrativity is not ex-
hausted by Hegel and Marx's own versions of it. That is, simply because previous rationalisms have not sufficiently embraced difference does not mean
that subsequent rationalisms must follow suit. The problem with abandoning metanarrativity—and with it comprehensive social theory that authors a
master narrative of social criticism and social change without ignoring difference—is that the alternative appears to be neoliberalism. This neoliberalism champions the various causes of multicultural and other groups without
developing a comprehensive theory and program of concerted social change

necessary to effect thoroughgoing radical change. Without "mediating" people's differences through a rationalist master narrative, we will never be able to articulate solutions to people's problems that really address the root causes of those problems, which, following Marx, I contend are structural in nature. The critique of metanarrativity dooms people to piecemeal solutions formulated within the local discourses and practices of exploited groups, thus failing to locate the source of their exploitation in structures such as capitalism, racism, and male supremacy, which are often quite invisible, especially to those who view the world from the ground up.

To say this in defense of mediation, rationalism, and master narratives is to risk accusations of elitism, prescribing solutions to problems from on high, with imperial disdain for people's practical wisdom. Although grounding and immediacy are "good" in the sense that theory cannot proceed without a foundation in lived experience, as leftist phenomenologists (Piccone 1971; Paci 1972) have argued, lived experience cannot be the destination of theoretical comprehension because it is too manipulated and partial to provide lasting solutions. That is, theory necessarily "narrates" the world from outside of conventional wisdom, custom, the everyday, mistrusting what people take to be their predicament, albeit without simply ignoring common sense. A hallmark of critical social theory is the contention that most people have been deprived of the capacity for "mediation," which would allow them to understand their small worlds in dialectical relation to the large world purposely obscured by ideology.

Critical theory educates without being didactic. It transcends particulars in search of universals, sometimes expressed in terms that challenge common sense. Without this ideology-critical function, people cannot be shown the power they have available to them to change their circumstances and to join with others in changing theirs. The Frankfurt theorists were too detached and ironic, convinced that virtually every critical idea gets blunted by ideological hegemony. I think other critical social theories such as feminism and cultural studies are overly preoccupied with the grounding of critique and liberation in people's everyday lives, missing the force of false consciousness and global structures that frustrate freedom at every turn. Theorists need to achieve a balance that does not sacrifice grounding to a global master narrative nor construct that narrative oblivious to people's particular pathos, experience, and discourse.

## RESPONDING TO ITS CRITICS

Although critical social theorists will never persuade its most unsparing critics, it can make some accommodations to various criticisms, especially addressing critics who are not wholly indisposed to it. Numerous empirical sociologists want to read and appreciate critical social theories and incorporate their insights into their own work. The real-sociology critique is certainly abundant in U.S. sociology, especially among academics in self-styled mainstream research departments where the currencies of the realm are publication in *American Sociological Review* and multimillion-dollar grant proposals. But academia is not seamless. People who work at what Terry Caesar (1992) ironically calls "second-rate institutions" (such as his home institution, Clarion College in Pennsylvania), at liberal arts colleges with progressive traditions, and even at research universities find that critical theory answers many of their criticisms of mainstream sociology and social science. People with unusual intellectual and political backgrounds are often favorably inclined to critical theory because they do not have deep investments in mainstream theory and method; they are iconoclasts with open minds. I regularly received manuscripts for the journal and book series I edited from people looking for answers to their concerns about social issues and their home discipline's lack of engagement with these issues.

When I deliver talks, I invariably find members of the audience who are hostile to critical theory. They rehearse all of the criticisms of critical theory discussed in this chapter. I also find people who are theoretical fellow travelers, both politically inclined in my direction and sometimes impressively self-taught. Almost every college and university campus collects small groups of people interested in "theory," broadly understood, thirsty for the latest insights from European theories such as postmodernism and French feminism. Some of them want these complex theories explicated. Others want to know how these apply to their own empirical research in a variety of social science and humanities disciplines.

Critical social theory appeals to people who feel constrained by the method and scope of their own disciplines, which are not amenable to interdisciplinary and critical approaches. Sociologists, political scientists, anthropologists, philosophers, geographers, psychologists, humanists in English and comparative literature, scholars in women's studies seek to know more about the relevance of critical social theories to their own disciplinary and interdisciplinary work. Critical social theories have two main flaws for many of these inquisitive minds—lack of accessibility, which I have already discussed, and insufficiently articulated empirical applicability. Many critical theorists need to write more clearly, taking the time to explicate their complicated concepts without feeling compromised or diverted from their intellectual project. They also need to make connections to disciplinary frameworks. The German and French theorists were relatively unfamiliar with the American university, in which strict disciplinary boundaries define academics' intellectual and discursive frameworks. Critical social theorists must make concessions to the disciplinary grounding of many people's interests in critical theory, both writing "for" them in terms of their own intellectual problems and developing the empirical implications of critical theory for writing and teaching. I am convinced that critical social theorists can make much headway into various disciplinary mainstreams by demonstrating their empirical applicability and their ability to solve intellectual problems in ways not ordinarily available to disciplinary scholars.

Critical theories have been of great interest, for example, to geographers dissatisfied with the ways in which those in their discipline have traditionally studied the city. Geographers such as Henri Lefebvre (1991), David Harvey (1989), and Edward Soja (1989) have integrated insights from the Frankfurt School and postmodernism in order to conceptualize urban space in critical ways. Their work has begun to reformulate the discipline of geography. It has also begun to induce critical theorists outside of geography proper to integrate theories of the city and spatiality into their own work. For example, Jameson in *Postmodernism, or, the Cultural Logic of Late Capitalism* (1991) makes use of both geographic and demographic insights, demonstrating the potential for interdisciplinary cross-fertilization.

The original members of the Frankfurt School did not sufficiently articulate the empirical implications of critical theory for people who work within particular disciplines. This was partly because their own interdisciplinary erudition prevented them from recognizing that others are more limited by their own disciplinary formations and organizational constraints. It was also because Adorno and Horkheimer did not confront the hegemony of empiricists and positivists in German academia and thus they did not feel compelled to translate their theoretical approach into empirically researchable terms. Finally, they were convinced that ground-up strategies of social change were not likely to succeed, thus allowing them to remain on a high level of abstraction in their analyses of late capitalism.

When critical theory crossed the Atlantic during World War II, it confronted political and intellectual conditions quite different from those in Germany. There was no tradition of organized Marxism and leftism in the United States. (There was a tradition of radical populism, which later became the basis of the New Left and women's movement; see Kann's *American Left* [1982].) Academia was rigidly organized around disciplines, with a sharp split between the humanities and social sciences. Most academics had little or no philosophical background and lacked cultural capital (see Bourdieu 1977), especially by comparison to European intellectuals, who were much more conversant with a wide range of philosophical and cultural issues and necessarily more interdisciplinary. Empirical methodologies, frequently quantitative, dominated the social sciences, reflecting the hegemony of positivism.

Adorno tried to deal with this new intellectual and political constellation by engaging in collaborative empirical research. Adorno worked with Paul Lazarsfeld, a noted sociological methodologist, on empirical studies of

mass media. Later, Adorno led a team of researchers, most of them empirical social psychologists, on the "California study," which produced a series
of publications on the nature of prejudice. The most famous of these studies was *The Authoritarian Personality* (Adorno et al. 1950), which attempted to examine the empirical roots of fascism in the social psychological dynamics of what Adorno and his group called authoritarianism. They
argued that the "authoritarian personality" is not peculiar to the German
"character" but is found in all sorts of capitalist societies in which relatively powerless people deal with their powerlessness by identifying with
and supporting charismatic fascist leaders.

Horkheimer worked closely with Adorno during their American exodus.
Their collaboration produced the important *Dialectic of Enlightenment*
(1972), which developed the culture industry theory discussed in Chapter
4. Barely accessible to atheoretical American readers, the book was written
in German and published by a Dutch house. Its English translation was not
published until 1972, as German critical theory was being discovered by
American New Leftists who found critical theory pertinent to the development of their own nonauthoritarian versions of Marxism. Horkheimer
gave a series of talks at Columbia that were published as a book entitled
*Eclipse of Reason* (1974). This book, aimed at American social scientists,
was far more easily understood than *Dialectic of Enlightenment*, and it remains perhaps the most accessible and comprehensive statement of the
Frankfurt School's critical theory.

The need for critical social theorists to translate their arguments into empirical terms is not only a function of the prevailing positivism in many
American social science disciplines. It also answers to the need of American
social scientists for grounded, politicized intellectual work that engages
with the exigencies of daily politics, organizing, and consciousness-raising.
Side by side with the positivism of many American social science disciplines such as sociology and political science is the bedrock populism that
distinguishes U.S. political culture from European political cultures, in
which one finds both a socialist tradition and more hierarchy. This populism is mistrustful of grand abstractions and insists on a political immediacy and engagement frequently neglected by European critical theorists:
Americans demand that theories be "grounded" in the sense I discussed
above. The American need for concreteness, specificity, and even data thus
has a positive as well as negative side, reflecting populism as much as positivism. The call for empirical applications of critical social theories is not
necessarily a capitulation to the hypersociologists who control the mainstream journals and departments but could also be heard as a call for engagement and relevance on the part of a populist left. In other words, critical theory must be shown to "matter" to the lives of ordinary people—a
distinctively American requirement.

CHAPTER 8

# Critical Social Theory
## Applications and Implications

### CRITICAL SOCIAL RESEARCH

In this chapter I explore a number of areas in social science within which
critical social theories, ranging from critical theory and cultural studies to
postmodernism and feminism, are being applied in empirical research. I
also discuss future research implications of these perspectives, where actual
work has not yet begun or is in its infancy. Although much of this discussion bears directly on sociology, it clearly overlaps other disciplines as well,
given the interdisciplinary nature of most critical social theories. This
chapter responds to the concern raised in the preceding chapter that European theories by and large have not yet sufficiently developed their empirical implications but remain rather removed from everyday research and
politics. I attempt to ground critical theory in concrete research projects,
both spelling out its possible engagements with research and society and
also translating critical theories into terms recognizable by mainstream social scientists, many of whom do not have the background or predilection
for working through Adorno's *Negative Dialectics* or Foucault's *Discipline
and Punish*.

Although, as I have been saying, critical social theories are purposely
and necessarily interdisciplinary, blurring disciplinary boundaries and interrogating singular disciplinary identities, it is also clear that many traditional disciplinary scholars have become interested in critical theory. These
scholars have begun to apply critical-theoretical insights in a variety of
subfields and topical domains in which they pursue their empirical research and teaching. Virtually every subfield in sociology, from family and
gender research to media studies, has been affected. Even the field of research methodology has seen the intervention of critical theorists who sug-

gest new, more critical ways of viewing and doing empirical social research (e.g., Morrow [1994], influenced by Habermas; Reinharz [1992], influenced by feminist theory). In this chapter I consider eleven venues in which critical social theories have been or could be applied to empirical research: the state and social policy; social control; popular culture, discourse analysis, and mass media; gender studies; social psychology; sociology of education; social movements; research methods; race and ethnicity; politics and micropolitics; and pedagogy.

All of the applications discussed in this chapter are relatively unencumbered by doctrine. They are necessarily heterodox (nondoctrinal and flexible) in the senses that they go beyond Marx and other foundational critical theories, they inform and sometimes revise theory with empirical research as well as frame research with theoretical constructs, and they provide an empirically differentiated account of domination, emancipatory possibilities, and new social movements. They are also nonpositivist. More than anyone else, Habermas has argued against theories that seek first principles and do not revise themselves with empirical evidence, in this process missing actual and possible attempts to effect radical social change. He maintained that the original Frankfurt theorists—his teachers—painted an overly monochromatic view of late capitalism, especially in *Dialectic of Enlightenment* (Horkheimer and Adorno 1972). Habermas framed his own body of work as a response to and revision of *Dialectic of Enlightenment*, which he thought was an overly undialectical work seeking first principles of domination. Habermas's two-volume *Theory of Communicative Action* intends not only to make possible the retrieval of the concept of rationality from the postmodernists (whom Habermas attacked in *Philosophical Discourse of Modernity* [1987a]) but also to provide an empirically differentiated account of domination, emancipatory possibilities, and new social movements that jettisons the one-dimensional gloom of Adorno, Horkheimer, and Marcuse.

Although I have taken issue with aspects of Habermas's reconstruction of critical theory as communication theory, especially his notion of the ideal speech situation as an ethical basis of a new society, I do not take issue with his attempt to create an empirical heterodoxy fertilizing and fertilized by empirical social research. Habermas in *Knowledge and Human Interests* (1971) distinguished between positivism and empiricism, suggesting nonpositivist empirical research strategies and methods that fulfill the promise of an empirically differentiated critical social theory that is less post-Marxist and postmodern than postorthodox. There is simply too much to be learned (and that has been learned) about the empirical modalities of structured social domination to dismiss the empirical social sciences as irremediably positivist, as Horkheimer and Adorno appeared to do in *Dialectic of Enlightenment*, where they said that "enlightenment behaves towards things as a dictator toward men" (1972: 9). Habermas wants to preserve the possibility of enlightenment—rational communication, based on the power of the strongest argument fueled by both reason and empirical evidence. Habermas more than anyone else has established the possibility of an empirical research method and substantive findings that derive from postorthodox critical social theories.

As such, much of the work discussed in this chapter, although "critical" in nature, does not position itself clearly with respect to one theoretical orthodoxy or another. Such research not only derives from theory but contributes to theory. Sometimes empirical social researchers are too busy with their investigations to label themselves as adherents of a particular theoretical school. Or they have overlapping orientations. Or they do not want to mislead their readers with overly rigid and constraining theoretical categories, preferring a more pragmatic approach to the blending of theory and research. What makes empirical social research "critical," in the absence of clear theoretical identification and affiliation, is the unmasking of aspects of domination, both material and cultural, that are regarded as grounded in history, not social nature. As I noted above, this unmasking of domination is necessarily conducted outside the framework of positivism, which freezes domination into eternal patterns or laws. Such work tends to be interdisciplinary, such as work on the state, and often it mixes theoretical orientations, such as work on gender and economic inequality.

Finally, critical social researchers may not concern themselves with establishing their theoretical affiliations because they recognize that there is a useful division of labor between research and theory. Unlike positivist social researchers, critical social researchers are much more likely to view theoretical work as legitimate and necessary, painting the big pictures framing research as well as developing "narratives" of possible social change, showing how the empirical illumination of domination suggests strategies for overcoming domination in terms of people's everyday lives. Positivists not only eschew theory (except in their prefatory reviews of the literature); they also object to what they regard as the untoward "politicization" of academic work by leftists who seek not to identify social laws but rather to wed theory and practice in order to effect social change.

## THE STATE AND SOCIAL POLICY

The theory and analysis of the state are perhaps the most obvious derivations and deviations from Marxist orthodoxy. After all, Marx wrote about the state, recognizing its structural importance as an agent of capital. Later, Rudolf Hilferding (1981), who provided an important economic foundation for the Frankfurt School, offered the term *organized capitalism* to describe the relationship between the state and society. Claus Offe (1984) discussed crises in the state-society relationship under the term *disorganized capitalism*, recognizing (with Hilferding) that capitalism requires state intervention in order to buffer and defer its tendencies toward structural crisis. As in the nineteenth century, the state continues to protect capitalism against its own contradictory nature and potential to produce economic, social, and political crises by greatly expanding its role. Habermas's *Legitimation Crisis* (1975) suggests new lines of research for students of the state, policy, and ideology. Capitalism has outlived Marx's expectation of its demise because the state massively intervenes to alleviate economic crises by creating jobs, stimulating economic growth through military and space expenditures, controlling the money supply, and engaging in deficit spending. Marx did not foresee the rapid growth of the state's role in the economy and society in post–World War II capitalism. Building on the foundation of neo-Marxist critical theory, Ralph Miliband (1969, 1982, 1983), Offe (1985), James O'Connor (1973), and Nicos Poulantzas (1973) have done important empirical and theoretical work on the state. The journals *Kapitalistaat* and *Politics and Society* are important outlets for this kind of work.

State policy is a rapidly growing field of sociological research (e.g., Skocpol 1992, 1995). Policies on old age (e.g., Quadagno 1982, 1988), health (Skocpol 1996), and welfare (Quadagno 1994) are frequent topics. Research on policies concerning work and family (e.g., Gerstel and Gross 1987) spring from feminist theoretical concerns. Work on poverty (e.g., Feagin, Tilly, and Williams 1972; Feagin 1975; Wilson, McFate, and Lawson 1995; Wilson 1987, 1996) is often conducted within a critical framework. All of these approaches share the common premise that the expansion of the state in late capitalism somewhat shifts the locus of class, race, and gender struggles from the economy per se to the realm of state policy and politics. Habermas in *Legitimation Crisis* argues convincingly that late capitalism has displaced but not resolved capital's "contradictions," shifting them from the economy to the state and culture, creating widespread legitimation and motivation crises, as he calls them. The state is responsible for ameliorating legitimation crises through democratic welfare state politics and policies, while the culture industry is responsible for ameliorating motivational and psychic crises.

This is not to say that capitalism is free of such crises as unemployment, inflation, a huge federal deficit, strikes, and homelessness. Rather, people "blame" these crises not on capital but on the federal state, which is supposed to resolve or at least soften these crises. The state, especially in an era of massive deficits, cannot resolve all these problems at once, reducing unemployment, mastering inflation, and dealing with other outgrowths of unequal economic distribution. Federal states in capitalist countries are thus in perpetual crisis, lurching from election to election as they variously succeed and fail in keeping what Marx viewed as the contradictory logic of capital at bay. People with false consciousness do not understand that the "real" problem is the logic of capital, not greedy or mischievous federal bureaucrats who, after all, occupy the structural position of what Marx called the executive committee of the bourgeoisie. Thus, in the early twenty-first century, voters have high expectations of politicians who are structurally constrained from dealing with crises of accumulation and distribution that, as Marx indicated, spring from the economy and not from federal policy, which is at best a stopgap.

This is not to deny that state policy is or should be a contested terrain, especially after Reagan in the United States, Thatcher in the UK, and Brian Mulroney in Canada demonstrated how far anti-Keynesian conservatives could go in dismantling state safety nets, cutting back federal spending, and slowing or altogether eliminating a variety of redistributive programs. The 1980s proved that there are real differences between neoconservatives and neoliberals (Republicans and Democrats, in the United States), notably in their conceptions of state responsibility for softening economic crises that flow from people's class positions, which are exacerbated by their race and gender positions. However, once the electorate "allows" political debate to shift from structural issues of the economy to issues of state policy, people will necessarily be frustrated by limits to state intervention, given the state's mediating role between capital and labor.

Much of this work is framed explicitly by Marxism, leading to neo-Marxist empirical research into state policy and state functioning. For the most part, this substantive research area has been best fertilized by Marxist critical theorists who retain a sharp economic and political-economic focus. Although the Frankfurt School theorists were quite traditional Marxists in economic terms (see Horkheimer 1973), much of their work presupposed Marxian economics and instead focused on issues of cultural theory and criticism. Although some (e.g., Slater 1977) contend that the Frankfurt theorists surpassed and thus betrayed Marxian economics in favor of idealism, Habermas's and Offe's work on legitimation and the state demonstrates convincingly that German critical theory need not forsake economic issues.

Critical social theories have been applied in the areas of policy analysis and political sociology in order to examine closely the relations between the state and society. Although Marx had a theory of the state, he simply could not have imagined the extent to which the state would become a key player in the struggle between capital and labor, especially as that struggle moved increasingly into an international arena. Skocpol (1979) has done important work on the relationship between the state and society, advancing the theory and analysis of the state significantly beyond Marx. Students of the state such as Skocpol contend that the state simultaneously enjoys relative autonomy from capital and yet supports the accumulation of capital in crucial ways. These state theorists and analysts sidestep the debate about whether state functioning can be reduced to the needs of capital "in the last instance," as Althusser phrased it, instead preferring to be agnostic about this issue of reductionism and mechanism in the interest of advancing empirical research and theory. It is clear that state theorists believe that one can no more analyze the modern state without examining capital than one can study the economy without also examining state functioning. Indeed, it is precisely the state's ideological mission to construct the appearance of its neutral, bilateral mediation between capital and labor in order to serve the needs of capital more capably, making any discussion of capital's determination-in-the-last-instance virtually irrelevant.

## SOCIAL CONTROL

Foucault's postmodernism offers valuable insights to scholars of social control. His *Discipline and Punish* (1977) revolutionizes the study of crime and punishment, particularly in his argument that criminology is a discourse/practice that creates the category of criminality in "disciplinary society." This discourse is then imposed punitively on behaviors that formerly were viewed as socially legitimate or simply ignored as bizarre. This analysis converges with sociological labeling theory (e.g., Goffman 1959, 1974; Becker 1963), although it gives labeling theory a firmer historical and political foundation. Foucault helps sociologists view deviance in terms of the experiences and meanings that construct it. But unlike labeling and social-control theories, Foucault's postmodern theory of discipline stresses the inherent resistances that people mount against their labeling and differential treatment. This is a theme that emerges very clearly in his *History of Sexuality* (1978), where he discusses ways in which women and homosexuals resist their societal disapprobation. Although Foucault is sometimes accused of having a sloppy and even contradictory method (see Best and Kellner [1991] for a discussion of his shift from "archaeology" to "genealogy"), he makes up for this in his extraordinarily imaginative use of historical and cultural data, which he assembles into a theory of social control that neglects neither macrolevel nor microlevel phenomena. The postmodern study of social control, inspired by Foucault, also has implications for research on organizations, as Cooper and Burrell (1988) have demonstrated.

Foucault argues that we construct deviance such as crime and homosexuality in order to "normalize" certain behaviors and discipline other behaviors. The social construction of deviance is never innocent inasmuch as it always implies value judgments about appropriateness, which reflect and reinforce power. Over time, he argues, "modernity" increases discipline, control, and surveillance through various technologies of domination and punishment. Enlightenment does not free people from constraints but instead increases them as "panoptical" techniques of surveillance become more efficacious and make way for more effective enforcement.

## POPULAR CULTURE, DISCOURSE ANALYSIS, AND MASS MEDIA

The Frankfurt School's critical theory, feminist theory, Derrida's poststructuralism, and Baudrillard's postmodernism enrich empirical cultural studies of television (Kellner 1981, 1992; Best and Kellner 1988a, 1988b), journalism (Hallin 1985; Rachlin 1988), and advertising (Kline and Leiss 1978; Williamson 1978; Wernick 1983; Ewen 1976; Leiss, Kline, and Jhally 1986) as literary works encoding powerful authorial claims about—and recommendations for—the social world. Denzin has read films in which alcoholics and alcoholism are depicted. Ryan and Kellner read blockbuster Hollywood films not only for their frozen representation of the present but also for their subversive suggestions of difference and resistance. All critical social theories theorize culture, discourse, and media as important political and economic factors in late capitalism that both enhance domination by promoting false consciousness and, through commodification, contribute to profit. Cultural studies, diversely understood, is an extremely rich venue for empirical work that criticizes dominant social and economic arrangements and also stresses possible resistances springing from the ground of everyday life.

## GENDER STUDIES

Feminist theory, especially feminist postmodernism, feminist social constructionism, and queer theory, offers valuable insights to students of the family (Chodorow 1978), social control and deviance (Jenness 1993), household labor (England and Farkas 1986), and many other sociological subfields. These feminist and gay and lesbian scholars examine the ways in which women and men define gender in terms of the cultural polarity of masculinity and femininity, which they deconstruct to reveal not only dichotomy but also hierarchy and subordination. Much empirical work on gender interrogates the "gendering" of social behavior as a political process supporting male supremacy or patriarchy, arguing instead for more flexible and nonbipolar constructions of women and men's subject positions.

A postmodern and poststructural feminism such as that of Kristeva, Irigaray, Cixous, Weedon, Flax, and Fraser suggests concrete empirical stud-

ies of the ways in which discourses such as film (Mulvey 1989) are structured by gendered themes. In particular, feminist cultural studies focuses
on the different power positions of women and men as these influence
writing and reading. With Lacan and Lyotard, these approaches to feminism reject the notion of a singular (male) vantage point (Derrida's phallo-
gocentrism) from which knowledge and discourse are developed. They at-
tune us empirically to the ways in which knowledge of the world is
structured by discourses and representations such as pornography that reflect conflict over power; they decode these discourses as politically salient.
Richardson (1990b, 1991a) has systematically developed the sociological
implications of poststructural and postmodern feminism with respect to
the ways social scientists tell their research stories. Fraser (1989) has
blended critical theory, feminist theory, and poststructuralism in her development of a theory and practice relevant to women as well as men.

Feminist theory has produced major changes in the sociological study of
the family, which is no longer viewed in Victorian and Parsonian terms as
the site of a "natural" sexual division of labor, with husbands earning the
family wage and women cheerfully bearing children and performing domestic labor in return for "love." Instead, the family is viewed as a contested
terrain in which the sexual division of labor disempowers and disadvantages women and reproduces rigidly bifurcated gender roles for boys and
girls (see Chodorow 1978). Indeed, the study of work and family links the
sexual divisions of labor in the household and labor market in order to
demonstrate empirically that gender-role differentiation in the family sets
the pattern for gender inequality in the labor force. Unlike Parsonian sociology of the family (Parsons and Bales 1955) and Becker's (1981) human-
capital approach to the family, feminist theory argues that the sexual division of labor is the site of serious inequalities between men and women,
problematizing and politicizing the family. As well, feminists contend that
there is no single "family" but many alternative family forms, ranging from
single-parent families and extended families to families headed by gay and
lesbian couples (see Blumstein and Schwartz 1983). Indeed, they demonstrate that the so-called nuclear family, with husband working for wages
and wife staying home, is very uncommon in the United States, forcing
changes in both our conceptions of family and the ways we study families,
acknowledging ample difference in people's conduct of their intimate lives.

Another offshoot of feminist theory is the rapid expansion of gay and
lesbian studies, which deals both theoretically (e.g., Di Stefano 1991; Seidman 1996) and empirically (Slater 1995) with the roles and families of
gays and lesbians. A focus of gay studies is the impact on gay men of AIDS,
as well as social and political movements to stop the spread of AIDS.
Books such as *Modern Homosexualities* (Plummer 1992) examine ways in
which gays and lesbians construct their lives and identities amid a "hetero-

sexist" society, both legitimating gay and lesbian sexual orientations and drawing sociological attention to a population estimated to make up at least 10 percent of the total U.S. adult population.

## SOCIAL PSYCHOLOGY

Critical theory, postmodernism, and feminist theory offer new perspectives on the self and interpersonal relations. Wexler's *Critical Social Psychology* (1983) "applies" Adorno to a social psychology that refuses positivism and instead attempts to enlarge the social space for autonomous subjectivity. Habermas, too, has called for a critical social psychology that mediates between the levels of self and society. Critical social psychologies are challenged by postmodernism, which abandons the concept of the stable, singular subject (self) of Western logocentrism, instead substituting the concept of people's subject positions, into which people are positioned by language, class, gender, and race. Although Laclau and Mouffe (1985) demonstrate that one can endorse the postmodern rejection of the subject and still develop a radical politics grounded in the lifeworld, for the most part postmodern theory's impact on social psychology has been indirect, focusing on the concept of "discourse" as an alternative to the study of subjectivity and intersubjectivity. Indeed, Wexler's own work has evolved from critical social psychology to *Social Analysis of Education* (1987), which moves in a decisively postmodern direction.

## SOCIOLOGY OF EDUCATION

Wexler is one of many to incorporate postmodern, critical-theoretical, and feminist themes into their work on the sociology of education (see also Morrow and Torres 1995). Since Apple (1979, 1982, 1996), Giroux (1981, 1994; Giroux and McLaren 1989), and Aronowitz and Giroux (1985), a good deal of work in the sociology of education has been decidedly critical, focusing on a host of issues all the way from curriculum (Goodson 1988) to literacy (Luke 1988). These and other scholars in education recognize that schooling is increasingly a contested terrain in late capitalism, making education a vital topic for critical scholars interested in both criticizing ideology as disseminated through schooling and reconstructing institutions and discourses of higher education. Like media and cultural studies, the critical sociology of education, much of which has migrated to the United States from the UK and Australia, is concerned not only to identify domination (e.g., Bowles and Gintis's [1976] classic work on what they call "the hidden curriculum") but also to identify and foster "resistances" both in the classroom and curriculum and in the ways educational administrators run their institutions. Much of the work in the critical sociology of education is interdisciplinary, drawing on and fertilizing work in sociology, cultural studies, and women's studies.

## SOCIAL MOVEMENTS

The "new social movements" theory of Habermas (1981b; see also Boggs 1986) offers theoretical insights to scholars of social movements who otherwise lack a larger theoretical perspective explaining where these movements come from and what sort of structural impact they might have. Finding a course between orthodox Marxist theories of class struggle and non- or post-Marxist perspectives on social movements, Habermas retains the Marxist vision of transformational sociopolitical action while significantly altering left-wing orthodoxy with respect to movements traditional Marxists deemed irrelevant, especially movements of people of color, feminists, gays and lesbians, anticolonialists, antinuclearists, environmentalists, and peace activists. Here, as in his analysis of the state's legitimation crisis, Habermas makes contact with venerable sociological concerns and places them in a larger historical materialist framework, recouping their most radical insights in spite of themselves (e.g., his reading of Parsons in *The Theory of Communicative Action* [1987b: 199–299]). Unlike most sociological students of social movements (and like Foucault in this respect), Habermas locates points of resistance against systemic domination that give his overall critical theory a certain practical intent as well as a multiperspectival focus, similar to the postmodern stress on polyvocality and small narratives.

## RESEARCH METHODS

Critical social theories have begun to transform research methodologies in significant ways. Feminist theory (Reinharz 1992; Smith 1990a; Williams 1989, 1993, 1995), critical theory (Morrow 1994), and postmodern narratives and ethnography (Richardson 1990a, 1990b; Clough 1992; Denzin 1992) all reject the notion that quantitative survey research is the only legitimate mode of sociological investigation. These perspectives valorize qualitative research as legitimate and necessary in order to understand "depth" aspects of everyday life and personal experience inaccessible to anonymous survey instruments. Indeed, critical social theories even have impact on the ways in which people conduct quantitative analysis, demonstrating the inherent "undecidability" of empirical operationalizations of variables (see Bose's [1985] critique of the gendered nature of status-attainment research in social stratification) as well as revealing the power motives behind sociological positivism, which both Foucault and the Frankfurt theorists addressed in their respective critiques of the disciplinary society and totally administered or one-dimensional society. Methodologists influenced by one critical social theory or another do not simply abandon empiricism but rather attempt to incorporate insights from critical theory into their own research and interpretation of data.

Perhaps the most important influence of critical social theory on research methodology is the valorization of narrative as a legitimate research tool (see Richardson 1990b; Clough 1992, 1994). Following both French feminists and male postmodern theorists such as Lyotard, social researchers treat people's words about their experiences not only as valid data sources but also as sources of theoretical insight. These theorists extend their critique of theoretical metanarrativity into a critique of research methods that privilege the voice and experience of the scientist and disqualify the voices and experiences of her research subjects. In this process the hierarchy of researcher over research subject is deconstructed, much as Derrida uprooted and reversed all "logocentric" hierarchies. Suddenly, the researcher loses epistemological privileges and the research subject is empowered to know and tell her story. Multicultural postmodern theory valorizes this polyvocal perspectivity and denies the logocentric, Eurocentric, androcentric privileging of the scientific perspective, which, in Derridean fashion, is revealed to be a power position from which people's everyday experiences of exploitation are either excluded entirely or forced into the dispassionate demographic categories of survey research. The strongest insight of narrativity is that all knowledge is expressed in narratives or stories, which are necessarily partial and fragmentary.

Postmodern and feminist narrativity, at once multicultural and polyvocal, is remaking the social sciences, which are being forced to confront challenges to the epistemological privilege of science. This does not mean that the narrativists reject empiricism. Rather, they link empirical research to perspectivity, which is now seen to be an inevitable feature of all subject positions and the discourses emerging from them. Perspectival knowledge, articulated in the small narratives of everyday experience and vernacular, is at once partial (nontotalizing) and inherently valid, given the intimate relationship between what Habermas called people's knowledge and interests. Once we become aware of the perspectivity of knowledge as it emerges through narrative, we must recognize the validity and limitations of all discourses and narratives, including quantitative survey research.

The strongest sociological expression of postmodern narrativity and perspectivity is in the growing tendency of empirical researchers to be bimethodological, using both qualitative and quantitative methods, or at least learning from both methods. This challenges the dominance of quantitative methods that, since Comte and Durkheim, were viewed as necessary features of "hard" science and hence enlightenment. As I said in my comments on the real-sociology critique of critical social theories, although many sociologists and social scientists do not question the privilege and hegemony of quantitative methodology, the real-sociology critique is being challenged as narrativity and perspectivity make headway in both research methodology and the philosophy of social science.

In this sense, more social scientists are becoming genuinely postpositivist, freeing them to valorize both quantitative and qualitative methods. The positivist equation of knowledge and quantitative method, modeled on the natural sciences, is being surpassed by a variety of critical developments in epistemology, methodology and the philosophy of science. In this context, predictably, defenders of the positivist faith feel increasingly embattled and aggressively oppose these new methodologies and epistemologies as nonsociology. There is as yet no consensus on the appropriateness of these changes in perspective, especially on the part of sociologists convinced that sociology should attempt to be a "science" in the positivist sense. But sociology conferences and publications reflect a flurry of inquiry into these largely European social theories that challenge traditional assumptions about both theory and method.

## RACE AND ETHNICITY

Postmodernism's critique of Eurocentrism has had significant impact on the ways in which sociologists study race and ethnicity. Much as feminist theory detects androcentric biases in traditional approaches to the study of gender, arguing that gender needs to be decoupled from sex and instead viewed as a social construction, postmodernism and multiculturalism raise important questions about the duality of white and colored as well as about First World and Third World, or colonizing and colonized, nations, groups, and people. Race and ethnicity are no longer viewed as essentially biological categories but, like gender, as subject positions, identities, and discourses constructed by oneself and others. Joe Feagin (Feagin and Hahn 1973; Feagin and Sikes 1994; Feagin and Vera 1995) has done important work on the ways in which critical social theories provide useful insights to students of race relations. Henry Louis Gates and Cornel West (Gates and West 1996) theorize race critically and from the implicit perspective of social constructionism, as do a variety of Africana feminists. Postmodern assumptions about narrativity and perspectivity, discussed in the previous section, inform much of this work, which critically displaces Eurocentric and androcentric discourses about race and ethnicity by arguing not only that people of color experience and narrate the world differently from dominant-group members but that these narrations have enormous utility for social science. Feagin, for example, examines the narratives middle-class African Americans tell about their daily experiences of racism, which he interprets within the framework of critical social theory with an eye to how these narratives reflect resentment and provide evidence of resistance.

## POLITICS AND MICROPOLITICS

Social researchers inspired by critical social theories not only emphasize the implications of their empirical work for social reform and social movements; they view their academic work itself as political action in the sense that it is a "narrative" told from a "subject position" with a certain political "perspectivity." This is not to suggest that critical social scientists collapse their academic work into their politics, abandoning objectivity and distance. Indeed, a hallmark of critical theories is their ability to make distinctions between objectivity and subjectivity, the "real" and the desirable, thus ensuring that their work will be rigorous, unsentimental, and hence persuasive. And yet critical social researchers want their work to raise people's political consciousness by demonstrating how domination operates and how domination can be resisted and overcome from within people's daily lives as well as from on high, by politicians and policymakers. The point of such social research is not mainly to earn tenure, build careers, and accumulate professional prestige but rather to have political impact.

Positivists respond by saying that facts and values must be strictly separated lest one lose perspective and confuse analysis and advocacy. Postmodernists and critical theorists rebut this by arguing that *all knowledge is perspectival and flows from certain metaphysical, epistemological, and political commitments.* One cannot legitimately claim to be free of values, even though one must rigorously distinguish between what "is" and what "should" be. But one can simultaneously intend and attempt objectivity—analysis and critique of the world as it is—and at the same time suggest that the world "as it is" is flawed, "contradictory," as Marx called it (using Hegelian terminology), and can be changed. Critical social theorists understand that objectivity in the social sciences is molten, not frozen, thus precluding lawful representations of society. They further see that objective analysis of society's crises and contradictions is a form of political action designed to raise consciousness and produce radical change. As a narrative representing change or stasis, social science either contributes to the change or stasis that it discloses. For example, when positivists suggest that there are certain "laws" governing gender relations, they contribute to that representation of gender by depressing people's attempts to do gender differently. By contrast, when feminists argue for the historicity of gender and suggest the possibility of gender equality, they help promote that equality by convincing readers to live different lives. In this sense, representation— here, social science—reproduces the world politically, even if it claims to transcend politics, advocacy, values.

For writers, such as positivists, to claim no values and no political desire is, as Derrida and Adorno both recognized, dishonest in the sense that such texts intend to represent an ahistorical "reality" precisely in order to repro- duce it, hence fulfilling its own prophecy. When writers claim that social- ism is impossible, they intend to ensure that impossibility by forestalling socialist political organizing. When writers defend the sexual division of la- bor, they intend to protect it by calling forth certain gendered behaviors. This is not to say that positivist social science is the most important form of ideology or the critique of ideology the most important form of political resistance. But it is to recognize that every text advocates for one world or another, one conception of being or another. It is in this sense that I suggest that "representation reproduces" a certain world either buried or disclosed in it.

Critical social scientists openly admit their political interests, which their work advances by representing domination and thus fostering resistance. This must not be confused with polemics or what Marx called "utopian socialism"—sheer fantasy-making about a future society. As a dialectical theorist, Marx wanted to trace the possibility of a different society to the contradictions of the present society, demonstrating how people can ex- ploit present contradictions in order to move society in a radically different direction. Critical social science is dialectical, not utopian; it concentrates on analysis and critique, not the drafting of blueprints of how people will live in a distant future. In these difficult political times, when violence and deprivation characterize life for many of the world's billions, critical social science does not echo with optimism, even though in principle optimism is always a dialectical possibility. Rather, critical social science portrays al- most unrelieved misery—homelessness, racial and sexual violence, poverty, AIDS, crack babies. At most it represents individuals' attempts to change their own lives as a beginning of overall social change, refusing to neglect the micropolitics of personal life. Postmodernism, critical theory, and femi- nist theory all agree that the personal is political, auguring new social movements that spring from the ground of people's attempts to achieve modest victories in their daily lives—forming unions, improving entitle- ment programs, achieving educational innovations, creating noncommodi- fied culture, organizing. Political victories are usually small ones, captured in the small stories told by people who do not live their lives according to metanarrative scripts in which, as Hegel noted, history is the slaughter bench of individuals.

Here in particular I agree with postmodern and post-Marxist theorists who eschew grand narratives that paint with a broad brush and thereby miss the quotidian. In demarcating the French structuralist left, which embraced the metanarrative of a Communist revolution, from the poststructuralist New Left, which embraced micropolitics, the 1968 May movement continues to have significance. The American New Left reinforced radical populism and through its own dialectical contradictions produced the women's movement, which was also committed to a micropolitics, women holding their New Left boyfriends accountable for their chauvinism (see Gitlin 1987). In this sense, one could map postmodern theory and postmodernity onto the late 1960s, perhaps even the particular year 1968, which brought not only the French May movement but also the Tet offensive in Vietnam and the assassinations of Robert Kennedy and Martin Luther King Jr., fatefully ending a millenarian conception of progress and simultaneously inaugurating a postmodern, post-Marxist era of micropolitics and new social movements.

In this context American sociology and social science became politicized alism. At the same time, they did not become Marxist in the classical metaalism. At the same time, it did not become Marxist in the classical metanarrative tradition but combined radical populism (such as that of C. Wright Mills, who inspired the Port Huron statement of the Students for a Democratic Society) and micropolitics (that the New Left and feminism advocated). Radical American sociologists did not have to position themselves as post-Marxist because most of them were never Marxist (see Gouldner's series of books, beginning with *The Coming Crisis of Western Sociology* [1970]) and thus never had to throw off the yoke of metanarrativity and political orthodoxy, as the French and German theorists did. Gouldner and his students came to Marxism through Western Marxism, translated by the journal *Telos*, founded in 1968, and by publishers such as Herder and Herder and Beacon Press, which issued translations of German critical theory in the early 1970s. (Merlin, a British house, published a translation of Lukacs's 1923 classic *History and Class Consciousness* in 1971; the nearly half century that elapsed between the original publication of Lukacs's book and its English translation represents a lost political generation for the American left.)

Thus, German critical theory hit U.S. shores *before* American academics and students had come to grips with Marx, giving American critical social science a strong foundation in nonauthoritarian, micropolitical, even postmodern theoretical constructs and political categories. Although postmodernism did not emerge in the United States until the 1980s (see Berman 1982; Harvey 1989), there were clear affinities between the New Left reception of Western Marxism, which viewed Soviet authoritarianism and Marxist structuralism as dismal failures, and the French theorists' stress on polyvocality, narrativity, micropolitics, and discourse analysis. And American feminist theorists were quick to appreciate the relevance of both German critical theory and French postmodern theory for their own nonauthoritarian, micropolitical project.

Critical social science (see Fay 1987) arose in a context inimical to authoritarian metanarrativity and the "old" social movements of traditional class politics. Free from doctrinal investments, critical sociologists could plunder European social theories for their empirical and political applications, giving their work more immediacy and practical relevance than German and French theory, which conducted its debates on a higher philosophical and cultural level. What European theorists gained in erudition they lost in concreteness, preventing them, at least until Habermas and Offe, from making connections with new social movements and micropolitics. Although Derrida and Foucault have been involved in various democratic left causes and social movements, little of this engagement surfaces in their writings, which, in Derrida's case, engage with philosophy, literature, art, and postcards. Baudrillard has become a caricature of himself (see Kellner 1989c), having abandoned the systematic theorizing of *For a Critique of the Political Economy of the Sign* (1981) and even *Simulations* (1983) for the wordplay and aimless cultural commentaries of *America* (1988), which, if anything, celebrates the commodification and mainstreaming of postmodernism. For their parts, Adorno and Horkheimer in the 1960s were openly hostile to the German New Left for its irrationalist authoritarianism, mistrust of theoretical distance, and downright cultural boorishness and hooliganism.

Although critical sociologists and social scientists have to contend with the positivists who control their disciplines, they do not bear the albatross of high-theoretical obscurantism even as they learn from the Germans and French. The positivists condemn the politicization of academia, dismissing critical social science as advocacy. But critical empiricism sticks close to everyday life and practical politics, framing research and social criticism with theoretical constructs borrowed from the German, French, and feminist theorists. Feminist theory and cultural studies have been particularly adept at mediating macropolitics and micropolitics, the political and personal, because their theoretical identities do not derive from metanarrative disputation about doctrine. Instead, they are theoretically eclectic and driven more by political and empirical concerns than by doctrinal questions. This is not to say that feminist theory and cultural studies are "ground level," implying that they are somehow less theoretically sophisticated than German and French theory. Rather, feminists and cultural studies proponents conduct theoretical argument much closer to the everyday and the empirical. More American and British, feminist theory and cultural studies are perhaps for that reason more pragmatic than the high theories developed by the German and French.

## PEDAGOGICAL APPLICATIONS: IMMANENT CRITIQUE, HISTORICITY, AND THE POLITICS OF CURRICULUM

Critical social theories are not only applied in empirical research projects conducted by critical sociologists and social scientists. They also inform curriculum and pedagogy, especially at the graduate level. This happens in five different venues. First, faculty who teach social theory introduce German and French theory, feminist theory, and cultural studies. Second, courses on research methodology and the philosophy of science contain critical-theoretical components as students are exposed to the possibility and practice of critical research methods. Third, "substantive" courses on various empirical subfields such as race and political sociology are informed by critical content. Fourth, interdisciplinary teaching treats critical social theories within the pandisciplinary contexts within which all of them were conceived. Fifth, critical theories can be presented as reflexive disciplinary critiques (much as my *Socio(onto)logy: A Disciplinary Reading* [Agger 1989c] tried to be).

Teaching critical theory is an important part of critical theories' own agendas inasmuch as these theories are concerned with the critique of ideology and consciousness-raising. In my own teaching, I try to strike a balance among the exposition of difficult critical-theory concepts that require the establishment of intellectual-historical and political contexts within which these ideas first emerged, the empirical application of critical social theories to various sociological subfields as well as to issues and practices of research methods, and, finally, the "immanent" disciplinary critique offered by various critical social theories. It is difficult to fit all of this into a single semester! However, one of the main intentions of the "totalizing" German theorists was to suggest theoretical, empirical, and political implications for a host of academic practices, including writing, teaching, and the organization of disciplinarity. Although my courses sometimes fail to go much beyond exposition, given time constraints as well as the intellectual formation of students, it is very important that students and colleagues do not view critical theories as esoteric perspectives belonging to the history of ideas, a kind of zoo that collects weird species. Critical social theories must be taught as if they are vital perspectives on a wide range of practices, discourses, literary styles, and methods.

The two best ways to demonstrate the vitality of critical theory in sociology is to suggest how critical theories can deal with issues, including empirical data, addressed in substantive courses on race, gender, social stratification, education, culture, and social psychology. This often proceeds by way of immanent critique, a critical interpretive method suggested by the Frankfurt School theorists that probes the internal inconsistencies and implications of various perspectives, both theoretical and empirical. This dealing-with-perspectives-in-their-own-terms is very similar to the deconstructive program, which also aims to bring assumptions and aporias to light. Immanent critique differs from most deconstructive readings in that it is quite explicitly political, demonstrating ideological implications of various theories, empirical approaches, and research methods. For example, in my own teaching I use feminist theory to suggest ways in which Parsons's depiction of the sexual division of labor as "functional" discloses his own interest in reinforcing male supremacy through positivist literary strategies intending to reflect or represent the invariance of the sexual division of labor as a way of bringing it about. I also read the first few pages of Durkheim's *Rules of Sociological Method* (1950), where he defines "social facts," to suggest that Durkheim accepted as invariant the notion that social forces, which "cause" various social facts such as suicide, must be seen essentially as coercive. Thus, the "immanent critique" of disciplinary work takes the form of historicizing readings of positivist writings and research that depict society in ontologically invariant terms precisely in order to bring about that supposed invariance—frozen capitalism, patriarchy, racism, the domination of nature.

Historicizing readings demonstrate the political interest of sociological writers in freezing society as well as the literary ways in which these depictions or representations are accomplished so as to conceal their interest. This approach to immanent reading is necessarily a "polyvocal" exercise in that it provides different possible accounts of empirical phenomena. It also provides insights into the rhetoric of representation that freezes society into permanent patterns such as alleged laws. When dealing with what I have called journal science (1989b), this type of rhetorical reading treats not only prose but also figures as relevant texts—forms of rhetoric that silently argue for one state of affairs over others. Journal article writers attempt to create what I earlier called a science aura by enmeshing their proseful arguments in the thick text of statistical, figural, and graphic display, appearing to represent reality in the same way the hard sciences do. In other words, immanent critiques inspired by critical theory treat methodology as an important argument in its own right, following the lead of Derrida, who implies that marginalia such as footnotes, indexes, tables, and article abstracts are a powerful subtext driving or even replacing narrative argumentation.

Positivism's rhetoric of representation involves reliance on lawlike discourse and on the methodologically driven science aura. Although the original positivists narrated their theories (for example, Comte with his law of the three stages), today most sociologists replace narrative argumentation with figural pyrotechnics, which both resemble hard science and produce a metaphoric representationality (e.g., graphs representing the physical patterns of the world out there). The science aura is produced by replacing prose with mathematics, which the logical positivists of the Vienna Circle identified as the essence of science. As I said earlier, sociology races to catch up to the physical sciences in its own mathematization, thus increasing disciplinary legitimacy and promoting a frozen view of society that precludes the possibility of radical social change. As well, journal article writers produce the science aura by labored close discussions of methodology and data analysis in the meaty "methodology" and "findings" sections of the article that follow the ritualistic opening section, where the authors ground their works in a Mertonian middle-range theory.

This analysis of journal rhetorics of representation does not require or presuppose authorial intention. After all, scholars learn the literary norms of positivism, especially reliance on method and mathematics, in graduate school and by imitation. Immanent critique does not have to establish "motive," especially where it can identify a literary culture of science that constrains authors. Nor is this a matter of infelicitous writing style (see Becker 1986)—jargon. Every language game, as Wittgenstein called it, employs "phrases" (Lyotard 1988) that signify its difference from other language games. Immanent critique need not oppose mathematics; rather, it would argue for critical, playful, nondeterministic uses of math and method that accentuate the indeterminacy and historicity of the social world. Methodology by itself neither resolves disputes nor solves intellectual problems; method is argument, which can be engaged once method is read as the rhetorical text it is.

Immanent critique is perhaps the best deployment of critical social theories in the classroom, disclosing what I am calling the positivist rhetoric of representation in close readings of other texts and techniques. This need not subvert the disciplinary canon of empirical and theoretical work but broadens it to include counterreadings and -writings, starting arguments over values and worldviews and thus enhancing the democratic public sphere advocated by most critical social theorists. It is very important that immanent-critical readings in the classroom not imply that empirical research per se is wrongheaded. Such Luddite stances are foreign to the pro-science tendencies of most theories discussed in this book, even postmodernism. The distinction between "theory" and "the empirical" obscures the fact that the classical theories, Marxist and non-Marxist alike, grappled with empirical topics ranging from economics to culture and religion. Weber and Marx did not view themselves as nonempiricists. They simply did not confront a generation of social scientists, such as the midwestern empiricists, who purge their writing of speculation and social criticism and thus foster the distinction between theory and empiricism as a distinction between speculation and valid science. By default, the project of theory, especially within the disciplinary context of sociology, has come to mean, as one of my former colleagues put it, "speculative bullshit," unsupported by the accoutrements and appurtenances of real science. Absent quantitative data, speculative sociology is denigrated as theory, when in fact the classical theorists were intensely interested in the empirical world and for the most part did not write metatheory (theory about theory).

Theory is denigrated by the real-sociology crowd if it does not produce testable hypotheses, get grants, or publish in a few vouchsafed mainstream journals. On this view, what distinguishes theorizing is *absence*, in Derrida's terms—what theory is *not*. In my "theoretical" teaching, I refuse this dichotomy/hierarchy of presence versus absence—empiricism versus theory—because I maintain that empirical work can be read immanently and critically (by "theorists") and theoretical work can be empirical, that is, it can and should have empirical topics and referents. The power of positivism is so great that many busy empiricists believe that theory is worthless if it cannot be "tested," as if such "testing" could be carried out and described in a discourse devoid of theorizing.

There are two relevant projects, then, for theoretical teachers and writers. First, they must defend the validity of teaching and writing theory against colleagues who view such work as extraneous. They must show the work theory can do in reading other texts and puncturing myths and misconceptions. Second, they must defend the empiricism of theory, on the model of the founders such as Durkheim, Weber, and Marx. Mathematical sociologists sometimes characterize their work as formal theory, meaning that their work is almost science, lacking only quantitative data. But this formal theory is heavily figural and lavishly mathematical, almost attaining the status of science and certainly distinguishing itself from speculative theory.

These two aims can be met contextually, within the courses taken by most American graduate students in sociology and neighboring disciplines. A theory teacher can show the good critical work to be accomplished by theoretically driven immanent critiques of the frozen, metaphysical work of the social physicists. I spend much of the semester in classical theory reading Durkheim's *Division of Labor in Society* (1956) as an almost Marcusean indictment of the "abnormal" division of labor, thus undercutting its patent apology for capitalism. I also demonstrate the ways in which theories have relevance not only for the advancement of empirical research but even for the practice and teaching of research methodology, which I ground in issues of epistemology, objectivity, and the philosophy of science. In these ways I relate the theory course to the other work that my students are doing in the same semester, making connections that demonstrate the relevance and vitality of theory and, perhaps most important, showing how theory is not something to be entombed in the history of ideas but to be unleashed in all sorts of rhetorical venues, from research methods to dissertation writing.

Finally, it is important for people who would defend the projects of theory to situate those efforts in the contested terrain of curriculum, thus defending their projects against empiricist detractors who would both reduce the curricular field of theory and isolate it, rendering it legitimate only as disciplinary curatorial work. Although it is important for students to know the history of their discipline, giving their studies depth as well as context, I teach theory in terms of historicity and in terms of its contemporary vitality and applicability. Not only do I fight to ensure that students take theory, including critical social theories, but I resist the framing of my courses as somehow extraneous to my department's programmatic center, which is said by some to be "mainstream" empiricism.

Given norms surrounding the notion of academic freedom in American universities, it is unusual for faculty instructors, especially in research universities, to be told "what" to teach in their courses. Thus, the politics of curriculum usually take place in three related venues—whether courses are required of students, how frequently these courses are offered, and which faculty members are assigned to teach them. Positivist departmental leaders decenter theory courses by failing to make them compulsory, by offering them infrequently, and by assigning them to faculty members who do not publish theory. In many quantitative sociology departments, graduate students are required to take only a semester of theory, sometimes taught by an instructor who is not a specialist in theory, whereas they are required to take many methodology and statistics courses. Required theory courses frequently cover only classical theory, from Comte to Marx. And Marx is treated misleadingly as a "conflict theorist" (Agger 1989c: 193–225). Sometimes theory courses are really courses in substantive areas, such as theories of social change. Sometimes theory courses are taught from so-called theory-construction perspectives, including rational choice theory, exchange theory, and other approaches to mathematical sociology.

## THE END OF THEORY OR THE RENEWAL OF SOCIOLOGY?

I have noted that Marx, Weber, and Durkheim wrote comprehensive social theories that bridged empirical concerns and speculative theorizing. In the previous section, I suggested applications and implications of critical social theories for empirical social research. Coupled with my earlier discussion of how scientific writing as "discourse" is already freighted with values and theoretical constructs, these observations might lead one to conclude that all writing is already theoretical and that theoretical writing is both in and of the empirical world. Indeed, the sociological duality of empirical research and theory is born of a peculiarly positivist notion of research as value and theory free and of theory as merely the historiography of the discipline. The arguments in this book lead inescapably to the conclusion that the empiricism-theory duality is false, thus calling into question the role of theory as a distinctive disciplinary specialty hermetically sealed off from the empirical core. Although I have just argued for the validity and viability of theory in the sociological curriculum, I cannot defend the compartmentalization and isolation of theory as if theory did not necessarily bleed into empiricism and empiricism into theory. Both are writing—versions of the social.

Perhaps it is better to say that empiricism is a version that is methodical and data-based, while theory is systematic and speculative. This denies neither method nor system. John O'Neill (1974) makes a similar argument, treating sociology not as a blank slate on which social facts are imprinted but as an everyday social activity that enjoys no epistemological privilege. He makes that argument from within social phenomenology, not postmodernism. This does not lead either of us to "end" theorizing, simply collapsing it into busy empiricism. If anything, theory gains new purchase once we recognize that empirical researchers always and already theorize when they design survey instruments, collect data, analyze them, and present them in journal-science form.

Theory is sociology's self-consciousness, its awareness of its own corrigible authorship. Writing does not end interpretation, with definitive clarifications and definitions removing all doubt as to meaning. Clarifications must be clarified—the hermeneutic circle. To theorize is to listen to sociological writing write, and in so doing to recognize that science—and thus society—could be written differently. Critical social theory is a way of listening to writing write that emphasizes the responsibility of writing to change the world—to pierce mythologies and ideologies, to debunk cant and dogma, to unpack cultural representations that reproduce the existing society, to make connections between oppressions. Above all, critical social theory rejects positivism on the ground that positivism is no less a form of writing than other texts. And as the Frankfurt School demonstrated, positivism is such a powerful ideology because it uniquely pretends to have broken with philosophical values and constructs, a value position in its own right. Positivist sociology is secret writing, copying "facts" in support of laws such as patriarchy, capitalism, and racism, intending its social text to become our social fate—domination. Critical social theory reads that secret writing for the polemic it is, thus undoing what Durkheim called social facts and the society they underwrite. Critical social theory does not attempt to become an *Urtext* in its own right, a definitive account. It is a way of reading writing that thaws the frozen social world into molten possibilities.

In this book I have introduced a number of critical perspectives on social theorizing. All of these perspectives originate outside of the boundaries of sociology but can inform and even transform sociology if sociologists learn from them. By now it is very difficult to avoid the conclusion that sociology is being challenged by questions as powerful as the questions asked of it during the 1960s, when its political role in the antiwar and civil rights movements was under debate. I remember taking an introductory sociology class at the University of Oregon in which the classroom atmosphere was electric with the demand for "relevance"; outside, the streets in Eugene were crowded with students, faculty, and citizens marching against the war in Vietnam. The year was 1968, two years before Alvin Gouldner published *The Coming Crisis of Western Sociology.*

Although the world has turned since then, with sociological scientism replacing activism and engagement, the postmodern turn in social and cultural theory poses no less significant a challenge to mainstream sociology than did the antiwar and civil rights movements. No longer can we simply accept the notion that "social facts" exist independent of theoretical frames and of writing. Social facts are produced by textual acts, forever changing the way that sociology understands itself. In the 1960s we understood that sociology is political. Now we understand that sociology is discourse. There is a connection here: I have argued elsewhere that the dawning of postmodernity could be traced back to the Tet offensive in 1968, when a ragtag army began to turn the tide in a war against a vastly better armed and more thoroughly militarized "modernist" opponent. In the 1960s sociology was at the end of its modernist phase, although it took another twenty years for the writings of Derrida to be translated into English, thus initiating the postmodern turn in social theory. In 1970, with remarkable prescience, Paul Breines, a young critical theorist inspired by the Frankfurt School, dedicated a book he had edited on Marcuse (P. Breines 1970) to Ho Chi Minh and Adorno, reflecting the conjuncture of the end of modernity and the emergence of postmodernity, which was anticipated by Adorno and his Frankfurt colleagues.

The 1990s are as exciting an era for sociology and social theory as were the 1960s. The text—science, culture, media—has been politicized and problematized: The text is a society through which power is transacted in the nucleic language games linking writer and reader. We need to remind postmodernists that society is not all text, however. Derrida recognized that every reading is a writing, a new version. Although this argument is resisted by sociological mainstreamers who continue to claim epistemological privilege for their methods, outside of sociology positivism has been vanquished. In this book I have made the argument that it is increasingly difficult for mainstream sociologists to defend the boundaries of the discipline against postmodern, critical, and feminist interlopers, who find common cause in their critique of positivist, patriarchal representation. The challenge for sociologists during the next decade will be integrating these extrasociological insights in ways that help us do better sociology and social science, albeit changing what it means to "do sociology." I hope that this book has raised fundamental questions about the sociological project without abandoning that project. As one with roots in sociology's activist era, I find it impossible to forget the promise that a critical sociology held in the late 1960s. Sociology then provided the best explanations of a host of social and political phenomena that would remake our world and our lives. It can do so again.

# CHAPTER 9

# The 1960s at Forty

## Renewing Public Sociology in the Twenty-first Century

Since the first edition of this book was published in 1998, mainstream American sociology has become more positivist and quantitative, at least judging from what is published in journals. In response, the nonpositivist rump is growing, both within and outside of sociology. Positivist sociology is becoming a contested terrain. I have called for the renewal of a "public sociology" that will return sociology to engagement with important public issues and will be cast in a language that is intended not only for sociological specialists who make use of sophisticated quantitative methods but also for a more general public (Agger 2000; also see Burawoy 2005). Although Burawoy and I have our differences about the exact meaning of public sociology (see Agger forthcoming)—I believe that his version is still more "mainstream" than it needs to be and assumes that mainstream positivists will amicably coexist with nonpositivist public sociologists—we agree that the journals and leading graduate programs have gone too far in the direction of mathematics and methodology.

In this book, I examine several varieties of critical social theory. I also examine the empirical implication of these approaches. Since the first edition was published, several changes in the discipline have taken place, although I hasten to add that these trends were already underway in the late 1990s, when the first edition of this book was issued. Theorizing in American sociology has declined further. Theory has become a low-status occupation, a trivial pursuit, compared to number crunching and statistical work. This subordination of theory can be defended by those who notice that there are few jobs in theory (a self-fulfilling prophecy, of course), few major departments that specialize in theory, few mainstream journals that publish theory, and, indeed, a diaspora of theory to other more humanistic social sciences and even across the campus to humanities departments and programs. Theory has moved to

English, comparative literature, women's studies, cultural studies, and queer studies, among other fields, losing its anchor in the grand narratives of nineteenth-century social theory of the kind written by Auguste Comte, Emile Durkheim, Max Weber, and Karl Marx. This is a matter of both pushes and pulls: Mainstream sociologists want to banish or at least compartmentalize theory (to a one-semester graduate course often taught by people with other "substantive" interests), and theorizing is now found in humanities programs in which there is already postmodern skepticism about grand narrativity and hence an aversion to sociological and Marxist versions of theorizing. Theory in many English departments (see Watkins 1989; Eagleton 2003) amounts to literary and literary-critical theory and not the critical social and cultural theory of the Frankfurt School and the Birmingham School. Although the quantitative center of the discipline still holds, there are more sociologists on the fringes of the discipline and protosociologists in other disciplines who are doing theory and qualitative work and who reject mainstream quantitative empiricism.

All of this is to say that the sociological and academic divisions of labor, since I published the first edition of this book in 1998, have become even more refined, with the mainstream discipline's version of theory no longer marching across the discipline, and even beyond disciplines, but remaining narrowly confined to specialized intellectual activities such as the interpretation of historical texts. This is an exegetical activity that in effect canonizes the sociological classics as important but archaic statements that have been surpassed by subsequent quantitative work. In short, American sociology has become even more positivist, technical, grant-oriented, and hostile to European intellectual sources. And yet, as I explore in this concluding chapter, the positivists' hold on disciplinary power has become tenuous; it is increasingly challenged by younger scholars and students trained in humanistic methods and intellectual traditions—especially those joined under the umbrella concept of cultural studies, a necessarily pandisciplinary project—who don't believe that SPSS yields the truth or that arguments without data are therefore flawed.

## THE HEGEMONY OF POSITIVISM, VIEWED AS DISCOURSE AND NOT DOCTRINE

In my studies of sociological journal writing (Agger 1989b, 2000) I have discovered that sociological positivism is less an explicit doctrine than a discourse, a mode of presenting and figuring an argument. This discourse puts prose in the background and foregrounds mathematics and methodology, which become the real subtext of the articles. This mode of literary presentation began to dominate American sociology during the 1970s, for reasons explored in the following section. Now, in the early twenty-first century, the leading journals and graduate programs stress the use of quantitative methods, compared to which other "softer" methods, let alone theory, are judged to be deficient, even to be nonsociology.

One of the ironies of this focus on quantitative methods is that perhaps the majority of working American sociologists (and the vast majority in Europe, the UK, Canada, Australia, and New Zealand) appreciate both qualitative methodologies and theory. Evidence of this is the recent elections of Joe Feagin, Michael Burawoy, and Frances Fox Piven as presidents of the American Sociological Association. Piven is an interesting case not only because her work is radical but also because she was photographed (and the photo was widely circulated) climbing into a window during the 1968 Columbia University student takeover while she was a young faculty member, suggesting a connection between the 1960s and the present that I explore later in this chapter. Enough disciplinary "outsiders" came forward from colleges and universities off the beaten path to elect these nonpositivist candidates; they bested the supporters of quantitative insiders for this high elective office. The discipline is still controlled by the number crunchers who chair and work in mainstream departments and who occupy positions on the ASA Council, but there are many sociologists in the field, especially on its periphery, who don't buy into the dominant consensus about method and mathematics.

As I have argued in my books on the sociology of sociology, a discursive positivism—transforming doctrinal positivism into a literary style proliferating in the journals—freezes the world, imitating Newton's model of the natural sciences. Comte's promise of sociology as social physics is still tantalizing to empirical sociologists working at public and private universities visited by budgetary cutbacks and the eroding prestige of sociology as a discipline. They feel that if they restore sociology's scientific legitimacy, which began to erode during and after the 1960s, they will build back sociology's position in the university and society at large—more students, more Ph.D.s graduated, more faculty hiring, more grant money. Sociology responded to the 1960s and its own partisan role as an opponent of the Vietnam War and a supporter of civil rights with regret and even shame, clamoring to get back on the scientific straight and narrow.

But this is a different positivism from the earlier positivism of the natural sciences. John Locke posited the mind as a blank slate on which sense data would imprint. Other positivists positioned knowledge entirely outside of the world, looking in with dispassion. Most positivists, following the lead of the physicist Robert Newton, set science the task of describing laws of motion in the natural world. From these influences, Comte derived the mission of a scientific sociology, applying the assumptions and methods of Newton's physics to the social sciences and to his own fledgling discipline of sociology, which he described as social physics.

The latter-day, post-1960s sociological positivists have little time to debate these epistemological doctrines. Instead, they are engineers (see Turner 1998) who scramble to get federal grant money with which they analyze large data sets and write journal articles. The heart of science for them is not epistemology (the theory of knowledge) but method and especially statistics. For today's positivists, improvements in knowledge come not from the testing of grand theory but from methodological and statistical innovations, which are lavishly displayed in the figural gestures of the journals. Indeed, these diagrams are the main text of journal sociology, by comparison to which the "content" of the article always seems quite mundane and even incidental.

As I explore below, the methodological bent of sociology since 1970 is partly a reaction to the engagements and partisanship of 1960s sociology, from C. Wright Mills (1959) to Alvin Gouldner (see Lemert 2005b). It is also partly a function of a technological determinism, according to which the investment in method and statistical techniques in effect breed themselves. People immerse themselves in these techniques because they can—the techniques are widely available, especially with desktop computing and canned programs such as SPSS. These advanced techniques, taught in graduate schools and then reproduced via imitation in the journals, fill a theoretical void left by the collapse of Parsonianism and its antithesis in radical, reflexive sociology (see Gouldner 1970; O'Neill 1972). Although there are still radical and reflexive sociologists afoot, the opinion makers in the discipline have worked hard to disqualify politically oriented versions of theoretical and qualitative sociology and also interdisciplinary work both within the social sciences and bridging the social sciences and humanities. The argument is often heard that sociologists require strong and singular disciplinary identities in order to right the ship of a sinking discipline. This was much the same argument made by Durkheim in *The Rules of Sociological Method* (1950) when he demarcated the new discipline of sociology from psychology and made its province the study of social facts, conceptualized as instances of people's determination by impinging social structure.

As I mentioned earlier, there are many younger sociologists as well as scholars and graduate students in neighboring disciplines such as anthropology and political science, and even in more distantly related disciplines such as English, who are interested in critical theory, postmodernism, women's studies, queer studies, postcolonial studies, and cultural studies. There has been a diaspora of theory (see Agger forthcoming) from sociology into these more humanistic fields. There is no shame in doing theory for faculty and students in English, comparative literature, and cultural studies programs. In fact, theory is a high-status occupation in these quarters. Only in mainstream sociology has theory been eclipsed by method, both to shun the 1960s and to try out the shiny new methodological and statistical machines that take a lifetime to master, given their complexity.

These methods and techniques have become the norm in mainstream journal writing. They thus reproduce themselves as "what it takes" to break into the pages of *American Sociological Review*. Although the mainstream journals try to avoid appearing monolithic by publishing the occasional qualitative or theoretical piece, they are controlled by editors, reviewers, and authors who believe that quantitative sociology is cutting-edge, more likely to be funded, and "real sociology." Graduate students, being "trained" and not educated, realize that in a crowded job market they must publish in the leading journals, so they take the road more traveled—quantitative method—and succumb to the figural language game of the discursive positivism abounding in the journals and disciplines. Even if they want to take the theoretical road less traveled, they are advised by their faculty mentors that they will have an easier time finding a job if they have quantitative "skills."

In *Public Sociology* (2000), I devoted a chapter to the analysis of hundreds of prepublication article reviews done for mainstream sociology journals. The vast majority of these reviews focused on methodological and technical issues in the submitted papers and not on issues of "substance." Indeed, it became clear to me that method *was* the substance of these papers and the reviews of them. Some of this is perhaps inherent in the complicated language game of journal positivism: Mastering the latest quantitative techniques is as arduous and fraught with difficulty as learning to play the cello. And so reviewers concentrated on these seemingly objective matters that could be addressed and remedied, rather than on the theoretical ideas underlying the data analyses (if there were any theoretical ideas underneath). In these ways, journal positivism has become less a doctrine based on certain clear-cut epistemological principles, as it was for Locke earlier, than a discourse governed by certain rules of presentation, including the lavish use of figures and other gestures, as I term them, that clutter the busy scientific journal page and squeeze out prose and, thus, theory.

## After Chicago, Kent State, and the Weather Underground, Sociologists Retreat from the Public Sphere

By the early 1970s, it was clear (see Marcuse 1973) that a counterrevolution had beaten back the New Left and reversed some of its important gains and goals. The 1960s ended in despair and retrenchment, perhaps symbolically on the day that the Weather Underground townhouse in Manhattan exploded, disqualifying the utopian idealism of the Students for a Democratic Society's (SDS) 1962 Port Huron Statement, written by Tom Hayden and then debated by nearly sixty students and academics at a United Auto Workers (UAW) summer resort on Lake Huron in Michigan. Or one might date the end of the 1960s from the time of the protests, during the spring and early summer of 1970, of the U.S. bombing of Cambodia, leading to the murder of college students at Kent State and Jackson State Universities. In the Port Huron Statement, Hayden drew liberally from C. Wright Mills as he envisaged a "new" left committed to participatory democracy, grounded in youthful vigor and experimentation, and not hamstrung by European and Soviet socialist infighting about political and theoretical correctness. The end of the 1960s probably began even earlier, at the Democratic National Convention in Chicago in 1968 (a year already marked by the assassinations of Bobby Kennedy and Martin Luther King Jr.), when the whole world watched (see Gitlin 2003) Chicago police club New Left demonstrators who opposed the war in Vietnam and especially Hubert Humphrey's pro-war candidacy for president. The Chicago convention was followed a year later by Days of Rage (see Ayers 2001; Varon 2004), when a few hundred Weatherpeople rampaged through the Chicago streets trying to destroy "pig city" via armed insurrection. They failed, and soon thereafter they went underground and devoted themselves to a campaign of strategic bombing of sacred American institutions such as the Pentagon and Congress.

In the midst of all this (see Turner and Turner 1990), American sociologists took stock. Sociology was bursting at the seams as a college major and a discipline during the 1960s, as students and young faculty sought answers and solutions for the burning issues of the time. By the time Nixon's counterrevolution got under way (for example, the FBI's systematic attempt to impose surveillance and capture on the New Left), sociology had begun a slow but decadelong decline in enrollment, number of Ph.D.s granted, funding opportunities, faculty hiring, and university prestige. The gray eminences who led the discipline, some of whom were already ambivalent about sociological activism during the 1960s, decided that sociology was suffering a decline in reputation because of its activism and needed to return to its original roots in science with Comte, Durkheim, and Weber.

The politically and intellectually fertile period of the 1960s saw American graduate students and younger faculty reading European texts of critical theory, phenomenology, postmodernism, and feminist theory. From these texts they developed an understanding of capitalist society relevant to the mid- and late-twentieth century. My own work springs mainly from the inspiration of the Frankfurt School, although I have also read in phenomenology, existentialism, and postmodernism. The journal *Telos* was started by a graduate student in philosophy at SUNY-Buffalo, Paul Piccone. *Telos* translated and explicated many of these European sources, from Martin Heidegger and Edmund Husserl to Georg Lukács and Theodor Adorno. These intellectual sources were relevant to young radicals inasmuch as they could explain the political opportunities and impasses of the moment, all the way from Vietnam and civil rights to the ossification of academic life. This was a period in which young scholars poured over European theoretical texts in order to build an American left grounded in democracy and humanism!

These German, French, Italian, and Hungarian sources of radical social and cultural criticism were extremely influential for a whole host of younger scholars who were in graduate school or in their undergraduate years during the 1960s. Russell Jacoby, Doug Kellner, Mark Poster, Tim Luke, Stanley Aronowitz, and I were all struggling during these years to understand our own alienation, the alienation of others (including working-class, black, female, and colonial others), and the newfound opportunities for left-wing social change that didn't exactly fit the template of traditional nineteenth-century Marxism. These intellectual influences have endured in American critical theory and cultural studies, which remain interdisciplinary projects, and in humanities disciplines such as English, comparative literature, and anthropology, all of which have embraced the critical-theoretical and postmodern projects, even if these disciplines haven't become monolithic.

American sociology reacted to the 1960s in a much different way. Empiricism and pragmatism—and the dreaded "p" word, positivism—were much more deeply entrenched in American sociology than in those humanities disciplines, mediating the influence of Comte through the applied sociology of the Chicago School. Although individual sociologists were activists during the 1960s, protested the war in Vietnam, and worked for civil rights, outside of Mills and Gouldner there were few who developed a radical critique of American society with which to replace Parsons's structural functionalism. By the time the 1960s had ended and the sociological establishment during the 1970s confronted the declining fortunes of sociology as a discipline, it became commonplace to blame sociology's misfortunes on its youthful engagements and enthusiasms during the decade that had just ended.

The sociological establishment thus turned its back on 1960s activism, on theory, and on critiques of objectivity and value-freedom, and it returned to science as a means of restoring the discipline's legitimacy. But it didn't return to the doctrines of positivism found in Locke, Comte, and the Vienna Circle. Such epistemological reflections were viewed as part of the problem in a discipline that had become too theoretical by the standards of pragmatic scholarship that seeks grants and impresses academic administrators with the promise of "external funding," the mythos of the privatized university. American sociologists replaced positivism as a doctrine with positivism as a discourse, a literary methodology that plays out in the ways authors compose mainstream journal articles and teach the discipline to their graduate students. The crux of this discursive positivism, designed to relegitimate sociology with deans and foundations, was a commitment to scientific method and mathematics as if the problem of sociology was the burdensome legacy of the 1960s.

For sociology to deny its recent activist past is part of a larger neoconservatism that shifts political discourse and debate further to the right. The Democratic Leadership Council wants the party to resemble the Republican Party in key symbolic ways, such as endorsing patriotism and a strong military. The equivalent of the DLC within sociology is the ASA Council and the host of mainstream journal editors and reviewers, who work overtime to deradicalize sociology and transform it further into what Comte originally called social physics. But this isn't the wordy and expansive social physics of the discipline's founders. It is a social physics that proceeds by indirection, using number and figure where before prose had stood. This is what I call journal science, grounded in a cumulative model of the progress of science that has been discredited since Albert Einstein and Thomas Kuhn. Theory is viewed as overly political and premethodological, returning to the old ways and discrediting a discipline that has worked hard to present itself as a science discipline.

This neglects the fact that there are different versions of science, just as there are different versions of the 1960s. Bill Clinton once said that people define themselves politically by whether they liked or disliked the 1960s, and the same could be said of contemporary sociologists. Those who trace their own intellectual and political genealogies from the 1960s without shame are more likely to read and write theory, do qualitative work, and engage unashamedly with political and social issues. Those who shun the 1960s, especially those of the younger generation of graduate students and junior sociologists for whom the 1960s represent a rumor of "classic" rock and marijuana, tend to view "real" sociology as quantitative and methods-driven, reject theory as ungrounded and speculative, and view politics as purely a private role.

Postmodernism has become a convenient target for mainstream sociologists, who disdain its sometimes convoluted writing style, its literary and philosophical bent, and its seeming rejection of science. "Postmodernism is not what you think," though, as Charles Lemert (2005a) has argued. It is a serious and systematic approach to a world that cannot be captured under glass, frozen in amber, or represented timelessly and causally on the journal page. Postmodernists such as Jacques Derrida and Michel Foucault, much like the Frankfurt School theorists, derive their perspective from Nietzsche, who argues that language is a prison, by which he means that language (including science) is an imperfect prism through which to view the world. Language is never totally precise, concise, without doubt. Indeed, our figures of speech, and our mathematical figures, often introduce ambiguity and obstruct meaning. For example, Marx and Weber both use the term *class,* but it has different meanings for each of them. Or methodologists might measure people's incomes as personal income, family income, or household income. All of these tropes (typical rhetorical gestures or figures of speech) can be defended. But what does this defending is theory, defined as the way that language understands itself understanding—its subtext, *Urtext,* or metatext.

Postmodernism notices that positivism is secret writing, pretending to have no author. That is the essence of journal science. The deauthored prose of the journals clogs the page with figure and number, hoping to convince the reader of its methodological purity. But the writer still surfaces in the undecidable, ambiguous prose that begs clarification. That is Derrida's point: Every act of reading writes in the sense that a reader's interpretation provides murky texts with necessary meaning. And texts are forever murky—all language is—because writing "defers" needed clarifications and definitions so that it can get on with the business of making sense within its chosen language game. Think of a nonnative speaker of any language thumbing through a dictionary looking for the word *supermarket*. She finds the definition but doesn't understand it fully, needing to look up the words *retail* and *commodities*. And so on, and so on. Positivism pretends that its writing is authorless, but in that respect positivism authors all the more forcefully because we believe (that is, choose to believe, as we have done since the Enlightenment) that scientific method and mathematics still the beating heart of authorial perspective and the necessity of readerly interpretation and intervention.

Postmodernism brings to light the power of perspective, which one would think is an eminently sociological contribution. But perspective, at least until Einstein and Kuhn, threatened the Newtonian worldview in which perspective, hesitancy, and ambiguity are viewed as error. Unfortunately, the philosophy of science since relativity theory, which is quite Derridean in unintended ways, has not been incorporated into American sociological methods writing and training. The sociological methodologists are nearly a hundred years out of date, relying on Newton's seamless universe. Enter postmodernism.

Using the 1960s as a model for a Mills/Hayden-like engaged and enraged sociology crosses over from nostalgia to innovation where we take stock of the 1960s in an accurate but sympathetic way. Kirkpatrick Sale (1973), Jim Miller (1987), Todd Gitlin (1987), Tom Hayden (1988), Tom Wells (1994), and Jeremy Varon (2004), among others, have offered both insider and outsider perspectives on this tumultuous but fascinating decade. None of them engages in a blind hagiography; all of them admit to failures and false starts just as they register real triumphs and the power of youthful political imagination. All of us believe that the legacies of the 1960s are still present in our political and personal worlds today, expressed in legislation, ongoing conflicts, and sensibilities that were opened and expanded during these times. Marcuse's pair of books on the 1960s, *An Essay on Liberation* (1969) and *Counterrevolution and Revolt* (1973), theorize both the highs and lows of this period. Marcuse grounds his appreciation of the 1960s "new sensibility" in Freudian Marxism, situationism, and critical theory, recognizing that the real power of the decade lay in its politics of everyday life, a theme of utmost importance for the SDS in the "values" section of the Port Huron Statement. Marcuse argues that one cannot postpone liberation to a distant future time without inviting authoritarianism. The long road to radical social change never seems to end; instead, one must prefigure the future in the small gestures and actions of the present.

The collapse of the Soviet Union is joined with the demonization of the 1960s as twin moments in a neoconservative backlash against progressive movements, women's liberation, gay rights, and good old-fashioned social- ism. Neocons such as Francis Fukuyama (1992) and Allan Bloom (1987) link the end of the USSR and the promise of the 1960s to their inherent flaws and then to the superiority of capitalism, patriarchy, Victorianism, and other traditional values. Although the SDS took issue with Stalinism, Hayden and his colleagues were careful to denounce American anticommunism as a reactionary posture, recognizing, with great insight, that the cold war was folly and that neither side deserved to "win."

I am not interested in resurrecting the Bolshevist model of democratic centralism, which turned out to be all centralism and no democracy. And yet there are real discontinuities between Lenin's *What Is to Be Done?* (1969) and Stalinism (see Marcuse 1958) that make a casual dismissal of the So- viet experience premature. In any case, as Mills, Hayden, and Dick Flacks recognized, the Soviet and central European experiences with socialism and Marxist theory are quite remote from American political culture and don't provide adequate reference points. For this reason, the Port Huron Statement didn't brand itself as socialist, even though it purposely positioned itself as on the left, albeit a "new" left.

The 1960s cannot be written off because they are in us. Generation and identity inform, and were affected by, our experiences of that decade, whether we were in high school, college, graduate school, or beyond. In a forthcoming book (Agger forthcoming), I explore the multiple meanings of the 1960s as I seek to establish possible relevances of that decade for the younger generations today, as well as for their parents. What we can learn from the 1960s above all is a politics of the personal, whether this has feminist or SDS connotations. And this politics of the personal includes our literary engagements, our rela- tionships to science and texts, and our perspectives on culture and media—all of which are issues for a positivist sociology that attempts to remove the self from its scribblings. As Marcuse indicates in *Essay on Liberation,* one of the central insights of the 1960s is that science and technology are not neutral, an issue stressed throughout the Frankfurt School's critique of positivism as a new ideology of domination since the Enlightenment. Marcuse goes fur- ther, positing a reconstruction and rehabilitation of science and technology as early-Marxist and neo-Freudian expressions of the life instincts—ways of being in the world that are playful and unconstrained.

This version of science has been criticized from within the Frankfurt School by Jürgen Habermas (1971), who dismisses the "heritage of mysticism" of the first generation of the Frankfurt theorists, including Marcuse. Habermas wants to reseparate technology/science and human interaction in almost Kan- tian fashion (see Agger 1976) in order to create a do-able, workable agenda for left social movements. Marcuse aimed higher, arguing that science is an expression of nonalienated labor, implicitly abandoning positivism, which makes of science simply a mirror of nature (see Rorty 1979). A public sociology does not abandon science so much as renders it dialectical, or undecidable in Derrida's terms. Science becomes a mode of being in the world, a project somewhat blind to itself. It becomes a language game, a nucleic society through which humanity and power are transacted. Science loses its special privilege with respect to fiction but becomes, unashamedly, a type of science fiction. This need not rob science of efficacy. Indeed, a version of science that admits its corrigibility and context is even more persuasive.

## ERODING SOCIOLOGICAL CONSENSUS IN THE POST-9/11 WORLD

American sociology, although still ruled by math and method, is slowly coming undone, experiencing the same type of decentering it experienced during the 1960s. This is in large part because the early twenty-first century is remarkably like the 1960s: The United States is embroiled in unwinnable foreign conflicts and military adventurism; the White House is controlled by a gang of reactionaries; the "silent majority," the 1960s term for middle-American Archie Bunkers who uncritically support right-wing elites and hate minorities and leftists, has returned with a born-again vengeance; and the United States is once again widely reviled abroad for its combination of arrogance and isolationism. All that is missing is a college-age generation of Tom Haydens armed with fresh ideas about participatory democracy in this Internet age. Although our college students are as yet quiescent by the standards of the mid-to-late 1960s, there is disquiet afoot on college campuses, as students listen to angst-driven music, worry about reinstatement of the draft, and oppose the White House. Decades and movements start slowly, without apparent cause and with unpredictable momentum.

On the intellectual scene, Russell Jacoby's (1987) argument for public intellectuals engaged with issues in broadly accessible vernaculars has taken hold, even if the academic left reacted defensively when *The Last Intellectuals* was first published. I have called for a public sociology that returns to Mills and the New Left for political verve and intellectual orientation. Quantitative method is rejected not for its particular techniques but as myth, a new religion that borders on ideology. There is nothing wrong with counting things, only with inflating the acts of counting and statistical operations into absolute truth, and a truth that displaces reason and prose. Judging by the outpouring of books on critical theory, cultural studies, postmodernism, and feminism, nonpositivist course curricula in sociology departments off the beaten path, and the ASA elections of renegades such as Feagin, Burawoy, and Piven, it appears that many younger, female, and nonwhite sociologists are ready to dislodge math and method as intellectual engines of sociology. Disciplinarity itself (see Klein 1990) is losing its grip as interdisciplinary projects such as cultural studies, women's studies, and queer studies make headway in universities. The very boundary between the social sciences and humanities is fading as people interested in "theory," broadly understood, combine their efforts and work and teach together.

The center of disciplinary power holds, but only tenuously. As our world burns, much as it did during the 1960s, sociologists and students of sociology are calling for *relevance,* that watchword of an earlier decade. It is not enough to write methodologically freighted articles for *American Sociological Review* that are written more for publication and the accompanying career capital than to be read; and it is not enough, in one's private life, to vote Democratic and engage in community and school activism. When urgent political and human problems abound, a methods-driven sociology is irrelevant, just as Mills and Hayden found Parsonian functionalism to be irrelevant toward the end of the Eisenhower presidency.

Addressing the changing demography of U.S. sociology, in which the occupants of the periphery now outnumber members of the positivist core, Joe Feagin made these observations:

> More than half the American Sociological Association voters in elections *now* are young people, grad students and young faculty, many of them idealistic in their general views (though pressed by their seniors to be good positivists to make tenure) and thus they have voted in several nonmainstream folks as president. A disproportionate percentage now are young women and young men of color. That is why I beat out the mainstream candidates and why Piven won. The old guard that runs most departments gets outvoted by those they oppress in the tenure process! These young people go into sociology mostly to change the world, but that old, mostly white, male positivist guard tries to beat that out of them as they become senior grad students and young faculty. The majority of young faculty live schizoid lives, trying to be progressive but forced to sell out for their degrees or tenure. The times are changing demographically [in the sociological professoriate], but the old guard is trying to impose the past on that present (Feagin 2005).

Just as our nation is deeply divided between blue and red states, sociology is enduring conflicts about method, theory, and partisanship. This is highly reminiscent of the 1960s, when entire departments were split over the war in Vietnam and over sociology's professional or public roles. George W. Bush and Karl Rove, with their lying, corruption, procorporate stance, and xenophobia, remind one of the Nixon White House, with its plumbers, dirty tricks, treachery, and dissimulation. Bush/Rove's attack on the Left takes the form of Homeland Security, where Nixon energized the FBI to seek out and destroy New Leftists and Black Panthers via the vehicle of COINTELPRO (FBI counterintelligence programs designed to repress political dissent). The times they are a-changin', but they are also staying the same in important ways. Perhaps all that is missing is the draft, which would spur millions of college students into activism and even militancy. As Wells (1994) indicates in his excellent study *The War Within,* the antiwar movement was scarcely imaginable without the threat that the draft posed to middle-class college students who were already sympathetic to the southern civil rights movement. Wells (2005) further speculates about the relevance of the 1960s for today, as do other authors, in a special issue of the journal *Fast Capitalism* (www.fastcapitalism.com) dedicated to discussing the 1960s at forty.

Sociology cannot remain on the sidelines and hope that the scientific method, now encoded in positivist journal discourse and its mathematical gestures, will bail it out. The Right controls the political agenda in America, and sociologists will need to take sides. It will not be enough for them to work for Democratic and even green candidates in their private lives while, in their public lives, they do disengaged science and build their careers. This schizophrenia of public versus private roles will cause sociologists great discomfort, especially if the Right continues to control the political agenda.

Michael Burawoy makes this clear in his work on public sociology, even though he, too, is ambivalent about what he calls "professional" (or positivist) sociology. Burawoy wants to preserve this version of sociology while carving out space for public and critical sociologies (which, for him, aren't the same thing). He believes that a sociological division of labor is workable, whereby some sociologists set up a firewall around their work and close it off from political contamination while other sociologists engage in advocacy work. He underestimates the professional/positivist group that controls the discipline's publication outlets, the ASA and its leading graduate programs. They won't tolerate public and critical sociologies because positivism by nature is imperialist and disqualifies nonpositivist knowledge as illegitimate. The positivist elite who control the discipline haven't opened up the journals, hiring, or graduate curricula even though they recognize that there are many challenges, both from within and outside the discipline, to what Burawoy calls professional sociology. Burawoy is unrealistic about this disciplinary elite's willingness to share power, method, publication opportunities, hiring, and graduate curricula. The elite will continue to demonize critical social theories, reserving special wrath for postmodernism, which, they fear, utterly abandons the project of science.

There are ironies here because, as I argue in my concluding section of this chapter, positivism and postmodernism share an apolitical stance, having rejected grand narratives of radical social change in favor of (in the case of positivism) mathematics and figural representation and (in the case of postmodernism) irony, wordplay, and an opposition to grand narratives. For that matter, phenomenology, too, before its social, political, and existential turn with Alfred Schütz, Jean-Paul Sartre, and Maurice Merleau-Ponty, resembles positivism in its desire to mirror the world without mediating representation (via the phenomenological reduction). These three "Ps" share the view that knowledge cannot and should not attempt to change the world, standing at one remove from it. Postmodernism and phenomenology differ from positivism, though, in that there are versions of each of these perspectives that allow for intersubjectivity, political action, and radical social change, even joining with Marxism and other versions of critical social theory.

Positivism hates postmodernism, and yet it shares with many postmodernisms a mistrust of utopia, of thinking the world otherwise. They together reject Marx, even though positivists mistrust postmodernism more for its apparent rejection of science. This is a jumble worth sorting out because it tells us a lot about our overall political cynicism and despair in the post-9/11 world (see Sloterdijk 1987). Postmodernism reads positivism as secret writing. Positivism rejects the supposed antiscience posture of postmodernism. Marxists and critical theorists reject both perspectives for their abandonment of utopia, of radical social change. Yet critical theorists learn from postmodernists about the power of culture and discourse to form the self. Kellner (1995), for instance, adapts the Frankfurt School's concept of the culture industry (see Horkheimer and Adorno 1972) by calling it media culture, drawing on various postmodern themes found especially in Baudrillard (1983; and see Kellner 1989c).

A Port Huron model of radicalism would reject the apolitical quietism of positivism and postmodernism, and it would also abandon the discourse of traditional male/European Marxism for its irrelevance to the American sensibility and political culture. This is why in the next section of this chapter I return to Mills and Hayden for imagination and inspiration at a time when the world seems girded for more poverty, starvation, ecological degradation, violence, and terror. And it is a time when the ideological polarity of blue and red, Left and Right, seems unbreachable.

## BEYOND POSITIVISM AND POSTMODERNISM (AND BACK TO MILLS AND HAYDEN FOR A PARADIGM)

In this era of post-9/11 fast capitalism in which class, race, gender, and global conflicts have resurfaced and are being played out on both global and local scales, sociologists disagree about the politics of epistemology, methodology, and theory. Like the 1960s, these times are volatile and unpredictable. Sociologists are challenged to make their work "relevant," again that 1960s word, and yet they don't share a common paradigm or framework. Quantitative method was never much of a paradigm because it deeply concealed its real support of the status quo, which must be divined deconstructively from the densely figured text of the scientific journal article. And this has always been a schizophrenic stance for sociologists who, since the 1960s, have been mostly progressive even as they profess math and method as panaceas for the passions of the 1960s that, they feel, led the discipline astray. Ex-1960s and post-1960s sociologists vote Democratic, work for social change, perhaps even smoke dope, and yet they build careers by apprenticing in top-twenty departments, publishing in the big three journals, and purveying quantitative method, which becomes a language game in its own right.

But method solves no intellectual problems, let alone political ones. The abundance of method cluttering the journal pages and driving graduate students to distraction in their many required methods and statistics courses reflects a discipline that has no theoretical center; the gap is filled with technique, which, as Heidegger always knew, is no solution because technique lacks ontology, a theory of being. Method especially lacks utopia, which abounded during the 1960s, especially in the Port Huron Statement and in the writings of Mills. Sociology needs to return to Mills as an example of an engaged intellectual who tested his intellectual work against the standard of relevance—to civil rights, the antiwar movement, the struggles of oppressed people everywhere.

Mills died far too early, in his forties, just as the SDS was gathering momentum and winning converts. Hayden, who wrote a thesis on Mills at the University of Michigan (forthcoming in book form [Hayden 2006]), where the SDS was originally centered, took over Mills's legacy of engaged intellectuality as he drafted the Port Huron Statement, which moved a whole generation into social and political action—easily the most important political manifesto of the twentieth century, rivaling *The Communist Manifesto* from the last century. In particular, Hayden agreed with Mills that people's private troubles needed to be understood in terms of larger public institutions such as the economy, the political system, international politics, class, race, and gender. (Gender, truth be told, was not a serious issue for the New Left until the girlfriends tired of their subordination to charismatic and macho male movement "heavies" [see Gitlin 1987; W. Breines 1982].) Feminists and critical theorists would add that public issues need to be understood as private issues, too, in that the self is always already somewhat removed from political and social determinations; the self is, and will always be, inevitably private even as it is also rendered public by the colonization of the lifeworld (see Habermas 1984, 1987b).

By returning to Mills I am not saying that we should spend more time poring over Mills's writings, combing *The Power Elite* (1956) and *The Sociological Imagination* (1959) for hidden code relevant to our times. I am suggesting that Mills's example of intellectual and political engagement, carried forward by the early SDS as it tried to reimagine European socialism as participatory democracy, is useful today at a time when the academic social sciences have little to say about our world and about what people can do to change it, and themselves. The last place one would go to find nostrums or manifestos is the mainline academic sociology journals, clogged with math and figures and statistical techniques. These deauthored texts are secret writing, to be sure, silently advocating one state of affairs over others—the present as a plenitude of social being. But it takes much deconstructive work to read scientific sociology as the subtly partisan project that it is, and it takes little work to read it as a dismal text devoid of authorial passion, perspective, and position. Where the Port Huron Statement, in mimeo form and selling for a quarter, circulated across American college campuses and started the political moment of the 1960s—and toppled a president and helped win civil rights for blacks and women—today the only possible public circuitry of such manifestos is found in the cables that deliver the Internet to many homes, offices, and coffee shops.

Mills and Hayden set an example of intellectuals and students who don't embrace either method or irony as adequate postures. Neither is positivist, nor postmodernist, even though Mills was the first to use the term "post-modern" in English. They are passionate, public, and committed. They also explore the interior lives of damaged selves who must deal with the gap between political and existential meanings; hence Hayden's interest in Albert Camus as well as in Mills and early Marx. Long after the 1960s had ended in Nixon's counterrevolution, Hayden took stock of the past in an autobiography entitled *Reunion* (1988). He followed this with a book on the existential meaning (for him) of being Irish, *Irish on the Inside* (Hayden 2001), in which he explores what it means to be an outsider, as he and Mills (also Irish) certainly were.

The problem with positivism is that it freezes the present into ontological amber, implying that the peaks and valleys of figured social inequality are the stuff of social nature, one day to be captured in Comtean social laws. The problem with postmodernism (although we can learn a lot from it about how culture and discourse enmesh the self) is that it denies a utopian future and thus shuts down political imagination as hubris. This was Jean-François Lyotard's point in *The Postmodern Condition* (1984). However, Frederic Jameson (1991), Douglas Kellner (1995), Timothy Luke (1989), and I have tried to narrow the distance between the concerns of German critical theory and French postmodern theory because, together, they coalesce into a powerful critique of the Enlightenment's arrogance about scientific method and mathematics as royal roads to truth. In denying the knowing self a privileged position outside of time and place, postmodernists such as Foucault and Derrida tend to deny all truths, even if these are provisional and conditional, especially political truths about the body politic and political bodies.

Late in his career, Derrida issued a book, *Specters of Marx* (1994), that actually situated his deconstructive project squarely within Marxism, arguing, as I have done in *Postponing the Postmodern* (2002), that Marx was already postmodern in that he recognized that truth telling is always infected with history ("historicity," in Hegelian language). This infection need not render all truths relative if we read history as having a meaning, as G. W. F. Hegel and Marx felt that it did. History spoils the truth only if we agree with the Greeks that truth is ahistorical. The New Left well understood that the truth is democratic in the sense that it needs to be achieved through open discussion, the changing of minds and building of consensus. Habermas has made much the same argument, although within the framework of communication theory and new social movements theory. This New Left truth—that humans are infinitely valuable and capable of managing their affairs—is inscribed in the Port Huron Statement, which was always intended to be a living document subject to revision and rethinking. Indeed, the draft of the manifesto that Hayden brought with him to the UAW camp was worked over and rearranged by the SDS campers, who had the wisdom to position the statement on values that made SDS famous at the beginning of the document. There was much debate over how to treat the Soviet Union and American anticommunist politics, again demonstrating that the New Left didn't close the book on truth but opened it.

Nostalgia for the 1960s (see Agger forthcoming) creates an anamnestic solidarity (Lenhardt 1976) with the dead and with survivors that renders liberation a transhistorical, intergenerational project. This is essential for countering the immediacy of fast capitalism, which leaves yesterday behind in its instantaneizing project. Nostalgia turns into a radical resource where it draws from the past models of engagement based on participatory democracy and the Marcusean new sensibility (Marcuse 1969) that prefigures large-scale change in the small choices people make in their everyday lives. U.S. sociology made a fateful mistake when it extirpated 1960s radicalism from the discipline, not returning to Parsons but leaping forward, or so it thought, into the mathematical metaphysics of a deterministic Newtonian universe left behind by Einstein in 1905, in his first paper on the special theory of relativity.

This is the heart of the matter: Positivist sociologists have been imitating a causal universe discredited in physics for a hundred years. Relativity theory parallels Derrida's later stress on undecidability, the notion that the text (here, of science) cannot exhaust the things it describes without trading on tropes (literary conventions) that themselves cry out for clarification. Try to define the meaning of a word without using other words that themselves must be defined, ad infinitum. But the literary positivists who clog their journal articles with the talismans of number and figure haven't read widely in the philosophy of science; they are pragmatists who "do" science but don't theorize it. Their positivism is a way of getting published and getting ahead, reproducing the normal science (Kuhn 1970) that was published last year, and the year before that. Literature—wide-ranging fiction and nonfiction that explores the human condition—has been truncated into literature reviews, brief discussions of articles on one's topic published in the last several years from which one derives a warrant for one's own research, which narrowly innovates in the treatment of that topic.

Reading science this way need not issue in the antiscience posture of many postmodernists (see Rosenau 1992) who, in establishing the indeterminacy and undecidability of all narratives, reject the grand narrative of truth out of hand. Lyotard goes so far as to link these grand narratives with Stalin, noticing that epistemological hubris underpins political arrogance. This is true, but Stalin is best read as a positivist Marxist, which he was. Marx wasn't to blame for Stalin, as the authors of the Port Huron Statement, in their youthful prescience, realized. Lyotard and his postmodern colleagues throw out the baby with the bathwater where they conflate positivism and Marxism. Postmodernism doesn't best positivism where it rejects truth, even grounded versions of it. Although Friedrich Nietzsche was correct that language is a prison house, confining as well as illuminating, we must still do the dirty and exhausting work of talking endlessly with our friends and allies—and even the opposition—just as the SDS campers at Port Huron did as they debated the meaning of participatory democracy and drew up their plans for a world-altering New Left.

Mills and Hayden remind us that sociology should be a partisan project, not disengaged contemplation or sheer technique. This model of engagement was born of the 1960s and in turn gave birth to the 1960s—its social movements and new sensibilities. This model of engagement also inculcated an intellectual sensibility dedicated to merging theory and practice, resonating with Marx and Engels's eleventh thesis on Feuerbach, where they argue that intellectual work should not only understand the world but also try to change it. This post-1960s generation of graduate students and young academics migrated into academia and began to occupy university faculty positions, as Jacoby documents in *The Last Intellectuals* (1987). This is my generation, and his. Unfortunately, this "academization" caused our own discourse to decline (see Agger 1990) as we lost the ability to be public intellectuals, writing accessible but pointed prose directed at an audience beyond the academy. Thus, academization became an occupational hazard for former New Leftists who learned critical theory and postmodernism in order to understand the turmoil of that tumultuous decade better.

Jacoby argues that ex–New Leftists who entered the university needed to restrict the codes of their writing in order to get published and, hence, tenured. Where Mills and Hayden wrote for millions, left-wing academics write for thousands and perhaps even only hundreds (given the restricted print runs of most academic books and monographs). This changes things for the Left, cutting it off from the body politic and reinforcing obscurantism—the practiced attempt to be obscure in one's writing! Although Adorno and his Frankfurt School colleagues were careful literary craftspeople and their sentences packed a dialectical punch, full of double entendres, circumspection, and doubling back and forward, Adorno is a difficult read for people who lack his enormous philosophical erudition. And Adorno was probably Jacoby's favorite philosopher and social theorist.

This is why New Left metaphors need to be tempered with the realization that Mills and Hayden were not writing for publication (although they both published). Nor were they writing for tenure (although Mills held it at Columbia University). They were writing *agitationally,* to enlighten, edify, enrage, and energize. These passions are lacking in the work products of contemporary sociologists who take it for granted that their codes will be restricted (see Bernstein 1975) and that their postures must appear cool and distant, objective and professional. In leaving behind the 1960s as a stain on sociological objectivity and hence legitimacy, contemporary sociologists also leave behind Marx (both early and late), Mills, and the SDS, all of whom both urged and exemplified the merging of theory and practice.

Positivists are not alone in stepping back from the theory/practice unity. Postmodernists, too, embrace detached irony as the appropriate stance of the world-weary intellectual who risks committing the sin of pride, hubris, that has gotten us into so much trouble since the Enlightenment. Adorno and Derrida shared a mistrust of what Adorno called "identity theory"—thought, including both dogmatic science and dogmatic theory, that pretends that its concepts and methods completely exhaust or represent the object world out there. Instead, Adorno indicates that there is an "indissoluble something" that concepts can never quite capture, a region of what Derrida calls "undecidability," the elusiveness of concepts and categories that refuse to be pinned down and completely drained of ambiguity and what he calls deferral—postponing the resolution of their quandaries of meaning until the future, when, presumably, all will become clear. Thus, the critique of positivism is owed to both critical theory and postmodernism, and it springs from the realization that some of the greatest atrocities have been committed in the name of absolute truth.

However, this critique of positive knowledge, math, and method need not lead to the sheer abandonment of truth and reason, as Lyotard, Jean Baudrillard, and other postmodernists seem to advocate. Critical theory (from Germany) and postmodernism (from France) have been sundered by both Lyotard (1984) and Habermas (1987a), losing the utopian and radical edge of postmodern theory that thinks and acts progressively on the boundary of positivist truth and reason. Foucault and Derrida were clearly on the side of left-wing progressive moments, and they participated in these movements as early as the 1960s and as recently as the 1980s and 1990s. But later postmodern theorists (Stanley Fish comes to mind) erect barriers and opposition between German and French versions of critique in the conviction that Marxism itself is a major part of the problems of hubris and authoritarianism.

This depends on whether one reads Marx (see Althusser 1970) as having implications for contemporary post-Fordist capitalism which has introduced the post-Marxist elements of the welfare state (O'Connor 1973 and Mandel 1978) and culture industry (Horkheimer and Adorno 1972).

Positivism and a quiescent version of postmodernism agree that left-wing thought and practice have become anachronistic in this age of the triumph of method and technique (for positivists) and the eclipse of grand narratives of liberation (for postmodernists). These scholars are not pursuing the next left, having consigned the New Left to the dustbin of social and intellectual history, which is an easy task once we consider the narcissism and social irrelevance of Sergeant Pepper and Woodstock and the unraveling of the SDS into the Weather Underground.

In a recent interview for my forthcoming book on "the 1960s at forty," Tom Hayden told me that he thought it was gratuitous to criticize Weatherman for its rather opportunistic and untheorized approach to late-1960s social change. He emphasized how defeated and depleted were the forces of the New Left by the time of Chicago and Columbia, as the Right gathered momentum. In discussing the history of the Left generally, Jacoby (1981) characterizes this tendency for the Left to lose as "the dialectic of defeat." Just because the Left has a righteous cause doesn't mean that it will always, or often, triumph. It is "Left" because the Right has captured the dominant middle; it is positioned and positions itself as the initially weaker and more disorganized force, even if, as a Hegelian Marxist would maintain, it has world-historical powers on its side, notably the power of a vast global majority of the powerless.

In examining the post-1970s history of American sociology, as well as American society generally, it is difficult to escape the impression that sociological liberals have jumped on the neoconservative bandwagon for reasons made clear in Adorno, Frenkel-Brunswik, Levinson, and Sanford's *Authoritarian Personality* (1950). They want to belong and to be on the winning side. The mathematization of the discipline in face of the defeat of the Left by the end of the 1960s was cowardly, capitulating to and hence accelerating trends such as the privatization of the corporate university. Sociologists should have stood their ground and not buried themselves in a methodologically oriented sense of disciplinary identity—"real" sociology demarcated from its imposter politically partisan versions—in order to buttress their departments, graduate programs, and grant opportunities in a political climate in which administrators and politicians blamed sociologists for the turmoil of the 1960s. After all, Mills was a sociologist, and Hayden studied him closely. Also, Dick Flacks, one of Hayden's closest confidants and a major figure in the Port Huron–era SDS, was and still is a practicing sociologist (working at the University of California–Santa Barbara).

Sociology during the 1960s was the most exciting place to be for students and faculty seeking answers to questions about social justice and social change. Today, politically and theoretically minded students are more likely to pursue studies in English and other humanities disciplines, where they can take courses and write theses on cultural studies, women's studies, post-colonial studies, and queer studies. In a curious reversal, English has become a protosociology discipline, with a decidedly theoretical bent, and sociology has become a protomathematics discipline. These disciplines recruit different sorts of students and younger faculty. The sociology initiates are more likely to be working-class, pragmatic, and oriented to an engineering view of the world and to possess little cultural capital. The English initiates are more likely to be middle- or upper-middle class, speculative and theoretical, and oriented to a humanistic view of the world and to possess significant cultural capital. These are basically class differences. Sociology has become a discipline of men (and women) in plaid, while English and related cultural fields have become disciplines of people who wear black. Were these generations transported back in time to Port Huron and Chicago, the hip English students and faculty would probably take the places of Mills, Hayden, and Flacks, and the sociology students might be the ones registering for the draft, holding onto their draft cards, and even fighting to keep university campuses free of outside agitators.

Returning to the 1960s as a model for an engaged sociology, a sociology patterned on Mills and Hayden and their political involvements, is ironic because it is those very 1960s engagements that scandalized the sober post-1970s discipline and moved it (back) toward science and method. The 1960s need to be reclaimed by the next New Left for their tremendous energy and vision as well as for their striking political gains, which changed the face of America for the better. This is not an exercise in nostalgia, although it is important to view the 1960s realistically and with a profound sense of gratitude for the gains accomplished. We must reclaim the 1960s for sociology so that sociology can be in the vanguard of the next New Left, refusing to remain the dismal science it has become since the hegemony of method was sealed during and after the 1970s.

A public sociology modeled on Port Huron's participatory democracy and New Left politics and organization would not fixate on method but would allow a hundred methodologies to bloom, including those from the humanities and interdisciplinary projects such as cultural studies. It would retain from Marx the merger of theory and practice—the eleventh thesis. And it would compose itself accessibly, trying to reach a broad audience. It would reach out to students not because teaching balances single-minded research agendas but because students have proven themselves to be a pivotal social agent, and they could become so again. Teaching should be dialogical, democratic, didactic if necessary. It should mobilize, energize, and inspire. One of the major insights of the Port Huron generation is that young people armed with concepts, energy, and passion can change the world. Academic administrators, fearing backlash from publics and politicians, want teaching to matter for all the wrong reasons. Teaching should matter because students do. Students, like our own children, are prisms through which we understand ourselves better. They also model democracy and play in ways that most sociologists have forgotten. Children are utopian agents, as they proved during the 1960s (see Agger and Shelton 2006).

During the seven years since the first edition of this book was published, suicide bombers crashed planes into the World Trade Center and the Pentagon, killing themselves and a few thousand others. In retaliation, the United States invaded Iraq, the wrong country. George W. Bush won reelection and the Christian Right—the New Wrong—dominates the American political agenda. The American Sociological Association passed a resolution (with a significant number of dissenters) against the war in Iraq. The 2004 annual meeting of the ASA was held under the banner of public sociology, which has become a rallying cry. And yet the mainstream journals and graduate departments are much the same as they were at the end of the last millennium. Students, although supportive of Kerry, the Democratic candidate for president, stayed away from the polls. Although there has been talk of reinstituting the draft, no political party wants that blame and no one (except the next New Left) wants the political consequences of radicalized youth.

During the 1960s the draft mobilized the young, who moved from draft protest to draft resistance, not only disrupting the American war machine but also drawing attention to the war's lack of popularity and to internal strife. Without the draft today, what can mobilize the young? Sexual McCarthyism is one possible answer. In particular, the Right's attack on gays and lesbians (think of the national drive to ban gay and lesbian marriage) and on women and their bodies (think of reproductive rights and abortion) could become the basis of a *sexual-political civil rights movement*. Gays and women are being "Othered" by the New Wrong, and this could provoke the type of mass resistance seen during the 1960s. College students are liberal, especially about issues of sexual politics. Although they don't identify themselves as particularly feminist, a term they view as an archaic remnant from a fractious and out-there radical 1960s, they are tolerant and even supportive of same-sex coupling and various nonmainstream sexual choices. They also support a woman's right to control her body, particularly abortion rights. The New Wrong's attack on gays and women could become the leverage for a new social movement designed to promote sexual-political civil rights, striking to the heart of the Right's repressive view of the family and of bodies. Queer studies within (e.g., Seidman 1997) and beyond (Sedgwick 1990) sociology could become a point of leverage for a new critical theory and social movement that addresses sexual politics as a moment of a larger critique of domination.

In this post-9/11 context, positivist sociology seems to be beside the point. It is self-referential, self-reproducing, and technical. Sociologists on the fringes of the discipline and protosociologists beyond the discipline reject the intellectual monolith of method and mathematics. They neither read the leading journals nor submit their work to them. Mainstream sociology is like the gas-powered automobile: It dominates the road today, and it will probably still dominate the road ten years from now, although there will be more hybrids inching along. But fifty years from now, scientific sociology, like the gas-powered car, will be a relic of a distant past. There will be many methods, literary styles, and political engagements, all traveling down the road in their own sweet time.

Image: Frances Fox Piven is a young faculty member at Columbia. The year is 1968, and the SDS's action faction, led by Mark Rudd, has taken over several administrative buildings in the university, protesting the university's plan to build a swimming pool on Columbia property in Harlem. Piven is being assisted by Tom Hayden as she climbs through a window to join the student protest and occupation of university buildings. (Her daughter is also perched in the window sill, which opens into the Math Building.) Today, Piven is president-elect of the ASA. She doesn't turn her back on the 1960s, and one hopes that she will appreciate the 1960s at forty as a critical intellectual and political resource today, as she steers the ASA away from the religion of science and toward the type of public engagement that she, Rudd, Hayden, and the other Columbia activists demonstrated nearly four decades ago. With the Bush gang in the White House, with an ascendant New Wrong that has mobilized evangelical citizens from middle America, with the quagmires of Iraq and Afghanistan, with a naked corporate agenda among the executive committee of the bourgeoisie, and with global inequalities that fester and become malignant, there is no reason why young and older Americans cannot mobilize around images of participatory democracy (perhaps now with a cyber component) and social justice. A public sociology can provide analysis and energy for this incipient movement, much as it did during the 1960s, when Paul Potter of the SDS urged people at a major 1965 demonstration in Washington, D.C., to name and analyze the system that oppresses them. No less is needed today.

Metaphor: Piven climbing into the Columbia building, to occupy it in solidarity with the students. Today, Piven seeks to occupy the house of sociology and to transform it. Hayden assisted her in 1968, and he can do so again if we take from him, Flacks, Mills, early Marx, and the civil rights movement an agenda for the next Left.

# Bibliography

Aaron, Jane, and Walby, Sylvia, eds. 1991. *Out of the Margins: Women's Studies in the Nineties.* London: Falmer.

Ackerman, Bruce. 1980. *Social Justice in the Liberal State.* New Haven, Conn.: Yale University Press.

Adam, Barry. 1995. *The Rise of a Gay and Lesbian Movement.* Revised edition. New York: Twayne.

Adorno, Theodor W. 1945. "A Social Critique of Radio Music." *Kenyon Review* 9:208–17.

———. 1954. "How to Look at Television." *Quarterly of Film, Radio and Television* 3:213–35.

———. 1973a. *Negative Dialectics.* New York: Seabury.

———. 1973b. *Philosophy of Modern Music.* New York: Seabury.

———. 1978. *Minima Moralia.* London: Verso.

———. 1984. *Aesthetic Theory.* London: Routledge and Kegan Paul.

Adorno, Theodor W., Else Frenkel-Brunswik, Daniel Levinson, and R. N. Sanford. 1950. *The Authoritarian Personality.* New York: Harper.

Agger, Ben. 1976. "Marcuse and Habermas on New Science." *Polity* 9:151–81.

———. 1979. *Western Marxism: An Introduction.* Santa Monica, Calif.: Goodyear.

———. 1989a. *Fast Capitalism: A Critical Theory of Significance.* Urbana: University of Illinois Press.

———. 1989b. *Reading Science: A Literary, Political, and Sociological Analysis.* Dix Hills, N.Y.: General Hall.

———. 1989c. *Socio(onto)logy: A Disciplinary Reading.* Urbana: University of Illinois Press.

———. 1990. *Decline of Discourse: Reading, Writing, and Resistance in Postmodern Capitalism.* London: Falmer.

———. 1991. "Critical Theory, Poststructuralism, Postmodernism: Their Sociological Relevance." *Annual Review of Sociology* 17:105–31.

———. 1992a. *Cultural Studies as Critical Theory.* London: Falmer.

———. 1992b. *The Discourse of Domination: From the Frankfurt School to Postmodernism.* Evanston, Ill.: Northwestern University Press.

———. 1993. *Gender, Culture, and Power: Toward a Feminist Postmodern Critical Theory.* Westport, Conn.: Praeger.

———. 1994a. "Derrida for Sociology?" *American Sociological Review* 59:501–5.

———. 1994b. "Marcuse in Postmodernity." In *Marcuse: From the New Left to the Next Left*, edited by John Bokina and Timothy J. Lukes. Lawrence: University Press of Kansas.

———. 1996. "Postponing the Postmodern." *Cultural Studies* 1:37–46.

———. 2000. *Public Sociology: From Social Facts to Literary Acts.* Lanham, Md.: Rowman & Littlefield.

———. 2002. *Postponing the Postmodern: Sociological Practices, Selves, and Theories.* Lanham, Md.: Rowman & Littlefield.

———. Forthcoming. *The Sixties at Forty: Generation and Identity among Sixties People.* Boulder, Colo.: Paradigm.

Agger, Ben, and Beth Anne Shelton. 2006. *Fast Families, Virtual Children: A Critical Sociology of the Family.* Boulder, Colo.: Paradigm.

Alexander, Jeffrey C. 1982. *Theoretical Logic in Sociology.* Vols. 1–4. Berkeley: University of California Press.

———. 1985. *Neofunctionalism.* Beverly Hills, Calif.: Sage.

Alexander, Jeffrey C., Bernhard Giesen, Richard Munch, and Neil J. Smelser. 1987. *The Micro-Macro Link.* Berkeley: University of California Press.

Alexander, Jeffrey C., and Steven Seidman, eds. 1990. *Culture and Society: Contemporary Debates.* New York: Cambridge University Press.

Althusser, Louis. 1970. *For Marx.* London: Allen Lane.

Anzaldua, Gloria. 1987. *Borderlands: The New Mestiza = La Frontera.* San Francisco: Spinsters/Aunt Lute.

———, ed. 1990. *Making Face, Making Soul = Haciendo Caras: Creative and Critical Perspectives by Women of Color.* San Francisco: Aunt Lute.

Apel, Karl Otto. 1980. *Towards a Transformation of Philosophy.* London: Routledge and Kegan Paul.

Apple, Michael. 1979. *Ideology and Curriculum.* London: Routledge and Kegan Paul.

———. 1982. *Cultural and Economic Reproduction in Education.* London: Routledge and Kegan Paul.

———. 1996. *Cultural Politics and Education.* New York: Teachers College Press.

Arendt, Hannah. 1958. *The Human Condition.* Chicago: University of Chicago Press.

Aronowitz, Stanley. 1981. *Class, Politics, and Culture in Marxist Theory.* New York: Praeger.

———. 1988. *Science as Power: Discourse and Ideology in Modern Society.* Minneapolis: University of Minnesota Press.

———. 1990. *The Crisis in Historical Materialism.* 2nd ed. Minneapolis: University of Minnesota Press.

———. 1992. *The Politics of Identity: Class, Culture, Social Movements.* New York: Routledge.

———. 1993. *Roll Over Beethoven: The Return of Cultural Strife.* Hanover, N.H.: Wesleyan University Press.

———. 1994. *Dead Artists, Live Theories, and Other Cultural Problems.* New York: Routledge.

Aronowitz, Stanley, and Henry Giroux. 1985. *Education under Siege.* South Hadley, Mass.: Bergin and Garvey.

Ashley, David. 1997. *History without a Subject: The Postmodern Condition.* Boulder, Colo.: Westview.

Atkinson, Ti-Grace. 1974. *Amazon Odyssey.* New York: Links Books.

Ayers, Bill. 2001. *Fugitive Days: A Memoir.* Boston: Beacon.

Bakhtin, Mikhail. 1978. *The Formal Method in Literary Scholarship: A Critical Introduction to Sociological Poetics.* Baltimore: Johns Hopkins University Press.

———. 1994. *The Bakhtin Reader.* Edited by Pam Morris. London: E. Arnold.

Barthes, Roland. 1975. *The Pleasure of the Text.* New York: Hill and Wang.

Baudrillard, Jean. 1981. *For a Critique of the Political Economy of the Sign.* St. Louis: Telos Press.

———. 1983. *Simulations.* New York: Semiotext(e).

———. 1988. *America.* London: Verso.

Beauvoir, Simone de. 1953. *The Second Sex.* New York: Knopf.

Becker, Gary. 1976. *The Economic Approach to Human Behavior.* Chicago: University of Chicago Press.

———. 1980. *Human Capital: A Theoretical and Empirical Analysis.* 2nd ed. Chicago: University of Chicago Press.

———. 1981. *A Treatise on the Family.* Cambridge, Mass.: Harvard University Press.

———. 1996. *Accounting for Taste.* Cambridge, Mass.: Harvard University Press.

Becker, Howard. 1963. *The Outsiders: Studies in the Sociology of Deviance.* New York: Free Press.

———. 1986. *Writing for Social Scientists.* Chicago: University of Chicago Press.

Behar, Ruth, and Deborah A. Gordon, eds. 1995. *Women Writing Culture.* Berkeley: University of California Press.

Bell, Daniel. 1960. *The End of Ideology.* Glencoe, Ill.: Free Press.

———. 1973. *The Coming of Post-Industrial Society.* New York: Basic.

Benhabib, Seyla. 1987. *Critique, Norm, and Utopia.* New York: Columbia University Press.

———. 1992. *Situating the Self: Gender, Community, and Postmodernism in Contemporary Ethics.* New York: Routledge.

Benjamin, Jessica. 1988. *The Bonds of Love: Psychoanalysis, Feminism, and the Problem of Domination.* New York: Pantheon.

Benjamin, Walter. 1969. *Illuminations.* New York: Schocken.

Berger, Peter. 1963. *Invitation to Sociology.* Garden City, N.Y.: Doubleday.

Berman, Marshall. 1982. *All That Is Solid Melts into Air.* New York: Simon and Schuster.

Bernard, Jessie. 1972. *The Future of Marriage.* New York: World Publishers.

———. 1981. *The Female World.* New York: Free Press.

Bernstein, Basil. 1975. *Class, Codes, and Control.* New York: Schocken.

Best, Steven, and Douglas Kellner. 1988a. "(Re)Watching Television: Notes Toward a Political Criticism." *Diacritics* 17:97–13.

———. 1988b. "Watching Television: The Limits of Postmodernism." *Science as Culture* 4:44–70.

———. 1991. *Postmodern Theory: Critical Interrogations.* New York: Guilford.

Blau, Peter, and Otis Dudley Duncan. 1967. *The American Occupational Structure.* New York: Wiley.

Bloom, Allan. 1987. *The Closing of the American Mind.* New York: Simon and Schuster.

Blum, Alan. 1974. *Theorizing.* London: Heinemann.

Blumstein, Philip, and Pepper Schwartz. 1983. *American Couples: Money, Work, Sex.* New York: Pocket Books.

Boggs, Carl. 1986. *Social Movements and Political Power: Emerging Forms of Radicalism in the West.* Philadelphia: Temple University Press.

Bose, Christine. 1985. *Jobs and Gender: Sex and Occupation.* New York: Praeger.

Bottomore, Tom. 1978. *Austro-Marxism.* Oxford: Clarendon.

Bourdieu, Pierre. 1977. *Outline of a Theory of Practice.* Cambridge, UK: Cambridge University Press.

———. 1984. *Distinction: A Social Critique of the Judgment of Taste.* Cambridge, Mass.: Harvard University Press.

———. 1988. *Homo Academicus.* Stanford, Calif.: Stanford University Press.

Bourdieu, Pierre, Jean-Claude Passeron, and Monique de Saint Martin. 1994. *Academic Discourse: Linguistic Misunderstanding and Professorial Power.* Stanford, Calif.: Stanford University Press.

Bourdieu, Pierre, and Loïc W. D. Wacquant. 1992. *An Invitation to Reflexive Sociology.* Chicago: University of Chicago Press.

Bowles, Samuel, and Herbert Gintis. 1976. *Schooling in Capitalist America.* New York: Basic.

Breines, Paul. 1970. *Critical Interruptions.* New York: Herder and Herder.

———. 1994. "Revisiting Marcuse with Foucault: *An Essay on Liberation* Meets *The History of Sexuality.*" In *Marcuse: From the New Left to the Next Left,* edited by John Bokina and Timothy J. Lukes. Lawrence: University Press of Kansas.

Breines, Wini. 1982. *Community and Organization in the New Left, 1962–68.* New York: Praeger.

———. 1992. *Young, White and Miserable: Growing Up Female in the Fifties.* Boston: Beacon.

Brodribb, Somer. 1992. *Nothing Mat(t)ers: A Feminist Critique of Postmodernism.* North Melbourne, Australia: Spinifex Press.

Brown, Richard. 1987. *Society as Text.* Chicago: University of Chicago Press.

Browne, Ray. 1989. *Against Academia: The History of the Popular Culture Association, 1967–88.* Bowling Green, Ky.: Bowling Green University Press.

Brownmiller, Susan. 1975. *Against Our Will: Men, Women, and Rape.* New York: Simon and Schuster.

Burawoy, Michael. 2005. "For Public Sociology." *American Sociological Review* 70:4–28.

Butler, Judith. 1990. *Gender Trouble: Feminism and the Subversion of Identity.* New York: Routledge.

Caesar, Terry. 1992. *Conspiring with Forms: Life in Academic Texts.* Athens: University of Georgia Press.

Callari, Antonio, and David Ruccio, eds. 1996. *Postmodern Materialism and the Future of Marxist Theory.* Hanover, N.H.: Wesleyan University Press.

Camic, Charles. 1987. "The Making of a Method: A Historical Reinterpretation of the Early Parsons." *American Sociological Review* 52:421–39.

Carver, Terrell, and Paul Thomas, eds. 1995. *Rational Choice Marxism.* Basingstoke, UK: Macmillan.

Castoriadis, Cornelius. 1984. *Crossroads in the Labyrinth*. Cambridge, Mass.: MIT Press.

———. 1987. *The Imaginary Institution of Society*. Cambridge, Mass.: Polity.

Chodorow, Nancy. 1978. *The Reproduction of Mothering*. Berkeley: University of California Press.

Cixous, Hélène. 1986. *Inside*. New York: Schocken.

———. 1988. *Writing Difference: Readings from the Seminar of Hélène Cixous*. Milton Keynes, UK: Open University Press.

Clough, Patricia. 1992. *The End(s) of Ethnography*. Newbury Park, Calif.: Sage.

———. 1994. *Feminist Thought*. Cambridge, UK: Blackwell.

Coleman, James S. 1990. *Foundations of Social Theory*. Cambridge, Mass.: Harvard University Press.

Coleman, James S., and Thomas J. Fararo, eds. 1992. *Rational Choice Theory: Advocacy and Critique*. Newbury Park, Calif.: Sage.

Colletti, Lucio. 1973. *Marxism and Hegel*. London: New Left Books.

Collins, Patricia Hill. 1991. *Black Feminist Thought*. New York: Routledge.

Comte, Auguste. 1975. *Auguste Comte and Positivism*. New York: Harper and Row.

Connell, Robert. 1987. *Gender and Power: Society, the Person, and Sexual Politics*. Cambridge, Mass.: Polity.

Cooper, R., and G. Burrell. 1988. "Modernism, Postmodernism, and Organizational Analysis: An Introduction." *Organizational Studies* 9:91–112.

Culler, Jonathan. 1982. *On Deconstruction*. Ithaca, N.Y.: Cornell University Press.

Dahrendorf, Ralf. 1968. *Essays in the Theory of Society*. Stanford, Calif.: Stanford University Press.

Dalla Costa, Mariarosa, and Selma James. 1973. *The Power of Women and the Subversion of the Community*. Bristol, UK: Falling Wall Press.

Delphy, Christine. 1984. *Close to Home: A Materialist Analysis of Women's Oppression*. London: Hutchinson.

de Man, Paul. 1986. *The Resistance to Theory*. Minneapolis: University of Minnesota Press.

Denzin, Norman. 1986. "Postmodern Social Theory." *Sociological Theory* 4: 194–204.

———. 1989. *Film and the American Alcoholic*. New York: Aldine De Gruyter.

———. 1990. "Reading Cultural Texts." *American Journal of Sociology* 95:1577–80.

———. 1991a. "Empiricist Cultural Studies in America: A Deconstructive Reading." *Current Perspectives in Social Theory* 11:17–39.

———. 1991b. *Hollywood Shot by Shot: Alcoholism in American Cinema*. New York: Aldine de Gruyter.

———. 1991c. *Images of Postmodern Society: Social Theory and Contemporary Cinema*. London: Sage.

———. 1992. *Symbolic Interactionism and Cultural Studies*. New York: Blackwell.

———. 1994. "Deconstructionism and Postmodernism." In *Postmodernism and Social Inquiry*, edited by David Dickens and Andrea Fontana. New York: Guilford.

———. 1995. *The Cinematic Society: The Voyeur's Gaze*. London: Sage.

Derrida, Jacques. 1973. *Speech and Phenomena*. Evanston, Ill.: Northwestern University Press.

——. 1976. *Of Grammatology*. Baltimore: Johns Hopkins University Press.

——. 1978. *Writing and Difference*. Chicago: University of Chicago Press.

——. 1981. *Positions*. Chicago: University of Chicago Press.

——. 1982. *Margins of Philosophy*. Chicago: University of Chicago Press.

——. 1986. *Memoires: For Paul de Man*. New York: Columbia University Press.

——. 1988. *The Ear of the Other*. Lincoln: University of Nebraska Press.

——. 1994. *Specters of Marx*. New York: Routledge.

Dews, Peter. 1984. "Power and Subjectivity in Foucault." *New Left Review* 144:72–95.

——. 1987. *Logics of Disintegration: Post-Structuralist Thought and the Claims of Critical Theory*. London: Verso.

Diesing, Paul. 1982. *Science and Ideology in the Policy Sciences*. Hawthorne, N.Y.: Aldine.

——. 1991. *How Does Social Science Work? Reflections on Practice*. Pittsburgh: Pittsburgh University Press.

Di Stefano, Christine. 1991. *Configurations of Masculinity: A Feminist Perspective on Modern Political Theory*. Ithaca, N.Y.: Cornell University Press.

Donovan, Josephine. 1985. *Feminist Theory*. New York: Ungar.

D'Souza, Dinesh. 1991. *Illiberal Education: The Politics of Race and Sex on Campus*. New York: Free Press.

Durkheim, Emile. 1950. *Rules of Sociological Method*. Glencoe, Ill.: Free Press.

——. 1956. *The Division of Labor in Society*. Glencoe, Ill.: Free Press.

Dworkin, Andrea. 1974. *Woman Hating*. New York: Dutton.

Eagleton, Terry. 1983. *Literary Theory: An Introduction*. Minneapolis: University of Minnesota Press.

——. 1990. *The Significance of Theory*. Cambridge, UK: Blackwell.

——. 2003. *After Theory*. London: Allen Lane.

Ehrenreich, Barbara. 1983. *The Hearts of Men: American Dreams and the Flight from Commitment*. Garden City, N.Y.: Anchor/Doubleday.

Eisenstein, Zillah, ed. 1979. *Capitalist Patriarchy and the Case for Socialist Feminism*. New York: Monthly Review Press.

Elshtain, Jean Bethke. 1981. *Public Man, Private Woman: Women in Social and Political Thought*. Princeton, N.J.: Princeton University Press.

Elster, Jon. 1986. *Foundations of Social Choice Theory*. New York: Cambridge University Press.

Engels, Friedrich. 1972. *The Origin of the Family, Private Property, and the State*. New York: Pathfinder.

England, Paula, ed. 1993. *Theory on Gender/Feminism on Theory*. New York: Aldine de Gruyter.

England, Paula, and George Farkas. 1986. *Households, Employment, and Gender: A Social, Economic, and Demographic View*. New York: Aldine.

Evans, Sara. 1979. *Personal Politics: The Roots of Women's Liberation in the Civil Rights Movement and the New Left*. New York: Vintage.

Ewen, Stuart. 1976. *Captains of Consciousness: Advertising and the Social Roots of the Consumer Culture*. New York: McGraw-Hill.

Faludi, Susan. 1991. *Backlash: The Undeclared War against American Women*. New York: Crown.

Fay, Brian. 1987. *Critical Social Science: Liberation and Its Limits*. Ithaca, N.Y.: Cornell University Press.

Feagin, Joe. 1975. *Subordinating the Poor: Welfare and American Beliefs*. Englewood Cliffs, N.J.: Prentice-Hall.

———. 2005. Private correspondence. May.

Feagin, Joe, and Harlan Hahn. 1973. *Ghetto Revolts: The Politics of Violence in American Cities*. New York: Macmillan.

Feagin, Joe, and Melvin Sikes. 1994. *Living with Racism: The Black Middle-Class Experience*. Boston: Beacon.

Feagin, Joe, Charles Tilly, and Constance Williams. 1972. *Subsidizing the Poor*. Lexington, Mass.: Lexington.

Feagin, Joe, and Herman Vera. 1995. *White Racism: The Basics*. New York: Routledge.

Featherman, David, and Robert Hauser. 1978. *Opportunity and Change*. New York: Academic.

Featherstone, Mike. 1991. *Consumer Culture and Postmodernism*. London: Sage.

Fekete, John. 1978. *The Critical Twilight: Explorations in the Ideology of Anglo-American Literary Theory from Eliot to McLuhan*. London: Routledge and Kegan Paul.

Feyerabend, Paul. 1975. *Against Method: Outline of an Anarchistic Theory of Knowledge*. London: New Left Books.

Fine, Gary Alan. 1995. *A Second Chicago School? The Development of a Postwar American Sociology*. Chicago: University of Chicago Press.

Firestone, Shulamith. 1979. *The Dialectic of Sex*. New York: Morrow.

Fish, Stanley. 1989. *Doing What Comes Naturally*. Durham, N.C.: Duke University Press.

———. 1995. *Professional Correctness: Literary Studies and Political Change*. New York: Clarendon Press.

Fiske, John. 1982. *Introduction to Communication Studies*. New York: Methuen.

———. 1987. *Television Culture*. New York: Methuen.

Fjellman, Stephen. 1992. *Vinyl Leaves: Walt Disney World and America*. Boulder, Colo.: Westview.

Flax, Jane. 1990. *Thinking Fragments: Psychoanalysis, Feminism, and Postmodernism in the Contemporary West*. Berkeley: University of California Press.

Foucault, Michel. 1972. *The Archaeology of Knowledge*. New York: Pantheon.

———. 1977. *Discipline and Punish: The Birth of the Prison*. New York: Pantheon.

———. 1978. *The History of Sexuality*. New York: Pantheon.

———. 1980. *Power/Knowledge*. New York: Pantheon.

Fraser, Nancy. 1984. "The French Derrideans: Politicizing Deconstruction or Deconstructing Politics." *New German Critique* 33:127–54.

———. 1989. *Unruly Practices: Power, Discourse, and Gender in Contemporary Social Theory*. Minneapolis: University of Minnesota Press.

Freire, Paulo. 1970. *Pedagogy of the Oppressed*. New York: Seabury.

Friedan, Betty. 1963. *The Feminine Mystique*. New York: Norton.

Friedman, Debra, and Carol Diem. 1993. "Feminism and the Pro-(Rational) Choice Movement: Rational Choice Theory, Feminist Critiques, and Gender In-equality." In *Theory on Gender/Feminism on Theory*, edited by Paula England. New York: Aldine de Gruyter.

Friedrichs, Robert. 1970. *A Sociology of Sociology.* New York: Free Press.

Frith, Simon. 1983. *Sound Effects.* London: Constable.

Fukuyama, Francis. 1992. *The End of History and the Last Man.* New York: Free Press.

Fuss, Diana, ed. 1991. *Inside/Out: Lesbian Theories, Gay Theories.* New York: Routledge.

Gadamer, Hans-Georg. 1975. *Truth and Method.* Evanston, Ill.: Northwestern University Press.

Game, Ann. 1991. *Undoing the Social: Towards a Deconstructive Sociology.* Milton Keynes, UK: Open University Press.

Garfinkel, Harold. 1967. *Studies in Ethnomethodology.* Englewood Cliffs, N.J.: Prentice-Hall.

Gates, Henry Louis, Jr., and Cornel West. 1996. *The Future of the Race.* New York: Knopf.

Gellner, Ernest. 1959. *Words and Things.* London: Gollancz.

Gerstel, Naomi, and Harriet Engels Gross, eds. 1987. *Families and Work.* Philadelphia: Temple University Press.

Giddens, Anthony. 1972. *Politics and Sociology in the Thought of Max Weber.* London: Macmillan.

———. 1984. *The Constitution of Society: Outline of the Theory of Structuration.* Berkeley: University of California Press.

Gilligan, Carol. 1982. *In a Different Voice.* Cambridge, Mass.: Harvard University Press.

Giroux, Henry. 1981. *Ideology, Culture, and the Process of Schooling.* Philadelphia: Temple University Press.

———. 1994. *Disturbing Pleasures: Learning Popular Culture.* New York: Routledge.

Giroux, Henry, and Peter L. McLaren. 1989. *Critical Pedagogy, the State, and Cultural Struggle.* Albany: SUNY Press.

Gitlin, Todd. 1987. *The Sixties: Years of Hope, Days of Rage.* New York: Bantam.

———. 2003. *The Whole World Is Watching: Mass Media in the Making and Unmaking of the New Left.* Berkeley: University of California Press.

Goffman, Erving. 1959. *The Presentation of Self in Everyday Life.* New York: Doubleday.

———. 1974. *Frame Analysis: An Essay on the Organization of Experience.* New York: Harper and Row.

Goldman, Robert. 1992. *Reading Ads Socially.* London: Routledge Chapman Hall.

Goldman, Robert, and Stephen Papson. 1991. "Levi's and the Knowing Wink." *Current Perspectives in Social Theory* 11:69–95.

———. 1994. "The Postmodernism That Failed." In *Postmodernism and Social Inquiry*, edited by David Dickens and Andrea Fontana. New York: Guilford.

———. 1995. *Sign Wars: The Cluttered Landscape of Advertising.* New York: Guilford.

Goldmann, Lucien. 1964. *The Hidden God: A Study of the Tragic Vision in the Pensées of Pascal and the Tragedies of Racine*. New York: Humanities Press.

———. 1972. *Racine*. Cambridge: Rivers Press.

———. 1975. *Towards a Sociology of the Novel*. London: Tavistock.

———. 1976. *Cultural Creation in Modern Society*. St. Louis: Telos Press.

———. 1981. *Method in the Sociology of Literature*. Oxford: Blackwell.

Goodson, Ivor. 1988. *The Making of Curriculum*. London: Falmer.

Gouldner, Alvin W. 1970. *The Coming Crisis of Western Sociology*. New York: Basic.

———. 1976. *The Dialectic of Ideology and Technology: The Origins, Grammar, and Future of Ideology*. New York: Seabury.

———. 1979. *The Future of Intellectuals and the Rise of the New Class*. New York: Seabury.

———. 1980. *The Two Marxisms: Contradictions and Anomalies in the Development of Theory*. New York: Seabury.

Graff, Gerald. 1992. *Beyond the Culture Wars: How Teaching the Conflicts Can Revitalize American Education*. New York: Norton.

Gramsci, Antonio. 1971. *Selections from the Prison Notebooks*. London: Lawrence and Wishart.

Green, Donald P., and Ian Shapiro. 1994. *Pathologies of Rational Choice Theory*. New Haven, Conn.: Yale University Press.

Greer, Germaine. 1971. *The Female Eunuch*. New York: McGraw-Hill.

Griswold, Wendy. 1986. *Renaissance Revivals: City Comedy and Revenge Tragedy in the London Theatre*. Chicago: University of Chicago Press.

———. 1994. *Cultures and Societies in a Changing World*. Thousand Oaks, Calif.: Pine Forge.

Grossberg, Lawrence. 1992. *We Gotta Get Out of This Place: Popular Conservatism and Postmodern Culture*. New York: Routledge.

Grossberg, Lawrence, Cary Nelson, and Paula Treichler, eds. 1992. *Cultural Studies*. New York: Routledge.

Habermas, Jürgen. 1971. *Knowledge and Human Interests*. Boston: Beacon.

———. 1975. *Legitimation Crisis*. Boston: Beacon.

———. 1979. *Communication and the Evolution of Society*. Boston: Beacon.

———. 1981a. "Modernity Versus Postmodernity." *New German Critique* 22: 3–14.

———. 1981b. "New Social Movements." *Telos* 49:33–37.

———. 1984. *Theory of Communicative Action*. Volume 1. Boston: Beacon.

———. 1987a. *The Philosophical Discourse of Modernity*. Cambridge, Mass.: MIT Press.

———. 1987b. *Theory of Communicative Action*. Volume 2. Boston: Beacon.

———. 1992. *Postmetaphysical Thinking*. Cambridge, Mass.: MIT Press.

———. 1996. *Between Facts and Norms*. Cambridge, Mass.: Polity.

Hall, Stuart. 1978. *Policing the Crisis: Muggery, the State, and Law and Order*. London: Macmillan.

———. 1980a. "Cultural Studies: Two Paradigms." *Media, Culture and Society* 2:57–72.

———. ed. 1980b. *Culture, Media, Language: Working Papers in Cultural Studies, 1972–79*. London: Hutchinson.

———. 1988. *The Hard Road to Renewal: Thatcherism and the Crisis of the Left*. London: Verso.

Hallin, Daniel. 1985. "The American News Media: A Critical Theory Perspective." In *Critical Theory and Public Life*, edited by John Forester. Cambridge, Mass.: MIT Press.

Harms, Steven, and Douglas Kellner. 1991. "Critical Theory and Advertising." *Current Perspectives in Social Theory* 11:41–67.

Hartmann, Heidi. 1979. "The Unhappy Marriage of Marxism and Feminism: Towards a More Progressive Union." *Capital and Class* 8:1–33.

Harvey, David. 1989. *The Condition of Postmodernity*. Oxford: Blackwell.

Hassan, Ihab. 1987. *The Postmodern Turn: Essays in Postmodern Theory and Culture*. Columbus: Ohio State University Press.

Hayden, Tom. 1988. *Reunion: A Memoir*. New York: Random House.

———. 2001. *Irish on the Inside*. London: Verso.

———. 2006. *Radical Nomad*. Boulder, Colo.: Paradigm.

Healey, Joseph E. 1995. *Race, Ethnicity, Gender, and Class*. Thousand Oaks, Calif.: Pine Forge.

Hebdige, Dick. 1979. *Subculture: The Meaning of Style*. London: Methuen.

———. 1988. *Hiding in the Light: On Images and Things*. New York: Routledge.

Hegel, G. W. F. 1967. *The Phenomenology of Mind*. New York: Harper and Row.

Hekman, Susan. 1990. *Gender and Knowledge: Elements of a Postmodern Feminism*. Oxford: Polity.

———. 1995. *Moral Voices, Moral Selves: Carol Gilligan and Feminist Moral Theory*. University Park: Penn State University Press.

Held, David. 1980. *An Introduction to Critical Theory*. Berkeley: University of California Press.

Hilferding, Rudolf. 1981. *Finance Capital: A Study of the Latest Phase of Capitalist Development*. London: Routledge and Kegan Paul.

Hoagland, Sarah Lucia, and Julia Penelope, eds. 1988. *For Lesbians Only: A Separatist Anthology*. London: Onlywomen.

Hochschild, Arlie. 1989. *The Second Shift: Working Parents and the Revolution at Home*. New York: Viking.

Hoggart, Richard. 1957. *The Uses of Literacy*. London: Chatto and Windus.

Holstein, James, and Gale Miller, eds. 1993. *Reconsidering Social Constructionism: Debates in Social Problems Theory*. New York: Aldine de Gruyter.

Homans, George. 1950. *The Human Group*. New York: Harcourt, Brace.

hooks, bell. 1984. *Feminist Theory: From Margin to Center*. Boston: South End.

———. 1989. *Talking Back: Thinking Feminist, Thinking Black*. Boston: South End.

———. 1990. *Yearning: Race, Gender, and Cultural Politics*. Boston: South End.

———. 1992. *Black Looks: Race and Representation*. Boston: South End.

———. 1995. *Killing Rage: Ending Racism*. New York: Henry Holt.

———. 1996. *Bone Black: Memories of Girlhood*. New York: Henry Holt.

Horkheimer, Max. 1973. *Critical Theory*. New York: Herder and Herder.

————. 1974. *Eclipse of Reason*. New York: Seabury.

Horkheimer, Max, and Theodor W. Adorno. 1972. *Dialectic of Enlightenment*. New York: Herder and Herder.

Hughes, H. Stuart. 1975. *The Sea Change: The Migration of Social Thought, 1930–65*. New York: Harper and Row.

Huyssen, Andreas. 1984. "Mapping the Postmodern." *New German Critique* 33:5–52.

————. 1986. *After the Great Divide: Modernism, Mass Culture, Postmodernism*. Bloomington: Indiana University Press.

Irigaray, Luce. 1985. *This Sex Which Is Not One*. Ithaca, N.Y.: Cornell University Press.

Jacoby, Russell. 1975. *Social Amnesia*. Boston: Beacon.

————. 1981. *Dialectic of Defeat*. New York: Cambridge University Press.

————. 1987. *The Last Intellectuals: American Culture in the Age of Academe*. New York: Basic.

————. 1994. *Dogmatic Wisdom: How the Education and Culture Wars Have Misled America*. New York: Doubleday.

Jaggar, Alison. 1983. *Feminist Politics and Human Nature*. Totowa, N.J.: Rowman and Allenheld.

Jameson, Fredric. 1971. *Marxism and Form*. Princeton, N.J.: Princeton University Press.

————. 1981. *The Political Unconscious: Narrative as a Socially Symbolic Act*. Ithaca, N.Y.: Cornell University Press.

————. 1984. "Postmodernism, or, the Cultural Logic of Late Capitalism." *New Left Review* 146:53–93.

————. 1991. *Postmodernism, or, the Cultural Logic of Late Capitalism*. Durham, N.C.: Duke University Press.

Jay, Martin. 1973. *The Dialectical Imagination*. Boston: Little, Brown.

————. 1984a. *Adorno*. Cambridge, Mass.: Harvard University Press.

————. 1984b. *Marxism and Totality*. Berkeley: University of California Press.

Jenness, Valerie. 1993. *Making It Work: The Prostitutes' Rights Movement in Perspective*. New York: Aldine de Gruyter.

Johnson. R. 1986–87. "What Is Cultural Studies Anyway?" *Social Text* 12:38–79.

Kann, Mark. 1982. *The American Left: Failures and Fortunes*. New York: Praeger.

————. 1991. *On the Man Question: Gender and Civic Virtue in America*. Philadelphia: Temple University Press.

Kellner, Douglas. 1981. "Network Television and American Society: Introduction to a Critical Theory of Television." *Theory and Society* 10:31–62.

————. 1989a. "Boundaries and Borderlines: Reflections on Jean Baudrillard and Critical Theory." *Current Perspectives in Social Theory* 9:5–22.

————. 1989b. *Critical Theory, Marxism and Modernity*. Cambridge, Mass.: Polity.

————. 1989c. *Jean Baudrillard*. Palo Alto, Calif.: Stanford University Press.

————. 1990. *Television and the Crisis of Democracy*. Boulder, Colo.: Westview.

————. 1992. *The Persian Gulf TV War*. Boulder, Colo.: Westview.

————. 1995. *Media Culture: Cultural Studies, Identity, and Politics between the Modern and the Postmodern*. New York: Routledge.

Kitzinger, Celia. 1987. *The Social Construction of Lesbianism*. Newbury Park, Calif.: Sage.

Klein, Julie. 1990. *Interdisciplinarity: History, Theory, and Practice*. Detroit: Wayne State University Press.

———. 1996. *Crossing Boundaries: Knowledge, Disciplinarities, and Interdisciplinarities*. Charlottesville: University of Virginia Press.

Kline, Stephen, and William Leiss. 1978. "Advertising, Needs, and 'Commodity Fetishism.'" *Canadian Journal of Political and Social Theory* 2:5–32.

Knorr-Cetina, Karin. 1977. "Producing and Reproducing Knowledge: Descriptive or 'Constructive'? Toward a Model of Research Production." *Social Science Information* 16:969–96.

———. 1979. "Tinkering toward Success: Prelude to a Theory of Scientific Practice." *Theory and Society* 8:347–76.

———. 1981. *The Manufacture of Knowledge: An Essay on the Constructivist and Contextual Nature of Science*. New York: Pergamon.

Kolodny, Annette. 1975. "Some Notes on Defining a 'Feminist Literary Criticism.'" *Critical Inquiry* 2:75–92.

———. 1980. "Dancing through the Minefields: Some Observations on the Theory, Practice, and Politics of a Feminist Literary Criticism." *Feminist Studies* 6(1):1–25.

———. 1984. *The Land before Her: Fantasy and Experience of the American Frontiers, 1630–1860*. Chapel Hill: University of North Carolina Press.

Korsch, Karl. 1970. *Marxism and Philosophy*. New York: Monthly Review Press.

Kowinski, William. 1985. *The Mailing of America*. New York: Morrow.

Kristeva, Julia. 1980. *Desire in Language: A Semiotic Approach to Literature and Art*. New York: Columbia University Press.

Kroker, Arthur, and David Cook. 1986. *The Postmodern Scene*. New York: St. Martin's.

Kuhn, Thomas. 1970. *The Structure of Scientific Revolutions*. 2nd ed. Chicago: University of Chicago Press.

Lacan, Jacques. 1977. *Écrits: A Selection*. New York: Norton.

———. 1982. *Feminine Sexuality*. New York: Norton.

Laclau, Ernesto, and Claude Mouffe. 1985. *Hegemony and Socialist Strategy*. London: Verso.

Lasch, Christopher. 1977. *Haven in a Heartless World: The Family Besieged*. New York: Basic.

Lather, Patti. 1991. *Getting Smart: Feminist Research and Pedagogy with/in the Postmodern*. New York: Routledge.

Lauretis, Teresa de. 1984. *Alice Doesn't: Feminism, Semiotics, Cinema*. Bloomington: Indiana University Press.

———. 1987. *Technologies of Gender: Essays on Theory, Film, and Fiction*. Bloomington: Indiana University Press.

Lefebvre, Henri. 1991. *The Production of Space*. Oxford: Blackwell.

Leiss, William. 1973. *The Domination of Nature*. New York: Braziller.

———. 1976. *The Limits to Satisfaction*. Toronto: University of Toronto Press.

Leiss, William, Stephen Kline, and Sut Jhally. 1986. *Social Communication in Advertising: Persons, Products, and Images of Well-Being*. Toronto: Methuen.

Lemert, Charles, ed. 1993. *Social Theory: The Multicultural and Classic Readings.* Boulder, Colo.: Westview.

———. 1995. *Sociology after the Crisis.* Boulder, Colo.: Westview.

———. 2005a. *Postmodernism Is Not What You Think.* 2nd ed. Boulder, Colo.: Paradigm.

———. 2005b. "Why Mills and Not Gouldner?" *Fast Capitalism* 1.2. www.fast-capitalism.com.

Lenhardt, Christian. 1976. "The Wanderings of Enlightenment." In *On Critical Theory,* edited by John O'Neill. New York: Seabury.

Lenin, V. I. 1932. *State and Revolution.* New York: International Publishers.

———. 1969. *What Is to Be Done?* New York: International Publishers.

Lewis, Lionel S. 1975. *Scaling the Ivory Tower: Merit and Its Limit in Academic Careers.* Baltimore: Johns Hopkins University Press.

———. 1996. *Marginal Worth: Teaching and the Academic Labor Market.* New Brunswick, N.J.: Transaction.

Lichtheim, George. 1971. *From Marx to Hegel.* New York: Herder and Herder.

Lorber, Judith. 1994. *Paradoxes of Gender.* New Haven, Conn.: Yale University Press.

Luhmann, Nicklaus. 1982. *The Differentiation of Society.* New York: Columbia University Press.

Lukacs, Georg. 1962. *The Historical Novel.* London: Merlin.

———. 1963. *The Meaning of Contemporary Realism.* London: Merlin.

———. 1964. *Essays on Thomas Mann.* London: Merlin.

———. 1971. *History and Class Consciousness.* London: Merlin.

Luke, Allan. 1988. *Literacy, Textbooks, and Ideology: Postwar Literacy Instruction and the Mythology of Dick and Jane.* London: Falmer.

Luke, Timothy W. 1989. *Screens of Power: Ideology, Domination, and Resistance in Informational Society.* Urbana: University of Illinois Press.

———. 1990. *Social Theory and Modernity: Critique, Dissent, and Revolution.* Newbury Park, Calif.: Sage.

———. 1992. *Shows of Force: Power, Politics, and Ideology in Art Exhibitions.* Durham, N.C.: Duke University Press.

———. 1999. *Capitalism, Democracy, and Ecology: Departing from Marx.* Urbana: University of Illinois Press.

Lyotard, Jean-François. 1984. *The Postmodern Condition: A Report on Knowledge.* Minneapolis: University of Minnesota Press.

———. 1988. *The Differend: Phrases in Dispute.* Minneapolis: University of Minnesota Press.

MacKinnon, Catharine. 1987. *Feminism Unmodified: Discourses on Life and Law.* Cambridge, Mass.: Harvard University Press.

———. 1993. *Only Words.* Cambridge, Mass.: Harvard University Press.

Mandel, Ernest. 1978. *Late Capitalism.* London: Verso.

Marcus, George, and Michael Fischer, eds. 1986. *Anthropology as a Cultural Critique: An Experimental Moment in the Human Sciences.* Chicago: University of Chicago Press.

Marcuse, Herbert. 1955. *Eros and Civilization: A Philosophical Inquiry into Freud.* New York: Vintage.

————. 1958. *Soviet Marxism, a Critical Analysis*. New York: Vintage.

————. 1960. *Reason and Revolution: Hegel and the Rise of Social Theory*. Boston: Beacon.

————. 1964. *One-Dimensional Man: Studies in the Ideology of Advanced Industrial Society*. Boston: Beacon.

————. 1968. "Industrialization and Capitalism in the Work of Max Weber." In *Negations*. Boston: Beacon.

————. 1969. *An Essay on Liberation*. Boston: Beacon.

————. 1970. *Five Lectures: Psychoanalysis, Politics, and Utopia*. Boston: Beacon.

————. 1972. "The Foundations of Historical Materialism." In *Studies in Critical Philosophy*. London: New Left Books.

————. 1973. *Counterrevolution and Revolt*. Boston: Beacon.

————. 1978. *The Aesthetic Dimension: Toward a Critique of Marxist Aesthetics*. Boston: Beacon.

Marx, Karl. 1964. *Early Writings*. Edited by Tom Bottomore. New York: McGraw-Hill.

————. 1967. *Capital: A Critique of Political Economy*. New York: International Publishers.

Marx, Karl, and Frederick Engels. 1947. *The German Ideology*. New York: International Publishers.

————. 1967. *The Communist Manifesto*. New York: Pantheon.

Masters, William H., and Virginia E. Johnson. 1966. *Human Sexual Response*. Boston: Little, Brown.

McInnes, Neil. 1972. *The Western Marxists*. London: Alcove Press.

Meese, Elizabeth. 1992. *(SEM)erotics: Theorizing Lesbian: Writing*. New York: New York University Press.

Mehan, Hugh, and Houston Wood. 1975. *The Reality of Ethnomethodology*. New York: Wiley.

Melman, Seymour. 1974. *The Permanent War Economy*. New York: Simon and Schuster.

Merleau-Ponty, Maurice. 1964a. *Sense and Non-Sense*. Evanston, Ill.: Northwestern University Press.

————. 1964b. *Signs*. Evanston, Ill.: Northwestern University Press.

Merton, Robert K. 1957. *Social Theory and Social Structure*. New York: Free Press.

Miliband, Ralph. 1969. *The State in Capitalist Society*. New York: Basic.

————. 1982. *Capitalist Democracy in Britain*. Oxford: Oxford University Press.

————. 1983. *Class Power and State Power*. London: Verso.

Miller, Jim. 1987. *Democracy Is in the Streets*. New York: Simon and Schuster.

Miller, Mark Crispin. 1988. *Boxed In: The Culture of TV*. Evanston, Ill.: Northwestern University Press.

Mills, C. Wright. 1956. *The Power Elite*. New York: Oxford University Press.

————. 1959. *The Sociological Imagination*. New York: Oxford University Press.

————. 1962. *The Marxists*. New York: Dell.

Morrow, Raymond. 1994. *Critical Theory and Methodology*. Newbury Park, Calif.: Sage.

Morrow, Raymond, and Carlos Alberto Torres. 1995. *Social Theory and Education: A Critique of Theories of Social and Cultural Reproduction*. Albany: SUNY Press.

Mulkay, Michael. 1979. *Science and the Sociology of Knowledge.* London: Allen and Unwin.

———. 1985. *The Word and the World: Explorations in the Form of Sociological Analysis.* Winchester, UK: Allen and Unwin.

Mullins, Nicholas C. 1973. *Theories and Theory Groups in Contemporary American Sociology.* New York: Harper and Row.

Mulvey, Laura. 1989. *Visual and Other Pleasures.* Bloomington: Indiana University Press.

Nelson, Cary, and Lawrence Grossberg, eds. 1988. *Marxism and the Interpretation of Culture.* Urbana: University of Illinois Press.

Nicholson, Linda, and Steven Seidman, eds. 1995. *Social Postmodernism: Beyond Identity Politics.* Cambridge, UK: Cambridge University Press.

O'Connor, James. 1973. *The Fiscal Crisis of the State.* New York: St. Martin's.

Offe, Claus. 1984. *Contradictions of the Welfare State.* Cambridge, Mass.: MIT Press.

———. 1985. *Disorganized Capitalism.* Cambridge, Mass.: MIT Press.

O'Neill, John. 1972. *Sociology as a Skin Trade: Essays in Reflexive Sociology.* New York: Harper and Row.

———. 1974. *Making Sense Together: An Introduction to Wild Sociology.* New York: Harper and Row.

———. 1986. "The Disciplinary Society: From Weber to Foucault." *British Journal of Sociology* 37(1):42–60.

Paci, Enzo. 1972. *The Function of the Sciences and the Meaning of Man.* Evanston, Ill.: Northwestern University Press.

Parsons, Talcott. 1937. *The Structure of Social Action.* Glencoe, Ill.: Free Press.

———. 1951. *The Social System.* Glencoe, Ill.: Free Press.

Parsons, Talcott, and Robert Bales. 1955. *Family, Socialization, and Interaction Process.* Glencoe, Ill.: Free Press.

Piccone, Paul. 1971. "Phenomenological Marxism." *Telos* 9:3–31.

Pleck, Joseph. 1981. *The Myth of Masculinity.* Cambridge, Mass.: MIT Press.

Plummer, Ken, ed. 1992. *Modern Homosexualities.* London: Routledge, Chapman and Hall.

Popper, Karl. 1959. *The Logic of Scientific Discovery.* New York: Basic.

Portoghesi, P. 1983. *Postmodern, the Architecture of the Post-Industrial Society.* New York: Rizzoli.

Poster, Mark. 1975. *Existential Marxism in Postwar France: From Sartre to Althusser.* Princeton, N.J.: Princeton University Press.

———. 1990. *The Mode of Information.* Princeton, N.J.: Princeton University Press.

Poulantzas, Nicos. 1973. *Political Power and Social Classes.* New York: Routledge and Kegan Paul.

Quadagno, Jill. 1982. *Aging in Early Industrial Society: Work, Family, and Social Policy in Nineteenth-Century England.* New York: Academic.

———. 1988. *The Transformation of Old Age Security: Class and Politics in the American Welfare State.* Chicago: University of Chicago Press.

———. 1994. *The Color of Welfare: How Racism Undermined the War on Poverty.* New York: Oxford University Press.

Rachlin, Allan. 1988. *News as Hegemonic Reality.* Westport, Conn.: Praeger.

Rawls, John. 1971. *A Theory of Justice.* Cambridge, Mass.: Harvard University Press.

Reinharz, Shulamit. 1992. *Feminist Methods in Social Research.* New York: Oxford University Press.

Richardson, Laurel. 1988. "The Collective Story: Postmodernism and the Writing of Sociology." *Sociological Focus* 21:199–208.

———. 1990a. "Narrative and Sociology." *Journal of Contemporary Ethnography* 19:116–35.

———. 1990b. *Writing Strategies: Reaching Diverse Audiences.* Newbury Park, Calif.: Sage.

———. 1991a. "Speakers Whose Voices Matter: Toward a Feminist Postmodernist Sociological Praxis." *Studies in Symbolic Interactionism* 12:29–38.

———. 1991b. "Value Constituting Practices, Rhetoric, and Metaphor in Sociology: A Reflexive Analysis." *Current Perspectives in Social Theory* 11:1–15.

Rorty, Richard. 1979. *Philosophy and the Mirror of Nature.* Princeton, N.J.: Princeton University Press.

———. 1989. *Contingency, Irony, and Solidarity.* New York: Cambridge University Press.

Rosaldo, Renata. 1989. *Culture and Truth: The Remaking of Social Analysis.* Boston: Beacon.

Rosenau, Pauline Marie. 1992. *Post-Modernism and the Social Sciences.* Princeton, N.J.: Princeton University Press.

Ross, Andrew, ed. 1988. *Universal Abandon? The Politics of Postmodernism.* Minneapolis: University of Minnesota Press.

———. 1989. *No Respect: Intellectuals and Popular Culture.* New York: Routledge.

Rubin, Lillian. 1983. *Intimate Strangers: Men and Women Together.* New York: Harper and Row.

Rule, James B. 1978. *Insight and Social Betterment.* New York: Oxford University Press.

Ryan, Michael. 1982. *Marxism and Deconstruction.* Baltimore: Johns Hopkins University Press.

———. 1989. *Politics and Culture: Working Hypotheses for a Post-Revolutionary Society.* Basingstoke, UK: Macmillan.

Ryan, Michael, and Douglass Kellner. 1988. *Camera Politica: The Politics and Ideology of Contemporary Hollywood Film.* Bloomington: Indiana University Press.

Said, Edward. 1978. *Orientalism.* New York: Pantheon.

Sale, Kirkpatrick. 1973. *SDS.* New York: Random House.

Sartre, Jean-Paul. 1956. *Being and Nothingness.* New York: Philosophical Library.

———. 1976. *Critique of Dialectical Reason.* London: New Left Books.

Saussure, Ferdinand de. 1983. *Course in General Linguistics.* London: G. Duckworth.

Schiller, Herbert. 1989. *Culture, Inc.: The Corporate Takeover of Public Expression.* New York: Oxford University Press.

Schroyer, Trent. 1973. *The Critique of Domination: The Origins and Development of Critical Theory.* New York: Braziller.

Schumacher, E. E. 1973. *Small Is Beautiful: Economics as if People Mattered*. New York: Harper and Row.

Schwalbe, Michael. 1996. *Unlocking the Iron Cage: The Men's Movement, Gender Politics, and American Culture*. New York: Oxford University Press.

Searle, John. 1979. *Expression and Meaning: Studies in the Theory of Speech Acts*. New York: Cambridge University Press.

Sedgwick, Eve. 1990. *Epistemology of the Closet*. Berkeley: University of California Press.

Seidman, Steven. 1991a. "The End of Sociological Theory." *Sociological Theory* 9:131–46.

———. 1991b. *Romantic Longings: Love in America, 1830–1980*. New York: Routledge.

———. 1994a. *Contested Knowledge: Social Theory in the Postmodern Era*. Oxford: Blackwell.

———. 1994b. *The Postmodern Turn: New Perspectives on Social Theory*. New York: Cambridge University Press.

———, ed. 1996. *Queer Theory/Sociology*. Cambridge, UK: Blackwell.

———. 1997. *Difference Troubles: Queering Social Theory and Sexual Politics*. New York: Cambridge University Press.

Sennett, Richard. 1977. *The Fall of Public Man*. New York: Knopf.

Shelton, Beth Anne. 1992. *Women, Men, and Time: Gender Differences in Paid Work, Housework, and Leisure*. New York: Greenwood.

Shelton, Beth Anne, and Ben Agger. 1992. "Shotgun Wedding, Unhappy Marriage, No-Fault Divorce? Rethinking the Feminism-Marxism Relationship." In *Theory on Gender/Feminism on Theory*, edited by Paula England. New York: Aldine de Gruyter.

Sherwood, Steven Jay, Philip Smith, and Jeffrey Alexander. 1993. Review of *The British Are Coming ... Again! The Hidden Agenda of "Cultural Studies,"* *Contemporary Sociology* 22:370–75.

Skocpol, Theda. 1979. *States and Social Revolutions*. New York: Cambridge University Press.

———. 1992. *Protecting Soldiers and Mothers: The Political Origins of Social Policy in the United States*. Cambridge, Mass.: Harvard University Press.

———. 1995. *Social Policy in the United States: Future Possibilities in Historical Perspective*. Princeton, N.J.: Princeton University Press.

———. 1996. *Boomerang: Clinton's Health Security Effort and the Turn against Government in U.S. Politics*. New York: Norton.

Slater, Phil. 1977. *Origin and Significance of the Frankfurt School*. London: Routledge and Kegan Paul.

Slater, Suzanne. 1995. *The Lesbian Family Life Cycle*. New York: Free Press.

Sloterdijk, Peter. 1987. *Critique of Cynical Reason*. Minneapolis: University of Minnesota Press.

Smith, Dorothy. 1987. *The Everyday World as Problematic: A Feminist Sociology*. Boston: Northeastern University Press.

———. 1990a. *The Conceptual Practice of Power: A Feminist Sociology of Knowledge*. Boston: Northeastern University Press.

———. 1990b. *Texts, Facts, and Femininity: Exploring the Relations of Ruling*. New York: Routledge.

Soja, Edward. 1989. *Postmodern Geographies: The Reassertion of Space in Critical Social Theory.* London: Verso.

Soothill, Keith, and Sylvia Walby. *Sex Crime in the News.* New York: Routledge.

Spivak, Gayatri. 1988. "Can the Subaltern Speak?" In *Marxism and the Interpretation of Culture*, edited by Cary Nelson and Lawrence Grossberg. Urbana: University of Illinois Press.

Stacey, Judith. 1990. *Brave New Families: Stories of Domestic Upheaval in Late Twentieth Century America.* New York: Basic.

Stalin, Josef. 1973. *Dialectical and Historical Materialism.* New York: International Publishers.

Steinem, Gloria. 1986. *Outrageous Acts and Everyday Rebellions.* New York: New American Library.

———. 1994. *Moving Beyond Words.* New York: Simon and Schuster.

Students for a Democratic Society. 1962. Port Huron Statement. www.coursesa. matrix.msu.edu/~hst306/documents/huron/html.

Teigas, Demetrius. 1995. *Knowledge and Human Understanding: A Study of the Habermas-Gadamer Debate.* Lewisburg, Pa.: Bucknell University Press.

Turner, Jonathan. 1998. "Must Sociological Theory and Sociological Practice Be So Far Apart? A Polemical Answer." *Sociological Perspectives* 41:243–58.

Turner, Stephen, and Jonathan Turner. 1990. *The Impossible Science: An Institutional Analysis of American Sociology.* Newbury Park, Calif.: Sage.

Varon, Jeremy. 2004. *Bringing the War Home: The Weather Underground, the Baader Meinhoff Faction, and Revolutionary Violence in the Sixties and Seventies.* Berkeley: University of California Press.

Walby, Sylvia, ed. 1986. *Gender Segregation at Work.* Milton Keynes, UK: Open University Press.

———. 1990. *Theorizing Patriarchy.* Oxford, UK: Blackwell.

Walters, Suzanna. 1992. "Material Girls: Feminism and Cultural Studies." *Current Perspectives in Social Theory* 12:59–96.

———. 1995. *Material Girls: Making Sense of Feminist Cultural Theory.* Berkeley: University of California Press.

Watkins, Evan. 1989. *Work Time: English Departments and the Circulation of Cultural Value.* Stanford, Calif.: Stanford University Press.

Weber, Max. 1946. "Science as a Vocation." In *From Max Weber*, edited by Hans Gerth and C. Wright Mills. New York: Oxford University Press.

———. 1947. *The Theory of Social and Economic Organization.* Glencoe, Ill.: Free Press.

Weedon, Chris. 1987. *Feminist Practice and Poststructuralist Theory.* Oxford, UK: Blackwell.

Wells, Tom. 1994. *The War Within: America's Battles over Vietnam.* Berkeley: University of California Press.

———. 2005. "Two Wars, Two Movements: Iraq in Light of Vietnam." *Fast Capitalism.* 1.2. www.fastcapitalism.com.

Wernick, Andrew. 1983. "Advertising and Ideology: An Interpretive Framework." *Theory, Culture and Society* 2:16–33.

———. 1991. *Promotional Culture: Advertising, Ideology, and Symbolic Expression.* Newbury Park, Calif.: Sage.

West, Cornel. 1988. *Prophetic Fragments*. Grand Rapids, Mich.: Eerdmans.
———. 1993. *Race Matters*. Boston: Beacon.
Wexler, Phil. 1983. *Critical Social Psychology*. London: Routledge and Kegan Paul.
———. 1987. *Social Analysis of Education: After the New Sociology*. London: Routledge and Kegan Paul.
Whitehead, Alfred North, and Bertrand Russell. 1962. *Principia Mathematica*. Cambridge, UK: Cambridge University Press.
Williams, Christine. 1989. *Gender Differences at Work: Women and Men in Nontraditional Occupations*. Berkeley: University of California Press.
———, ed. 1993. *Doing "Women's Work": Men in Nontraditional Occupations*. Newbury Park, Calif.: Sage.
———. 1995. *Still a Man's World: Men Who Do "Women's Work."* Berkeley: University of California Press.
Williams, Raymond. 1958. *Culture and Society*. New York: Columbia University Press.
Williamson, Judith. 1978. *Decoding Advertisements: Ideology and Meaning in Advertising*. London: Boyars.
Willis, Paul. 1977. *Learning to Labour: How Working Class Kids Get Working Class Jobs*. Farnborough, UK: Saxon House.
———. 1978. *Profane Culture*. London: Routledge and Kegan Paul.
Wilson, William Julius. 1987. *The Truly Disadvantaged: The Inner City, the Underclass, and Public Policy*. Chicago: University of Chicago Press.
———. 1996. *When Work Disappears: The World of the New Urban Poor*. New York: Knopf.
Wilson, William Julius, Katherine McFate, and Roger Lawson, eds. 1995. *Poverty, Inequality, and the Future of Social Policy*. New York: Russell Sage.
Wittgenstein, Ludwig. 1976. *Philosophical Investigations*. Oxford: Blackwell.
Wolf, Naomi. 1993. *Fire with Fire: The New Female Power and How It Will Change the Twenty-first Century*. New York: Random House.
Woodiwiss, Anthony. 1993. *Postmodernity USA: The Crisis of Social Modernism in Postwar America*. London: Sage.
Wright, Erik Olin. 1985. *Classes*. London: Verso.
———. 1987. "Reflections on *Classes*." *Berkeley Journal of Sociology* 23:19–49.
Wuthnow, Robert. 1987. *Meaning and Moral Order: Explorations in Cultural Analysis*. Berkeley: University of California Press.
———. 1989. *Communities of Discourse*. Cambridge, Mass.: Harvard University Press.

# Index

Adorno, Theodor W., 78–80, 83, 165–66, 168, 196, 208–9; accessibility of writings, 158; on culture industry, 89–93; on domination, 84–87; and German New Left, 182; and "high" culture, 126–27; on identity theory, 85–86; on politics, 11; on progress, 38–39; on technology, 84–85

advertising. *See* culture industry; mass media; television

*The Aesthetic Dimension* (Marcuse), 91–93

*Aesthetic Theory* (Adorno), 91–93

affirmative culture, 127

Africa, ix

Africana feminism, 109, 113–15

AIDS, ix

Alexander, Jeffrey, 27, 131

alienation, 197; Marx's theory of, 82, 127

alterity/presence dichotomy, 57

Althusserian structuralism, 64–65

Althusser, Louis, 80, 130

*America* (Baudrillard), 139, 142

American Sociological Association, 193

American Sociological Association Council, 198

*American Sociological Review,* 195, 202

applications of critical social theory, 167–90; historicity, 183–84; immanent critique, 183–85; politics of curriculum, 187; politics and micropolitics, 179–82; race and

ethnicity, 178–79; research methods, 176–78; social control, 172–73; social movements, 116–18, 176; social psychology, 175; sociology of education, 175–76; the state and social policy, 169–72

Aronowitz, Stanley, 197

*The Authoritarian Personality* (Adorno et al.), 166

Bakhtin, Mikhail, 37

Bales, Robert, 117

Baudrillard, Jean, 36, 45, 68, 139–43, 159, 173, 204, 209

Becker, Gary, 118, 155–56

*Being and Nothingness* (Sartre), 7

Bell, Daniel, 68

Benjamin, Walter, 128

Best, Steven, 44

"beyond-bitch" feminism, 120

the Bible, 59–60

Birmingham School, 128–34, 192

bisexuality, 104–5, 117, 137

Bloom, Allan, 200

Bowling Green group, 133–34

*Boxed In* (Miller), 132

Brownmiller, Susan, 120

Burawoy, Michael, 191, 193, 201, 203

Bush, George W., x, 201, 202–3, 212, 213

Camus, Albert, 206

capitalism, 8; culture industry, 90; fast, 125, 140–41; Habermas on, 94–95,

233

# About the Author

**Ben Agger** is professor of sociology and humanities at University of Texas at Arlington. His recent books include *Postponing the Postmodern, The Virtual Self,* and *Speeding Up Fast Capitalism.* Agger is completing a book entitled *Fast Families, Virtual Children* (with Beth Anne Shelton) and a book on the 1960s entitled *The Sixties at Forty: Generation and Identity among Sixties People.* He edits the journal *Fast Capitalism* (www.fastcapitalism.com).